Transforming European Employment Policy

Transforming European Employment Policy

Labour Market Transitions and the Promotion of Capability

Edited by

Ralf Rogowski

Professor of Law, University of Warwick, UK

Robert Salais

Fellow at the Institute of Advanced Studies, Nantes and a former Director of the CNRS Research Centre, Institutions et Dynamiques Historiques de l'Economie, Cachan, France

Noel Whiteside

Professor of Comparative Public Policy, University of Warwick, UK

Edward Elgar

Cheltenham, UK • Northampton, MA, USA

Published by
Edward Elgar Publishing Limited
The Lypiatts
15 Lansdown Road
Cheltenham
Glos GL50 2JA
UK

Edward Elgar Publishing, Inc.
William Pratt House
9 Dewey Court
Northampton
Massachusetts 01060
USA

A catalogue record for this book is available from the British Library

Library of Congress Control Number: 2011932891

ISBN 978 1 84980 256 7 (cased)

Typeset by Columns Design XML Ltd, Reading
Printed and bound by MPG Books Group, UK

Contents

v

Acknowledgements

This book is the final outcome of two seminars. The first one ('Coping with Social Risks: Capabilities and/or Transition Securities?') was held at the Wissenschaftszentrum zu Berlin (WZB) on 7 June 2007, initiated and organised by Robert Salais, then guest researcher at the WZB, and Günther Schmid (WZB). The second one ('Governing Social Policy in Europe: the Promotion of Capabilities and Transitional Labour Markets') was held in Venice at the Palazzo Pesaro-Papafava (University of Warwick) on 10–11 April, 2008, organised by Noel Whiteside (University of Warwick) as part of the ESRC Seminar Series, *Coping with Uncertainty: European labour markets and the politics of social reform in comparative perspective* (RES 451-26-0429) and sponsored by Warwick University's Institute for Advanced Study. We wish to thank all institutions and sponsors involved for their support and help in organising these seminars.

We also acknowledge support from the European Commission's 6th Framework Programme project CAPRIGHT *Resources, rights and capabilities: in search of social foundations for Europe* (contract no. 028549-2). Discussions within this project over developing the capabilities approach have created the background for findings presented in several chapters of this book. The views expressed in these chapters are those of the authors and do not necessarily reflect legal or political views of the European Commission, and the European Commission is not responsible for any use that might be made of the information presented in this publication.

We wish to thank Dr Alice Mah for editorial assistance, Falk Maede-Heck for help with the index and Amy Margaret Morley and Victoria Surtees for help with translations.

Figures

Tables

Contributors

Peter Auer is Senior Fellow of the International Institute for Labour Studies of the ILO in Geneva, having previously worked there as Chief of Employment Analysis and Research and as Head of the European Employment Observatory. He has worked extensively on labour market developments and on labour market policy and regulations and his recent research focuses on a new framework for labour market security in response to the challenges of globalisation.

Jean-Michel Bonvin is Professor of Sociology and Social Policy at the University of Applied Sciences Western Switzerland and Founding Member of the Center for the Study of Capabilities in Social and Health Services (CESCAP). His research focuses on labour market policies, organisational innovation in the management of the public sector and of firms and theories of justice. Recent publications include *Amartya Sen, une politique de la liberté* (2008, with Nicolas Farvaque) and numerous articles in international journals.

Colin Crouch is Professor of Governance and Public Management at the Business School of Warwick University. He is External Scientific Member of the Max-Planck-Institute at Cologne and a Fellow of both the British Academy and the Academy of Social Sciences. He works on comparative European sociology and industrial relations, on economic sociology and on contemporary issues in British and European politics. His books include *The Responsible Corporation in a Global Economy* (2011, with Camilla Maclean); *The Strange Non-Death of Neo-Liberalism* (2011); *The Diversity of Democracy: Corporatism, Social Order and Political Conflict* (2006, with Wolfgang Streeck); *Capitalist Diversity and Change: Recombinant Governance and Institutional Entrepreneurs* (2005); *Post-Democracy* (2004); *Are Skills the Answer? The Political Economy of Skill Creation in Advanced Industrial Countries* (2001, with David Finegold and Mari Sako); *Citizenship, Markets and the State* (2000, with Klaus Eder and Damian Tambini); *Social Change in Western Europe* (1999); *Political Economy of Modern Capitalism: Mapping Convergence and Diversity* (1997, with Wolfgang

Streeck); *Organized Industrial Relations in Europe: What Future?* (1995, with Franz Traxler) and *Industrial Relations and European State Traditions* (1993).

Simon Deakin is Professor of Law at the University of Cambridge. He has written widely on labour law, corporate governance and private law from an empirical and social science perspective. His publications include *Labour Law* (5th ed. 2009, with Gillian Morris), *Capacitas: Contract Law and the Institutional Preconditions of a Market Economy* (2009, with Alain Supiot) and *The Law of the Labour Market* (2005, with Frank Wilkinson). He has recently been awarded the ECGI and Allen & Overy prizes for corporate governance research.

Claude Didry is Senior Researcher and Director of the CNRS research centre Institutions et Dynamiques Historiques de l'Economie in Cachan, France. His research, using an institutional perspective, focuses on industrial relations and labour law issues at national and European levels. His recent publications include *L'entreprise en restructuration: Dynamiques institutionnelles et mobilisations collectives* (2010, with Annette Jobert).

Bernard Gazier is Professor of Economics at the University of Paris-I (Panthéon-Sorbonne), a researcher at the Centre d'Economie de la Sorbonne, a member of the Institut Universitaire de France and the President of the *Société de Port-Royal*. His publications include *Les stratégies des ressources humaines* (2010), *Restructuring work and employment in Europe* (2008, with Frédéric Bruggeman), *Vers un nouveau modèle social* (2005), *Tous 'Sublimes': Vers un nouveau plein-emploi* (2003) and *The Dynamics of Full Employment: Social Integration Through Transitional Labour Markets* (2002, with Günther Schmid).

Petra Kaps was a Research Fellow at the Social Science Research Centre (WZB), Berlin from 2004 to 2008 and until recently at the Institute for Employment Research (IAB), Nuremburg, Germany. She has published on issues of governance, social politics and welfare reform and is currently completing her PhD on basic income for jobseekers.

Ralf Rogowski is Professor of Law at the School of Law at the University of Warwick. He has worked extensively on European labour law and labour market policy and regulations. His publications include *The European Social Model and Transitional Labour Markets: Law and Policy* (2008), *The Shape of the New Europe* (2006, with Charles Turner), *Labour Market Efficiency in the European Union: Employment Protection and Fixed Term*

Contracts (1998, with Klaus Schömann and Thomas Kruppe) and *Reflexive Labour Law: Studies in Industrial Relations and Employment Regulation* (1994, with Ton Wilthagen).

Robert Salais is Fellow at the Institute of Advanced Studies, Nantes and a former Director of the CNRS Research Centre, Institutions et Dynamiques Historiques de l'Economie (IDHE), Cachan, France and currently Research Associate at the French-German Centre Marc Bloch (CMB), Berlin. His research focuses on institutional economics, employment and labour issues in historical perspective. He served as coordinator of several European research projects dedicated to the development of the capability approach and its application to European employment and social policy. His publications include *Développer les capacités des hommes et des territoires en Europe* (2006, with Robert Villeneuve and Odile Quintin), *Europe and the politics of capabilities* (2005, with Robert Villeneuve), *L'action publique et ses dispositifs: Institutions, économie, politique* (2005, with Elisabeth Chatel and Thierry Kirat), *Governance, Industry and Labour Markets in Britain and France: The Modernizing State* (1998, with Noel Whiteside), *Les mondes de production: Enquête sur l'identité économique de la France* (1993, with Michael Storper) and *L'invention du chômage: Histoire et transformations dune catégorie en France des années 1890 aux années 1980* (1986, with Nicolas Baverez and Bénédicte Reynaud-Cressent).

Günther Schmid served as Director of the Research Unit 'Labour Market Policy and Employment' at the Social Science Research Centre Berlin (WZB) until 2008 and is Emeritus Professor of Economic Theory of Politics, Free University, Berlin. He has been a pioneer in research on transitional labour markets. His publications include *Übergänge am Arbeitsmarkt: Arbeit, nicht nur Arbeitslosigkeit versichern* (2011), *Full Employment in Europe: Managing Labour Market Transitions and Risks* (2008) and *The Dynamics of Full Employment: Social Integration through Transitional Labour Markets* (2002, with Bernard Gazier).

Holger Schütz was a Research Fellow at the Social Science Research Centre (WZB), Berlin, from 1997 to 2008 and is currently project manager and researcher at the Institute for Applied Social Research (infas) in Bonn, Germany. His main research areas include implementation and evaluation of labour market policy, job placement and counselling, controlling and reform of public employment services in comparative perspective.

Noel Whiteside is Professor of Comparative Public Policy at the University of Warwick and Fellow of the Royal Historical Society. She works on issues of employment and social welfare in historical and comparative perspective. Recent publications include *Britain's Pensions Crisis: History and* *policy* (2006, with Hugh Pemberton and Pat Thane) and *Pension Security in the 21st Century: Redrawing the Public-Private Debate* (2003, with Gordon L. Clark).

Philip Wotschack is Research Fellow at the Research Unit 'Skill Formation and Labour Markets' of the Social Science Research Centre Berlin (WZB). His research focuses on working time, work organisation, work–life balance, further training and lifelong learning. Recent publications include *Household Governance and Time Allocation. Four Studies on the Combination of Work and Care* (2009).

Bénédicte Zimmermann is Professor at the Ecole des Hautes Etudes en Sciences Sociales in Paris. She is the author of *Ce que travailler veut dire. Une sociologie des capacités et des parcours professionnels* (2011), *La constitution du chômage en Allemagne* (2001) and *La liberté au prisme des capacités* (2008, with Jean de Munck). Her current research is on moral ethnography of work and public action.

1. Introduction

Robert Salais, Ralf Rogowski and Noel Whiteside

Over the last twenty years, European employment and social policy have undergone a dramatic transformation. The burden of labour market adjustments was transferred to the individual employee or welfare recipient via activation policies. Attention has shifted from the provision of social protection to the promotion of employment: new forms of governance, accompanied by the introduction of new forms of policy delivery and audit, have emerged as central characteristics of the new European Employment Strategy (EES). One main focus of this book lies in addressing the limitations of this approach, limitations which became particularly apparent during the financial crisis since 2008. The book's aim is to provide ideas for an alternative European reform agenda that employs insights from two influential theoretical approaches, the transitional labour market approach and the capabilities approach, drawn from the work of Amartya Sen.

The two theoretical approaches share the fate of being known in Brussels, but misunderstood and neglected as far as their implications for European policy are concerned. This observation is especially pertinent for the capabilities approach but also holds true for the transitional labour markets approach, despite the influence it has had on the EES.[1] The neglect is in part related to a drift from policies designed to substantially affect social reality to measures that are merely intended to amplify political communication, a trend that is gaining ground in Europe (and which would merit further study but lies beyond the confines of our book). Announcing a rising employment rate is much more satisfactory in terms of communication than undertaking far-reaching action that truly improves the employment situation but fails to grab media headlines. The flexicurity concept promoted by the European Commission seems to us an example for this trend; in any case, as Günther Schmid shows in Chapter 3, this concept, if misunderstood, bears the danger of increasing employment precariousness rather than securing transitions in labour markets.

The objective of our book is to make proposals for the transformation of content and method of European employment policy. The transformation requires clearly defined concepts and innovative empirical work and implies a two-pronged approach: criticism and proposals that reciprocally support each other. The book is organised in two parts, both demonstrating how the twin approach of criticism and proposal can be used in specific areas. Part I describes and compares the two theoretical and political approaches covered by the book, the transitional labour market approach (Chapters 2 to 5) and the capabilities approach (Chapters 6 to 8), and Part II (Chapters 9 to 12) presents implications for European policy which include the need for new welfare typologies that are capable of apprehending real differences in national welfare models; the necessity of a new reflexive law and support for soft law solutions like codes of conduct and other mechanisms of self-regulation; and promotion of constitutive conventions for the common market of goods, capital, services and employment in Europe. From these policy implications emerges the outline of an 'integrated approach to employment' that thoroughly renews the bases of the current approach.

PART I: SECURING TRANSITIONS AND PROMOTING CAPABILITIES

Of the four policy agendas – flexibility, flexicurity, capabilities and transitional labour markets – that Peter Auer and Bernard Gazier outline in Chapter 2, the last two deserve close attention for the future of employment in Europe, and these two perspectives are explored in this book. As regards the first two policies, one – flexibility – contradicts the objectives of the other – flexicurity. The flexibility agenda that emphasises deregulation of the labour market, external numerical flexibility (instantaneous adjustment of the amount of work to the vagaries of the economy) and weakening or elimination of legal and social protection in the event of redundancy is diametrically opposed to the flexicurity agenda as pursued in the EU's EES and Lisbon strategy of 2000 and the ILO's Decent Work Agenda of 1999. However, questions are beginning to emerge about the adequacy of the flexicurity agenda in light of the current crisis. It is an open question if flexicurity represents a way out of the crisis, or simply goes hand in hand with this situation.[2]

The topic of reconciling flexibility and security dates back to debates surrounding the launch of the EES at the Luxembourg summit meeting in 1997. Günther Schmid and Robert Salais emphasised in similar vein but from separate perspectives the possibility and political advantages of this positive dynamic relationship in their contributions to the research conference that accompanied the 1997 Luxembourg summit, Schmid from the point of view of transitional markets and Salais from that of capabilities.[3] The concept of flexicurity has evolved considerably since then. From the initial idea of a mutual reinforcement of employment security and internal flexibility of companies, the debate has gradually turned to the realistic assessment of a trade-off between security and flexibility. The idea of trade-off is central in EU documents like the 2007 Green Paper on modernising labour law. According to the authors of this paper, labour laws should be amended in key areas to meet the European companies' increasing needs for flexibility, which in return, it is suggested, leads to firmer growth in employment.

Securing Transitions

A key concept in the discourse over European employment policy has been the concept of 'transitions', not only in relation to flexicurity. The concept creates the core idea of an alternative labour market policy concept known as the transitional labour market approach which served not only as a key theoretical concept of several European research projects since 1996 but has been most influential in the design of the European Employment Strategy.[4] Bénédicte Zimmermann reminds us in Chapter 6 how the Commission links the concept of transitions to the flexibility discourse: 'Flexibility ... is about successful moves ("transitions") during one's life course: from school to work, from one job to another, between unemployment or inactivity and work, and from work to retirement...'. But what have the policies aiming at easing transitions accomplished in fact? Chapters 3 to 5 attempt to answer this question. They focus on the many ways in which transition policies have been implemented (Günther Schmid) and on the assessment of two prominent measures: the reform of placement services (Petra Kaps and Holger Schütz) and working-time savings accounts (Philip Wotschack).

In Chapter 3 Günther Schmid makes a number of concrete suggestions of how transition policies can achieve positive combinations of employment security and operational flexibility within a company. His starting point is the assumption that the increasing diversity of forms of employment leads to greater risk for workers and that different countries engage in different flexicurity practices. If designed well, transition policies ease passages between different positions in the labour market and help to build sustainable careers via 'social bridges' and stepping stones.

Schmid's comments are based on experience with the German model of employment protection and its adaptation to contemporary circumstances and European requirements. The transitional labour markets approach considers job quality and enhancing chances for the acquisition of professional qualifications through training both as central normative goals and as practical proposals. These proposals are meant to combat inequality in a world of work in which professional requirements are increasingly exacting and employment is becoming precarious. If these ideas are applied in evaluating European policies it can be asked what the EES and the European flexicurity policies have done to achieve these goals. The answer has to be precious little, as the increasingly critical studies on the EES are beginning to show.

One of the central objectives of the EES is to enhance the efficiency of public employment services and a crucial indicator used to evaluate national strategies is how quickly the unemployed return to work. The Commission, as in the case of financial matters, is in this context thoroughly convinced by the theories of market efficiency, and supports contracting out of placement services, a policy that has rapidly spread across European countries. Great Britain was the pioneer in establishing 'quasi markets' with their job centres, followed by Germany in 2003 implementing the so-called Hartz reform programme, Italy experimenting with a voucher system[5] and France where public employment placement and unemployment compensation services (UNEDIC) merged in 2008. The aim of all these reforms is to put public placement services in competition with private enterprises which are publicly funded and selected by tender based on cost and performance criteria. The competition is meant to induce greater efficiency, because service vendors are evaluated and risk financial penalties or non-renewal of their contracts if their performance is deemed inadequate. Petra Kaps and Holger Schütz in Chapter 4 present the results of empirical research evaluating the effectiveness of privatising employment services in Germany, and compare these results with those of similar work in other countries. Their criteria are those of transitional markets (some of which are also found in the capabilities approach): individual autonomy, solidarity, effectiveness, efficiency. The research does not confirm the expectations of the advocates of privatisation. Instead, their results confirm fears that competition increases 'selection of the fittest' effects and the pressure to accept the lowest bids; neglects criteria that determine the quality of insertion and that credible management tools are absent; and priority goes to those deemed at the outset to be most employable and that little freedom of choice is left to 'clients'.

In Chapter 5 Philip Wotschack evaluates the use of working time accounts in German companies. This flagship measure of the flexicurity programme allows employees, by accumulating time (overtime, shorter holidays) during their working life, to free up paid working time that can be used for activities that they value: training, parenting of children, volunteer and civic activities. Several different approaches to labour market reform come together in this measure: transitional labour markets, capabilities, organisational approaches to life-long working careers.[6] Ideally working time accounts are personal rights that supplement collective rights and do not replace them. The first step to ensure a real freedom of choice for employees is that they receive income (equivalent to their basic salary) for these periods devoted to other activities.

Wotschak shows convincingly that the idea is a good one, but much remains to be done. There is also disappointment. Since this option became available in 2005 in German companies only a few employees have taken advantage of it. Where accounts were created, it was often at the employer's request to compensate for periods of unemployment or in connection with preparations for retirement. Many difficulties are still to be resolved: portability and preservation of rights when changing employer; protection of accounts against the temptation to use them to bridge periods of 'partial unemployment'; wider availability and true freedom of choice for account holders in how they use their rights; public subsidy to top up the amounts of accumulated resources, in particular for low-income workers. As is often the case (for instance, in ongoing training in companies) those who have the greatest need – those with low wages and/or intermittent jobs – do not benefit from the measure.

From the beginning the flexicurity agenda has been highly ambiguous, oscillating between neoliberal attempts to make the labour market more flexible and a reorientation towards institutional reform focusing on transitions as recommended by the transitional labour markets agenda. Chapters 3 to 5 contain a number of arguments to suggest that the balance has swayed in favour of the neoliberal flexibility agenda. The EES from the outset focused on individual employability and on the speed with which the unemployed return to work, rather than on the vulnerability of jobs to the vagaries of the economy or on the need for companies to prepare their employees for coming changes in work (and hence to invest in their professional development). These choices were made prior to the Luxembourg process and without public debate in Europe. During this period the European Commission funded research and reports on employability conducted mostly by mainstream economists and political inspiration came from, among others, the US-EU Working Group on Employment and Labor-Related Issues that was created in 1996 'to establish cooperation in providing a climate for job growth'. One of the first outgrowths was a symposium on Employment Policy and the Promotion of Employability Security held in Washington DC in May 1997.[7] Its message was rather one-sided, centring on the supply of work from individuals (employability) leaving demand for work to the initiative of companies, framed by a policy of deregulation. Given these ideological inputs it can be concluded that the European Commission has from the beginning of the EES made an unbalanced and instrumentalised use of the transitional labour markets agenda, largely neglecting its critical message and proposals.

Promoting Capabilities

In comparison with the transitional labour market approach the capabilities agenda has not yet truly been taken up at the European level, despite its relevance and proximity to European policies in other areas such as gender equality, life-long learning and social rights. The idea was supported in the 1999 report coordinated by Alain Supiot[8] whose authors endorsed a capabilities development policy and envisioned positive synergies between security and flexibility. However, the fact that it has been confined to poverty and under-development issues has undoubtedly contributed to its poor treatment by the European Commission, in contrast to the ILO, where along with other sources it serves to underpin the Decent Work Agenda. It is also conceivable, paradoxically, that the emphasis on true freedom of choice and action in the capabilities agenda has created a negative aura around this approach, because of its seeming similarity to neoliberal positions, although, among others, it differs radically from and is even diametrically opposed to neoliberal doctrine by its insistence on the conditions that make this freedom effective.

The situation is gradually changing. The misconception regarding the meaning of the capabilities approach is challenged by a number of research programmes on the capabilities approach which are currently developed in several European countries.[9] Chapters 6 to 8 engage with theoretical and practical difficulties of the approach and show the operational richness of the capabilities agenda. The areas addressed include vocational training and professional development in enterprises (Bénédicte Zimmermann), activation policies (Jean-Michel Bonvin) and public and social services (Noel Whiteside).

In Chapter 6 Bénédicte Zimmermann discusses the lack of European law and policy in addressing duties of companies for the professional development of their employees, in particular in relation to improvement of skills and planning of careers. Companies rarely feel pressurised by labour market conditions or by organisational needs to invest in the professional development of their employees and tend to refuse responsibility in this area, preferring to leave it to their employees or the state.[10] In line with Sen and Vygotski, Bénédicte Zimmermann insists that the development of capabilities transcends the world of work and brings work and economic activity back into the full set of each person's activities, framing these activities in the context of human development policy that has at its core true freedom and personal accomplishment.[11] The chapter demonstrates the operational dimensions of such a policy through a discussion of 'employee quality...produced by capabilities made available by the company in the areas of work, training, employee participation and work/life balance'.[12] Security is seen as dependent on acquisition of real freedom of choice in choosing one's work, and more generally in choosing the place that work occupies in one's life. Flexibility is possible on this basis, and a positive loop can be put in place between security and flexibility for both partners in the work relationship: motivation and efficiency on one side, true freedom and potential for accomplishment on the other. There is more at stake here than just the labour market. The obligation to put each individual in a situation of capability leads to another model of economic development. We will come back to this topic at the end of this introduction.

In Chapter 7 Jean-Michel Bonvin addresses a key element of the new European social policy called activation policies. Activation is achieved either through incentives ('making work pay') or through constraint ('workfare' schemes). In times of austerity and reduction of public policies, activation is seen by the European Union and its member states as a cost-effective solution. The chapter reviews through the prism of the capabilities approach a range of activation policies that have been implemented in the European Union. It seeks to define and specify evaluation criteria and methods that could be used to assess existing activation programmes and reform them to move in this direction.

Following Amartya Sen, Bonvin goes beyond short-term economic performance measures alone in defining the criteria for evaluating activation programmes. These criteria should assess the social opportunities created by the programmes and consider how much attention is given to the beneficiaries' participation. They should also look at ways in which the programmes augment political voice and the public debate on the fundamental motives, objectives and methods, thereby fostering public reasoning that is as broad and open as possible. One of the most sensitive issues is the place and role assigned to local actors and agencies. In line with Chapters 3 and 4, Bonvin shows in Chapter 7 the contradictions in which the programmes inspired by New Public Management become entangled when they seek to transfer state responsibilities to the market. Alternative pathways are suggested which include leaving room for local initiatives; preference for a participatory approach by letting some objectives remain undefined by the central authority; modifying evaluation criteria (that today focus on maximising the employment rate and rapidity of return to work) in favour of criteria that give priority to beneficiaries' autonomy, support capacity-building and emphasise a long-term vision over a short-term view. Holding individuals responsible for their employment situation and insisting that they take charge of their own future in the labour market has become the main justification for activation policies. However, exercising responsibility assumes conditions that allow individuals to use this responsibility in ways that respect the motivations and values in which their life and work choices are grounded. A space of genuine freedom and choice must be created for each individual, in other words a 'capacitation' policy must be instituted.

Noel Whiteside demonstrates in Chapter 8 how reflection on historical precedent stimulates fertile thinking about 'situated' action. Assessing today's work in the light of yesterday's experience should be at the heart of public reasoning, and the lessons learned should help decision-makers realise that, today as yesterday, there is no one single path (the market) but several ways forward. No one path is intrinsically better from an economic standpoint. Each one offers possibilities and carries constraints. A lot depends on the scope and quality of the democratic practices that preside over public decisions, on the way in which the issue is framed to make it relevant and the level of collective decision-making at which it is posed.

As Europe becomes more and more engaged in distant macro political governance and member states abdicate their social responsibilities, many questions can be raised about situated public action. By 'situated' public action we mean public action that is carried out by autonomous actors in the field who possess practical knowledge of the situation and who are able to raise issues and pose solutions in ways that are most appropriate for achieving the common good.[13] It is implemented via democratic deliberative processes that follow their own evaluation criteria and methods of amendment. The effectiveness of situated public action (in terms of both economic effectiveness and social justice) depends on choosing the most pertinent level of collective decision-making with respect to a given issue, using the subsidiarity principle in a discerning and flexible way. When engagement takes place at the appropriate level, situated action can develop a collective capacity to address and solve problems, a capacity that is independent of the market and of direct state intervention.

Noel Whiteside shows that at the turn of the last century the major cities of Europe successfully experimented with public services and social policies in this way. The political agendas were not always the same, and the beneficiaries varied, but these achievements have the common characteristic of coordinating social policies (social assistance, unemployment benefits, labour market policies) and public services (transport, electricity, sanitation, urban planning, housing) at the local level. These urban policies remind us that there are pathways other than importing market principles into the sphere of public services. Above all, they were developed by local authorities in the wake of the flagrant failure of market solutions that even the most ardent advocates of market orientations like the city corporation of Birmingham were forced to recognise.

PART II: WHAT FUTURE FOR EUROPEAN EMPLOYMENT POLICY?

A full-scale implementation of the principles for reforming the work and employment market that satisfy the two approaches of transitional labour markets and capabilities requires a profound change of European policies, in particular methods and the ways in which policies are combined. For example, New Public Management governance methods (steering according to performance indicators; competition between public agencies and private companies; privatisation of social services; absence of participation by beneficiaries; denial of real local autonomy) often hinder or contradict the recommendations that stem from these two approaches. New governance techniques are spreading fast and shape not only most European policies but also the content of the 2020 Agenda and, for example, the Competitiveness Pact suggested by France and Germany and attempts to reduce public deficits as a result of member state efforts to rescue the banking industry. Furthermore, citizens increasingly perceive the European Union as a configuration of actors orbiting like satellites in outer space. What is needed is bringing Europe 'back down to Earth' through systematic intervention of their representative bodies at intermediate levels in favour of employment for European citizens. This intervention should be the core of a reformed integrated approach to employment.

The contributions in Chapters 9 to 12 provide the base for this new approach to employment. They offer new typologies of welfare regimes that are able to apprehend national circumstances (Chapter 9); they rehabilitate the role of law as a driving force in Europe through promotion of reflexive law (Chapters 10 and 11); they request other constitutive conventions for the single market (Chapter 12).

European authorities make extensive use of welfare typologies and national models for benchmarking. The practice is inconsistent, one day promoting a national model (for instance, the Danish model taken as the paragon of flexicurity) and the next day preferring competition between national models as a way to select the lowest social bids. Colin Crouch shows in Chapter 9 that welfare typologies, including those based on the welfare models made popular by Esping-Andersen, while not totally use-less, are at best fragile, often fabricated from only a few macro indicators. Esping-Andersen's work is indeed inconclusive. An analysis of the data he conveniently published in his work reveals that they do not support his typology; in particular the group of so-called 'corporatist-continental' countries is in fact a hodgepodge of countries that have nothing in common.[14] Crouch extends this analysis to all the countries in geographical Europe, towards the east (the former USSR and ex-socialist republics) and the south (including Turkey). By also including sectors, paying close attention to services to enterprises and to collective and individual social services that grow in importance in terms of employment, he arrives at an alternative, more realistic cluster of welfare regimes. However, the political or operational relevance of societal typologies can be questioned. For example the alleged superior nature of free-market economies when it comes to innovation and employment can be called into doubt.

All chapters in Part II concur with the observation that social Europe is incomplete and threatened with disintegration under the advancing encroachment of market principles. The importance attached to European social policy and employment law during the Delors Presidency has vanished. Economic freedoms increasingly prevail over national social law, a trend that culminated in new rulings of the Court of Justice of the European Union (CJEU). Furthermore with the increase in soft law European law loses its binding force, and unclear legal terms, for example introduced in framework agreements, leave room for interpretation to member states and to the CJEU that sometimes produce outcomes contrary to the legislators' intentions. In addition countries with large Euro-sceptical populations are increasingly prone to use their right to opt out.

A way ahead for European law lies in reflexive law. A key notion of reflexive law is the ability to understand and make creative use of the limits of regulation. It proposes the magic formula of regulation of self-regulation and corporate social responsibility (CSR) is a prominent example in the field of corporate and labour law. CSR is an instrument that, if not exactly an alternative to law, is at least of a nature to remedy failures or absence of legal standards. Claude Didry reminds us in Chapter 10 that the ILO (Tripartite Declaration, 1977), the UN (Global Compact, late 1990s) and the OECD (1976 Guidelines, revised in 2000) all preceded the European Union on this path. CSR was, in the first instance, aimed at multinational corporations and intended to accompany and 'moralise' the growing wave of job displacement and transfers to countries with weak legislation, low labour costs and working conditions reminiscent of the first industrial revolution. Data compiled by the ILO on codes of conduct reveal that very different motives guided multinational corporations in adopting CSR.

Didry distinguishes four firm strategies in using CSR: an integrative approach that aims at addressing a whole range of actors internal to the company as well as in the business or other environment; a merchant firm approach that focuses on observance of fundamental rights in outsourced manufacturing facilities; a supervisor firm approach that encourages employees to take part in the implementation of CSR; and a knowledge firm approach that pays particular attention to intellectual property and protection of immaterial assets. Didry emphasises a number of weaknesses associated with CSR: codes of conduct do not have the effectiveness of legally binding standards; multinational corporations rarely draw up codes of conduct on their own initiative; strong motivating factors have to be labour unrest and action of movements in civil society that base their campaigns on national and international law or case law. The contribution of CSR to employment policy is marginal; it will never be able to compensate for the absence of political will and sufficient resources to maintain and develop employment throughout the European Union.

The last two contributions, Chapter 11 by Simon Deakin and Ralf Rogowski and Chapter 12 by Robert Salais, share the view that the one-sided turn towards a neoclassical market approach since the Maastricht Treaty of 1992 has broken the previous compact of a balance between the economic and social dimensions of the European project and that pursuing the construction of Europe calls for new foundations which uphold this compromise. The two chapters propose methods that provide new solutions for foundational challenges. They introduce reflexive law as an alternative method of governance and conventions as alternative to the neoclassical theory of the perfect market. Although far from encompassing, these alternative approaches indicate directions and open a discussion of new agendas for both research and action. They are based on a combined capabilities and transitional labour market approach which is suited to address issues that go beyond the labour market.[15]

Simon Deakin and Ralf Rogowski discuss in Chapter 11 how the approach of reflexive labour law can be applied to the study of European law. Reflexive law is both an empirical and a normative project. Deakin and Rogowski discuss the theoretical basis of reflexive law in the concept of autopoietic law developed by Niklas Luhmann and Gunther Teubner and propose as particularly relevant for an analysis of European law the insights of reflexive law on regulation. They detect a number of reflexive processes in European law and suggest a programme to implement the orientations and substance of the capabilities approach through the mechanisms of reflexive law. Although the emphasis is on procedure and the methods of reflexive law do not make assumptions about the content to which they apply, reflexive law is nevertheless compatible with the capabilities approach. If the capabilities approach is chosen as a European orientation, application of the methods of reflexive law would mean that the potential ramifications in terms of justice and democracy that underpin the approach would have to be allowed to freely develop.

European labour law is currently at an important turning point. With the economic crisis hopes of convergence between the economic, political and social structures of European countries have largely vanished. The original project of introducing a floor of rights at the level of the European Union associated with the 1989 Community Charter of the Fundamental Social Rights of Workers has largely been substituted by a new focus on employment and measures to combat unemployment. Article 151 of the current Treaty on the Functioning of the European Union (TFEU) (ex Article 136 TEC) still contains an impressive programme for European labour law.[16] However, implementation of these objectives through legislation, which in any case does not imply homogenisation of national labour laws,[17] has largely come to a standstill. Opponents of European labour law like the United Kingdom insist on using opt-outs. Finally, the CJEU has turned in the notorious *Laval* and *Viking* rulings against social freedom in support of economic freedom of companies. In short, employment protection for workers has been replaced at the European level by measures that favour employment promotion and support for companies in the hope that these measures lead to job creation.

The recent trend of using New Public Management governance mechanisms in employment policies, such as the open method of coordination, should make us particularly wary. This governance mechanism has little in common with reflexive law. These methods use batteries of aggregated indicators (such as the employment rate) to guide action in member states. The quantitative targets to be pursued, and if possible attained, are set by the European Commission on the basis of performance indicators. The Commission uses targets to evaluate national strategies and pit them one against the other. National governments are in fact given incentives, not to attempt to actually apply the underlying goals recommended by European policies, but to seek measures that directly boost their scores on evaluation scales. In addition, goals for social justice and democratic deliberation are shunted aside in favour of a top-down steering process.[18] For those with a bit of memory, this unhappily recalls the techniques employed by Soviet planners, with the results we have seen (perfect on paper but in fact masking a deteriorating situation in reality).

Robert Salais, in Chapter 12, argues that the capabilities approach places these two fundamental principles of justice and democracy at the centre of employment policy and ensures that they are truly taken into account in the economy, in law and in social protection. Justice holds that employment, its content and evolution, favours the development of each individual's capabilities, understood as the space of effective freedom of choice and action. The principle of democracy is to ensure that decisions that have an effect on employment, whatever they may be and at whatever level, must be subject to the procedures of democratic deliberation.

Although not central for the early construction of the European Union, the Treaty of Rome nonetheless introduced a rudimentary social dimension, centred on the principle of equality of treatment between men and women. What is at work here is a principle of justice, and not a question of distortion of competition. Furthermore this principle can be interpreted as seeking to establish equality of capabilities between men and women. Recognition of the need for democratic deliberation, both inside and outside of companies, on economic decisions affecting employment was introduced into the European debate in the 1970s, with the prospect of European works councils (leading to a directive more than 30 years down the line).[19] The outline of a principle of democracy glimpsed here should be brought in full into the debate in Europe.

What is the main obstacle blocking the way forward to implementation of these principles of justice and democracy? It is less an absence of political determination than poor choices in terms of constitutive market conventions, with effects that have accumulated over the course of time. In Chapter 12 'market convention' is defined as the interpretative framework that is applied to the functioning of actual markets and that serves as the basis for economic and social legislation, and subsequently for jurisprudence. The European Union never put the principles of justice and democracy high on the agenda in the construction of Europe, neither at the beginning in the 1950s nor in the 1980s with the institution of the single market. The ordo-liberal market convention kept questions of social justice at the national level and held that the creation of an efficient economic order did not require democratic legitimacy. By contrast, this convention was much more favourable to efficient economic integration of growth and employment than was the neoclassical convention of the perfect market introduced by the Single European Act and the Maastricht Treaty. For, unlike the neoclassical convention, ordo-liberalism (particularly at the time of its origin) does not seek to render the economy homogenous by considering that diversity and the quest for advantages in terms of quality and innovation, and not just price advantage, are obstacles to competition (on the contrary they are a driving force in the economy). The jurisprudence of the European Court of Justice since 2000 demonstrates the harmfulness of this neoclassical market convention. It deems national law and social protection systems to be obstacles to economic freedom, and as such to be eliminated, or at the very least deprived of their sustenance. From indifference at the European level we now encounter hostility to the principles of justice and democracy. The tendency is to see national sovereignty as an obstacle to European economic integration. To recreate a positive feedback loop between the economic and social spheres, each benefiting the other, and thus contribute to the progression of the European project, Chapter 12 proposes that the European Union undertakes to find a synthesis between ordo-liberalism (economic efficiency) and the capabilities approach (justice and democracy). In sum the European Union should return to its original sources, updated and inspired by a vision of the future. This would involve engaging in a wide-ranging and profound revision of the interpretation of fundamental economic freedoms, linked to an enrichment of the social sections of the Treaty, through integration of the capabilities development objective, so that economic freedoms and capabilities for all become mutually reinforcing. This would ensure a solid political status for the Charter of Fundamental Rights and would spearhead the move to adopt binding requirements for justice and democracy within the European Union.

TOWARDS AN INTEGRATED AND SITUATED APPROACH TO EMPLOYMENT

We end this introduction by expressing our collective astonishment at the inaction of the political classes, not least the European Commission, in the face of the financial crisis of 2008. The collapse of the banks and their subsequent bailout has transformed private into public debt. Were the catastrophe to be repeated (and, at the time of writing there is no reason why it should not) these vast pre-existing public debts would mean that, far from being too big to fail, some banks could be too big to rescue. In the meantime, the financial sector has little incentive to resist the more problematic and risky transactions that caused the problem in the first place, as taxpayers underwrite any unforeseen consequences.

Public debt has generated unprecedented cuts in public expenditure, creating widespread redundancy in all sectors of employment. Subsequent crises in the Eurozone have fostered further retrenchment, reducing the security and incomes of current and future working generations for decades to come. No European authority has put forward any new initiatives with which to tackle this emergency – or to prevent its recurrence. Instead we are offered more of the same. Recent EC proposals to reform economic governance to restore confidence in the financial system demand yet further public sector retrenchment, more privatisation of services, ever less support or protection for those seeking work or in precarious jobs. Europe's employment strategies and their targets for 2020 – their training requirements and other employment integration mechanisms – lie stranded in the backwaters of Europe's political agenda. The cure for a crisis created by the market apparently lies in a further extension of market disciplines and market mechanisms.

The ever-increasing belief in the merits of markets has been accompanied by growing faith in corporate management strategies in recent years; this has eaten into the heart of the European project. New Public Management (NPM) and its associated systems have been derived from business practices designed to meet short-term targets in order to secure shareholder value and, with this, the corporate bonus for successful executives. This does not represent a sound blueprint to secure Europe's future. The corporate executive aims at short-term success to win promotion to a higher position elsewhere; the shareholder is free to withdraw investment and the worker to change job, but the taxpayer cannot refuse to pay her taxes, nor can the citizen easily change her domicile. Devoid of any long-term objective or vision, NPM's top-down approach is necessarily autocratic and oligarchic. It understands citizens as customers, consumers or clients – not political beings capable of participating in democratic deliberation about how Europe can or should develop. The European Commission is not a management board and cannot run Europe's affairs as if it were one.

The tension between state sovereignty (reflecting the sovereignty of the citizenry) and what is seen as the growing encroachment of the EU's managerial authority lies at the heart of the problems with securing political acceptance of the EU in the member states. The economic crisis has revealed this contradiction. The legitimacy of the continual corrosion of state prerogatives is increasingly called into question, notably in respect to its democratic justification (which is indeed very weak). The major and almost sole instrument of this advance – the extension of economic freedoms in a perfect market to all domains of public action – has seriously disturbed Europe's construction, weakening it economically as well as politically and socially.[20] This encroachment tends to be seen as a threat. It increasingly rules out any positive cooperation between member states, as well as between European authorities and member states. The ruling of the German Federal Constitutional Court on 30 June 2009 on the constitutionality of the Lisbon Treaty addresses the problem head on. It states forcefully the limits of the European project: 'If in the framework of the evolution of European integration, a disproportion were to appear between the nature and scope of sovereign rights on the one hand, and the degree of democratic legitimacy on the other hand, it would be incumbent on Germany to change this situation and as a last recourse refuse to continue to participate in the European Union.'[21]

The purpose of our book is to demonstrate how successful integration of working people into viable and meaningful working lives requires proper co-ordination – real public action and clear pathways – if it is to be effective. The continuing policy freefall towards preference for markets above all else fosters general austerity programmes, increasingly transfers social protection (notably pensions) to commercial agencies and weakens the authority of public actors. In other words, it fractures social and economic development. These changes, to a greater or lesser extent, are provoking resistance in the vast majority of European countries. As like causes produce like effects, Europe is purely and simply facing a threat of economic, social and political decline. The reawakening of the European project, if not its very reconstruction, has to be addressed now. This reawakening is not going to come from either the Commission or from the European Central Bank in their current composition and orientation.[22] It is up to researchers and actors in the civil, economic and social spheres to take responsibility for opening up new paths and publicising them so that fellow citizens can appropriate them.

More specific commitments are beyond the scope of this book; here the aim is to show that other paths are possible, first and foremost to make readers aware of the urgent need to shake off the drowsiness induced by dogmatic thinking and to abandon the well-trodden route that is leading us nowhere. It is not as difficult as one might think to achieve this awakening. Our collective work enables us to go a bit further, because it makes us aware that a head-on contradiction is developing between two principles of action within the European Union.

The first principle, dominant at present and outlined above, is present in the ongoing crisis. It is reflected in the obstinate recourse to methods of governance that are increasingly disconnected from social reality. These refuse to acknowledge the impact that the financial crisis and the ways it has been handled have had on the degradation of working and living conditions experienced by Europe's citizens. The second principle stems from a diametrically opposite system of evaluation, to create an integrated approach to employment founded on entirely new assumptions compared to current policy. The effectiveness of a policy is evaluated not on the basis of abstract aggregated indicators defined at the European level, but on the basis of observation of its concrete effects on the life and work trajectories of each individual. Does the policy put the individual in a situation of capability? In other words, does this policy improve or degrade individual and collective itineraries, in terms of realising desired accomplishments and aspirations to participate in public affairs? How should current policies be modified, and using what methods? The idea is not to transfer responsibility for the vagaries of economic and social circumstances to individuals, who must then struggle along by whatever means they can in a battle of all against all. Placing people in situations of capability implies a profound change in the criteria and implementation of public policies, whether with respect to individuals, employment and enterprises, the economy or society. This also involves finding new dynamics for the development of the European project. Let us look briefly at this scenario and its step-by-step progression towards a general policy.

Let us start with people who are out of work. Currently, as attested in their practices, the agencies that are active in the labour market, whether in social assistance, placement or training, seek above all to attain quantitative performance targets that are constantly being modified or raised to higher levels, in keeping with NPM practices. Consequently an unemployed person must contribute to meeting a target: she must accept whatever job is offered or at the very least be removed from the claimant count (disqualified because she has a live-in lover, or misses an appointment with the agency concerned). The more costly the assistance claimed, the more severe her reception becomes. This goes hand in hand with the abandonment of job quality objectives, and more broadly of the goal of full employment. Using a contrasting approach, the main objective of these agencies should be to make each jobseeker capable of long-term placement in work. Attention should focus closely on the individual, and evaluation must consider her aspirations. This supposes entirely new management rules, a genuine dialogue between the jobseeker and the agency, more substantial and better calibrated resources.

But what is the point if there are no jobs or only poor ones? To create good jobs companies must take the potential of their employees and their local environment into consideration when developing their economic strategies. Their internal organisation should go to great lengths to give all employees a job and work situation that fosters progress in capabilities, participation and freedom of choice. In consequence, companies will gain in quality, motivation and efficiency. Economic choices must look to the future, in terms of sectors, products and services, knowledge and know-how. How can this be achieved if the member states and the European Union do nothing to oppose job displacement, and offer no policy measures in favour of industry and innovation to support and develop the economic foundations of Europe? Work groups and communities at different levels and with different competencies must have the rights, resources and means for intervention that enable them to influence corporate decision-making. There is no lack of money for sufficient employment (given the rate at which currency is produced) but it must be put into productive investment in Europe, not into speculation on stock markets. It must be devoted to renewal of traditional activities and to new activities: to promote a more environmentally sustainable society, for example. Thus a simple but fundamental requirement that public policy at all levels should enhance capabilities would lead, step by step to a new model of economic, social and political development.

This basis for evaluation works just as well as the other model. But it would be derived through different instruments, namely a social survey in which the various groups involved should be invited to participate, at different levels of aggregation, to elaborate the enquiry and interpret its results. In some senses, this offers a framework for assessing social well-being and happiness, recently a pre-occupation among politicians who have discovered that simple wealth does not achieve this objective. This second principle of action underlies the proposals elaborated in the chapters of this book. It accommodates the expectations of the beneficiaries of the measures studied and of the personnel in the institutions that implement them. Its implementation is supported by deliberative democracy at all levels that extends to the process of apprehending what collective problems need to be resolved and who should be charged with their resolution. Noel Whiteside reminds us how, at the end of the nineteenth century, this multi-faceted political problem was tackled by European metropolitan elites – coming to grips with social reality, reaching agreement on the issues, discovering appropriate ways to treat them, implementing solutions, a set of problems the author summarises in the concept of an informational basis for judgement in justice, borrowed from Amartya Sen.

The crisis has made the contradiction between the two modes of policy action and evaluation outlined above more visible, one abstract and disembodied, the other situated and democratic. The widening gap between these two modes can only augment collective awareness of the tensions they generate. The distant governance that is light-years away from people's urgent needs for social protection and employment is a source of incomprehension and growing hostility to European authorities and national governments alike.

Making situated evaluation an absolute priority does not mean that public actors must disappear and be replaced by self-assessment carried out by the actors themselves in the absence of guidelines or benchmarks. On the contrary, it means first and foremost that all responsibility for decisions affecting employment will be transferred to the level that is closest to the actual economic and social situations where the future of employment hangs in the balance. This will have a positive effect on the outcome of this action. For demands for employment will be more clearly heard. More importantly, local deliberation allows decision-making to be informed on all sides: people become better acquainted with constraints and feasible options; methods will be decided with total autonomy by actors at all levels;

stakeholders will be more easily and more fully included in deliberative procedures. Depending on circumstances the proper echelon may be the company, the territory, the corporate group, the economic sector. This same downward movement towards actors best acquainted with a given situation inspires the suggestion to adopt the techniques of reflexive law in European law.

Giving priority to situated evaluation entails a true commitment to responsibility at central level. Far from disengaging itself, the central authority must take the initiative to define major orientations, to assign effective rights of deliberation to actors at intermediate levels, to make sufficient resources available to support effective use of these rights. The European Union has more techniques available to achieve these goals than one might think. If the political philosophy of subsidiarity were taken seriously, and not reduced to a bureaucratic refinement, we would see that this principle encompasses all that is needed to implement situated evaluation based on needs and legitimate claims at the levels at which they are expressed.

Despite appearances, apparent unanimity in favour of maintaining the current course can unravel at the European level. A conflict focusing on political and democratic legitimacy is developing between three bodies of opinion: the Commission and the European Central Bank (ECB) on one side, the European Council and its Presidency on another and lastly the European Parliament. Since Maastricht the Commission and the ECB have been primarily responsible for the drift towards abstract, distant and quantitative methods of governance: seeing in these methods a way to compensate for their lack of democratic legitimacy. The political failure of these methods, if it is confirmed, spells defeat for the Commission and the ECB. The return to an intergovernmental mode, visible in the increasing weight carried by the European Council, is a return to haggling between national interests and allows certain countries to mark their Euro-scepticism. But at the same time it testifies to the renewed attention, although still inadequate, that is now being paid to economic and social reality on the ground, expressed at national level. As for the European Parliament, it could, as is in its interest, bolster the legitimacy bequeathed to it by the direct democratic process (legitimacy contested by the European Council which retains an indirect and fuzzy claim) by acting as a spokesperson for the expectations of European citizens on the issues of employment and social protection. From the complex interplay between these institutions, from the pressure of reality and of Europe's citizens may emerge a situation that is more open and propitious for the new ideas espoused in this book.

NOTES

1. See Rogowski, 2008.
2. Jørgensen and Madsen, 2007, and Burroni and Keune, 2011.
3. In his 1998 seminal WZB working paper, Günther Schmid advocated a new policy of full employment which goes beyond traditional labour market policy that idealises permanent dependent full-time employment and integrates various types of employment and social inclusion (Schmid, 1998). The capabilities approach advocated by Robert Salais constitutes, for the most part, the subject matter of Chapter 7 of the Supiot report, entitled 'Law and economic performance' (Supiot, 2001 [1999]). Salais' presentation was the first appearance of the concept of capabilities in the European debate.
4. Rogowski, 2008. See also Gazier, 2003 and Barbier, 2008.
5. See De Leonardis, 2009.
6. For example, Anxo and Boulin, 2006. The Supiot report (Supiot 2001 [1999]) takes these time accounts as an example of a broader move to social drawing rights.
7. This group was the first initiative of the New Trans-Atlantic Agenda (NTA), signed in December 1995 between the President of the United States, the Prime Minister of Spain in his capacity as European Council President and the European Commission President. See the document 'History of the US-EU Working Group on Employment and Labor-Related Issues 1996–2008', available at www.dol.gov/ilab/programs/oir/PDF/2008EU-History.pdf (accessed 15 August 2011).
8. Supiot, 2001 [1999].
9. A number of research centres are engaged in applying the capabilities approach to European policies. These include the Bielefeld Centre for Education and Capability Research (University of Bielefeld, Germany); Centre for Business Research (University of Cambridge, UK); Centre de Recherches sur l'Emploi et les Qualifications (CEREQ, France); Centre de Recherches Interdisciplinaires sur l'Allemagne (CRIA, EHESS, France); CriDIS (University of Louvain-la-Neuve, Belgium); Centre 'Institutions et Dynamiques Historiques de l'Economie' (IDHE, CNRS, France); Soziologisches Forschungsinstitut Göttingen (SOFI, University of Göttingen); and the research team led by Jean-Michel Bonvin at the University of Lausanne (Switzerland).
10. A point that is also emphasised by Philip Wotschack in Chapter 5.
11. See also Chatel, 2001.
12. A detailed discussion of 'employee quality' can be found in Chapter 6 by Zimmermann.
13. See for details Salais and Storper, 1993, part IV.
14. Salais, 2005.
15. Chapter 12 makes the proposal that the transitional labour markets approach could be integrated into the capabilities approach, the first one moving focus from employability to capability, the second one adopting an expanded approach including transitions.
16. *Article 151 TFEU* (ex Article 136 TEC): The Union and the Member States, having in mind fundamental social rights such as those set out in the European Social Charter signed at Turin on 18 October 1961 and in the 1989 Community Charter of the Fundamental Social Rights of Workers, shall have as their objectives the promotion of employment, improved living and working conditions, so as to make possible their harmonisation while the improvement is being maintained, proper social protection, dialogue between management and labour, the development of human resources with a view to lasting high employment and the combating of exclusion.
17. See Syrpis, 2007.
18. For a critical analysis of the open method of coordination as applied to the European Employment Strategy, Salais, 2006.
19. Council Directive 94/45/EC of 22 September 1994 on the establishment of a European Works Council; Directive 2002/14/EC of the European Parliament and of the Council of 11 March 2002 establishing a general framework for informing and consulting employees in the European Community.

20. For suggestions of a new approach in economic governance see Jabko, 2011.
21. BVerfG, 2 BvE 2/08 vom 30.6.2009, Absatz-Nr. 264; BVerfGE 123, 267 (381 f.).
22. The term 'reawakening' is borrowed from Alain Supiot, 2010, 'Réveiller l'Europe', *Lecture introductive*, final conference, 'Remettre l'Etat dans le jeu? Promouvoir le développement des capacités pour tous en Europe', CAPRIGHT, Nantes, 2–3 December 2010.

BIBLIOGRAPHY

Anxo, D. and J.-Y. Boulin (2006), 'The Organisation of Time over the Life Course', *European Societies*, **8**(2), 319–334.

Barbier, J.-C. (2008), *La longue marche vers l'Europe sociale*, Paris: Presses Universitaires de France (PUF).

Burroni, L. and M. Keune (2011), 'Flexicurity: A conceptual critique', *European Journal of Industrial Relations*, **17**(1), 75–91.

Chatel, E. (2001), *Comment évaluer l'éducation? Pour une théorie sociale de l'action éducative*, Neuchatel: Delachaux and Niestlé.

De Leonardis, O. (2009), 'Organization matters. Contracting for Service Provision and Civicness', in T. Brandsen, P. Dekker and A. Evers (eds), *Civicness in the governance and delivery of social services,* Baden-Baden: Nomos, pp.125–152.

Gazier, B. (2003), *Tous 'Sublimes' – Vers un nouveau plein-emploi*, Paris: Flammarion.

Jabko, N. (2011), 'Which Economic Governance for the European Union? Facing up to the Problem of Divided Sovereignty', Report No. 2 March 2011 of the Swedish Institute for European Policy Studies, Stockholm: Swedish Institute for European Policy Studies, available at http://www.sieps.se/sites/default/files/2011_2_0.pdf (accessed 15 August 2011).

Jørgensen, H. and P.K. Madsen (eds) (2007), *Flexicurity and Beyond. Finding a new agenda for the European Social Model,* Copenhagen: DJØF Publishing.

Rogowski, R. (2008), 'The European Social Model and Law and Policy of Transitional Labour Markets in the European Union', in R. Rogowski (ed.) *The European Social Model and Transitional Labour Markets: Law and Policy*, Aldershot: Ashgate, pp.9–28.

Salais, R. (2005), 'Décrire et évaluer la pluralité des modèles sociaux en Europe', in E. Chatel, T. Kirat and R. Salais (eds), *L'action publique et ses dispositifs*, Paris: L'Harmattan, pp.163–188.

Salais, R. (2006), 'Reforming the European Social Model and the politics of indicators', in M. Jepsen and A. Serrano Pascual (eds), *Unwrapping the European Social Model*, Bristol: Policy Press, pp.189–212.

Salais, R. and M. Storper (1993), *Les mondes de production. Enquête sur l'identité économique de la France*, Paris: Editions de l'Ecole des Hautes Etudes en Sciences Sociales.

Schmid, G. (1998), Transitional Labour Markets: A New European Employment Strategy, *WZB Discussion Paper*, 98-206, available at: http://bibliothek.wzb.eu/pdf/1998/i98-206.pdf (accessed 15 August 2011).

Sen, A. (1999), *Development as Freedom*, Oxford: Oxford University Press.

Sen, A. (2009), *The Idea of Justice*, London: Allen Lane.

Supiot, A. (ed.) (2001), *Beyond Employment. Changes in Work and the Future of Labour Law in Europe*, Oxford: Oxford University Press (original version in

French in 1999: *Au-delà de l'emploi. Transformations du travail et devenir du droit du travail en Europe*, Rapport pour la Commission Européenne (dir.), Paris: Flammarion).

Syrpis, P. (2007), *EU Intervention in Domestic Labour Law*, Oxford: Oxford University Press.

Vygotski, L. (1985 [1934]), *Pensée et langage*, trans. F. Sève, Paris: Messidor.

PART I

Securing transitions and promoting capabilities

Section 1.1

Securing Transitions through Flexicurity Policies, Placement Services and
Working-time Accounts

2. Social and labour market reforms: four agendas

Peter Auer and Bernard Gazier

INTRODUCTION

The number of declarations, communications and decisions of the EU Commission, and of numerous reports and articles on flexicurity in Europe, bears witness to the success of this concept in European employment policy debates. Even in the USA the (Danish) model was enthusiastically discussed by prominent commentators and academics such as Robert Kuttner and Dani Rodrik. The concept is now as well known in other parts of the world as in Europe and flexicurity seminars have taken place in such diverse countries as Argentina, Australia, China, India and Vietnam. Indeed, it becomes increasingly difficult to count the number of papers and events related to this buzzword. Furthermore and most importantly, flexicurity is nowadays institutionalised in the EU in which a proportion of the budget of structural funds is devoted to it and where this concept has become the overriding guideline for labour market reform.

There are remarkably few critical comments. Employers seem to support it. However, both from academia and from the unions, there emerge critical voices. For example, the Swedish labour economist Lars Calmfors criticises the fact that important trade-offs are 'swept under the carpet' in an illusion of a win-win situation. He underlines the danger 'that the practice of trying to subsume a number of different policy approaches under the common heading of flexicurity leads to less clarity regarding the policy options' (Calmfors, 2007, p.1).

Indeed, flexicurity as a concept is vague. It suggests something that is always desirable (achieving a flexible and secure state of the economy and the society) without indicating how to deal with concrete problems that need to be addressed. Nevertheless, numerous attempts have been made at clarifying the various interpretations, meanings and uses of the term (e.g. Jørgensen and Madsen, 2007; Wilthagen, 2007; Schmid, 2008). The last words in terms of definition of the concept are the eight 'common principles of flexicurity' that the Lisbon ministerial council adopted in 2007 (European Commission, 2007a).[1]

The chapter, contrary to the official view of the Commission, considers flexicurity as only one of several policy agendas which are currently under discussion, and among which it is situated. This departure point has two main advantages. First it intends to clarify the very nature of the flexicurity approach, which is neither a fully integrated theoretical perspective nor a set of independent policy prescriptions; second, it reintegrates it into a wider policy debate, dominated for some time by the pressures in favour of flexibility, and the reactions they trigger or foster.

The argument will be organised as follows: the first section will deal with methodological considerations; the second section will present in a relatively homogenised way the contents and rationales of four policy agendas, one of them being flexicurity. The third section discusses the results of these agendas, thereby using a cluster analysis of 15 European countries' performances regarding work and social indicators. Such an analysis is intended to shed some light on the place and meaning of flexicurity compared to other rival or convergent policy perspectives.

SOCIAL AND LABOUR MARKET REFORMS: FOCUSING ON POLICY AGENDAS

A regional bloc like the EU, consisting of countries that are jealous of their prerogatives and right to sovereignty, has to observe the subsidiarity principle and to rely on soft laws. This is particularly true for the areas of social, employment and labour market policies and their reforms.[2] It is in this context that 'soft' steering devices like the 'open method of coordination' and 'bottom-up' policy implementation (with an active role played by national/local actors at every level of responsibility) are a politically feasible approach for country-specific policies. Another common feature, that applies also to international organisations that often have virtually no grip on their member countries other than peer pressure (except in areas where binding minimum rules and follow-up are agreed upon) is to develop policy agendas and strategies. They are usually not binding but may achieve some convergence in policies by setting targets, developing guidelines and recommendations and proceed also by 'do-as-your-neighbour-does' policies, peer pressure and incentives. While the European Employment Strategy is the most developed of these strategies, similar strategies have been developed by other international organisations such as the OECD jobs strategy (1994, reassessed in 2006) or the decent work agenda of the ILO of 1999, which has also an employment strategy arm, the global employment agenda (GEA).

These strategies go beyond a simple collection of proposed measures with a timetable (a 'plan'), and are tantamount to proposing an organised set of reasons and measurements underlying several measures and 'plans'; they are not directly deduced from one precise and unique theoretical perspective, nor simply emanating from practice and experience. Policy agendas may be considered as an *intermediate* body of more or less strictly interrelated arguments indicating and illustrating one broad policy direction and classifying priorities accordingly, in a more or less strict hierarchical order.

Defining Policy Agendas as Cognitive and Normative Frameworks

In our view, a set of policy perspectives can become a policy agenda if three conditions are met:

1. It has managed to develop three dimensions: ends, means, and indicators;
2. It has managed to integrate them in a relatively autonomous way;
3. It has managed to develop arguments and indicators that provide evidence for favouring a particular policy option.

Policy agendas as they appear nowadays can be usefully compared with the concept of 'systems of references' (in French: 'référentiel') used by some political scientists (Jobert and Muller, 1987; Muller, 2005). In initial formulations, the system of reference has two different meanings. First, the 'global system of references' is a dominant world view; second, 'normative' or 'sectoral systems' of references are a set of representations and principles of action that provide an overall orientation for a given economic or social sector. Public policies are then understood as the result of an adjustment process of the normative/sectoral systems of references to the global one. In more recent elaborations (Muller, 2005), 'systems of reference' comprise values, norms and causal relationships that actors adopt when they confront their interests. They are normative and cognitive frameworks which, once adopted, seem evident to concerned actors. This conception however seems to put a very strong emphasis on the unconscious or preconscious dimension of representations and policy options and may sound over-deterministic.

Policy agendas may be seen as deliberate interventions aimed at transforming existing 'systems of references' by giving them a new direction.

They have much in common with 'normative/sectoral systems of references': they intend to provide a form of policy evidence through concepts, values and evaluations. But there are some differences: as we have seen they are more or less deliberate, emanating from pronouncements of experts and policymakers and are then refined in debates; they appear in a pluralistic and less determinate context, which implies that they are diverse and also competing with each other. Compared with 'systems of references', policy agendas are often more explicit in giving reasons and providing measurements for policy change. Flexicurity is a good example that illustrates the complexities of references.

Diversity of Political Agendas

Comparing four different policy agendas allows taking into account the set of constraints and power relationships underlying policy options, while escaping from an over-deterministic vision, and putting the emphasis on possible stabilities and changes in the realm of policy prescription. This plurality of perspectives and proposals may be especially useful in the case of flexicurity and its surprising success.

One may identify two main sources of diversity of political agendas: the first is their external connection to more global representations, and in particular their hierarchical position within them; the second is their internal consistency and degree of homogeneity.

External Consistency: Flexicurity in the Strategies of the ILO and the EU Commission

At what level does an agenda appear? We take the example of the place taken by flexicurity in two wider policy approaches, developed by the European Union and the ILO.

As a concept that includes all four objectives of the 'decent work' agenda (workers' rights, employment, social protection and the social dialogue) flexicurity is on the one hand in line with 'decent work', but seems sometimes to be as encompassing as 'decent work'. However, a short comparison with prevailing EU strategies shows that while it contributes to achieving 'decent work' (or in the case of the EU, concretising the Lisbon agenda), it is hierarchically placed well below the overall 'decent work' agenda and is part of the 'global employment agenda' (see Figure 2.1) but relates more to the other strategic objectives of 'decent work'.

Indeed, 'decent work' is the overall strategy for improving workers' rights, employment and working conditions in the world. The ILO's objective today is to 'promote opportunities for women and men to obtain

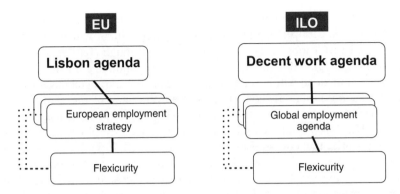

Figure 2.1 The connection between flexicurity and wider policy agendas in the EU and the ILO

decent and productive work, in conditions of freedom, equity, security and human dignity' (ILO, 1999) and this objective is to be achieved through four strategic objectives: international labour standards, employment, social protection and social dialogue.

The overall strategy of the European Union is associated with the EU's Lisbon agenda, which is a broad strategy with the ambitious objective to transform Europe into 'the most productive knowledge economy in the world by 2010' and includes all economic and social policies that might contribute to this aim.

There are indeed many differences between the two overall strategies, decent work and the Lisbon agenda, the most important being that the EU includes as principal part a macroeconomic strategy for its 27 member states, which aims at some economic (and social) convergence. Convergence pressures are stronger in the economic field (e.g. in monetary and fiscal policy, not least through a monetary union with a central bank that covers part of the union). It has economic targets and for the observance of these, a potential for sanctions. It has also some convergence instruments at its disposal, such as the structural funds.

This economic dimension is absent at the ILO. The overall integration of economic and social policies that the ILO supports at the national level is achieved at the multilateral level by all agencies (and their coordination) in the multilateral system, including the Bretton Woods institutions.

This of course is an important difference. The EU supports decent work as one of its goals and in the 27 European Union countries (but also beyond as can be seen in the development aid activities of the EU); the implementation of the Lisbon agenda will contribute to the implementation of the decent work goal.

There is similarity between some pillars of the Lisbon strategy, in particular the European employment strategy, the aim of which is to create more and better jobs in the EU and proceeds through eight employment guidelines integrated with 18 micro and macroeconomic guidelines. Flexicurity is embedded within the EES as witnessed by employment Guideline 21[3] and should therefore contribute to the overall aim of more and better jobs, which in turn contributes to the overall goals of the Lisbon agenda.

The ILO has a similar employment strategy in the employment pillar of decent work, the Global Employment Agenda, adopted by the ILO's governing body in 2003, which integrates flexicurity as one of its tools under core element 7 (active labour market policies) and also under the social protection chapter. Flexicurity is contributing to the aims of the GEA, of creating more and better jobs, which is a necessary element of decent work.

Seen from the hierarchy of strategies, flexicurity is thus placed at about the same level, namely as one policy area in the employment strategies that both organisations pursue as part of their larger agendas. And it is a means rather than an end, the end being the results of the overall strategies: for Lisbon the realisation of making the EU 'the most dynamic and competitive knowledge-based economy in the world capable of sustainable economic growth with more and better jobs and greater social cohesion, and respect for the environment by 2010' and for decent work: a maximum number of people should find 'sustainable opportunities for decent work'.

While flexicurity is part of the global employment agenda, it is linked in many ways to the ILO's four other strategic objectives as well. In particular, social protection and the social dialogue,[4] as well as norms and standards. This overlap also holds true for the EU.[5] There is another important difference for the sustainability of strategies: the EU has, contrary to the ILO, a method of follow-up (the open method of coordination with targets, guidelines, benchmarks, national reform plans, joint Lisbon reports, recommendations, peer reviews etc.). While the method can be considered 'soft' with no potential for sanction, and is based on goodwill and the effects of 'peer country pressure', the ILO's GEA so far has not developed any substantial follow-up instruments other than periodical updates presented in the Employment and Social Policy committee of its governing body.

Internal Consistency

An obvious second source of diversity for political agendas is of course their content and their possible internal heterogeneity. As we already observed, they are not integrated theories but more or less complex sets of arguments, sometimes grounded on several theories. They may appear at quite different levels of sophistication, of elaboration, and exhibit more or less internal consistency. This line of analysis leads us to the next section.

THE CONTENT OF FOUR AGENDAS

We select four agendas for a closer examination: Flexibility, Flexicurity, Transitional Labour Markets and Capabilities. Let us consider their content and put the emphasis on commonalities and differences.

All these are 'reform agendas', or at least reform proposals. They present policies which are combined in wider programmes that address major labour market challenges both at the macro and the micro level. They have as objectives to cure labour markets from 'ills' like unemployment, low employment rates, low pay, inequality; ills, which are all thought to be amplified, if not caused by, globalisation, technological change and other factors. The only 'reform agenda' that does not per se aim at better labour market functioning is capabilities. This is an important difference which certainly impacts on any comparison between these different approaches. In the following, we focus first on priorities and their justifications, then their practical meaning in terms of existing national experiences or references. We leave aside temporarily the question of indicators (see below).

Flexibility

Neo-liberalism is acknowledged by many as the dominant[6] reform agenda, which proposes administering strong doses of flexibility as a cure. The claim that in a period when all other markets (goods, services and financial) are increasingly liberalised, labour markets cannot remain regulated as changes in the other three spill over to them, has some logic. However, it ignores that a particular 'good or service' is exchanged on labour markets, which cannot be isolated from the individuals that offer their services for money on which their and often also their families' livelihood and psychological, social and economic well being is dependent.[7] For this reform stream, markets (workers) have to adapt and the preferred adaptation channel in the absence of total wage flexibility is (external numerical) mobility of workers and smooth workers' reallocation, preferably unhindered by government intervention.

The US labour market seems still to hold as a model for this (see the 2003 IMF world economic outlook, which predicts gains in growth and employment and decreases in unemployment were Europe to adopt the US type of low level of labour market regulations). A low level of regulation is also a condition for being well ranked on the World Bank's doing business indicators (World Bank, 2003 to present). Of particular concern here is the employing workers indicator (EWI), a set of regulations concerning flexibility/rigidity in terms of working hours and hiring and firing. These indicators (and the ranking) very strongly suggest that regulations of the labour market are a pure cost to doing business.[8] Considering ranking of countries in the EWI, the old USA flexibility/Europe sclerosis debate has resurfaced. For example Germany and France are ranked 137 and 144, while the US comes in rank 1.[9]

The flexibility reform agenda is in the realm of commodification (Esping Andersen, 1990) treating exchanges on the labour market just as any other exchange of goods. It is not particularly concerned with employment security and welfare (or decent work) or any (wage) distribution policies as they would distort the market. The proponents of the 'flexibility' doctrine are not necessarily proponents of an anti-worker attitude (but anti-union, certainly) as in their equations more flexibility equals increased welfare of workers: benefits will simply trickle down from improved economic and labour market performance due to enhanced adjustment capacities of labour markets. Their approach can be captured by the formula 'Easier firing brings about easier hiring', which enhances chances of job creation and diminishes unemployment. The market will bring the best of all worlds, whereas interventions to correct market failures will not work and thus there is little space for polity, policy and ethics. Surely this picture is a caricature of the complexities of thoughts and methods that this stream has developed, but these basic premises capture the core of the flexibility approach.

Flexicurity

A second labour market reform agenda is flexicurity, born as an alternative concept to 'flexibility only'. This buzzword seems for the time being to have won the politico-academic debate on how to organise (or only to coin?) the new securities that come together with an increasingly unstable labour market in Europe. Here from the start there is a concern that flexibility could undermine security if institutions are not made compatible with changes in the labour market. Changes towards increased flexibility, which are either 'deliberately sought'[10] or already existing,[11] should be compensated or accompanied by better (new or reformed) security devices inside and outside firms. The concrete forms of institutions providing external numerical flexibility is subject to debate but there is a certain agreement that unemployment benefit schemes, education and training, work and training schemes, job counselling and workers' accompaniment and place-ment, workers reallocation in restructuring situations, etc. are the core providers of this external form of security. The concept also gives a large place to negotiations between the social partners as the main avenue to manage change.

As Gazier (2008) observes, there are more or less encompassing concepts of flexicurity. Sometimes the concept is of 'reduced form' comprising a 'golden triangle' of external adjustment between (loose) employment pro-tection, generous unemployment benefits and active labour market policies, whose congruence is negotiated by the social partners (e.g. the Danish model as in Madsen, 2003). Sometimes it includes a whole array of institutions and social rights as in the recently developed concept of 'common principles of flexicurity' of the EU Commission (European Commission, 2007a). The common principles comprise new contractual arrangements, active labour market policies, life long learning and a mod-ern social protection system (which in itself is composed of an array of policies) and the preferred way to arrive at positive and congruent policy combinations and outcomes is the social dialogue between the social partners. It includes internal and external flexibility, insiders and outsiders, and should be gender sensitive and cost effective.

Ethically, allowing for adjustment, while giving security to workers is interpreted as a win-win game, a sort of 'Pareto-optimal' and even 'Rawls-optimal' setting of labour market institutions.[12] Another important ethical dimension consists of rights and duties and therefore individual responsi-bility (Dworkin, 2000). Economics needs politics for equitable outcomes and there is a belief in correcting or at least accompanying the market.

Transitional Labour Markets

Many of the above hold true for the TLM approach, which can be considered as a variant of the flexicurity approach (or is flexicurity a variant of TLM?), but while the flexicurity roots are dominantly economic and sociological with a strong connection to labour law[13] and an ethical dimension in the form of rights and duties added, the TLM roots are more diverse and integrate a range of disciplines (Schmid and Gazier, 2002, Gazier and Gautié, 2008): economics (and here not so much different from the flexicurity approach grounded also in the economy of institutions and in human resource management (the latter brought in strongly by Gazier)), political theory (and here based on Schmid's and also Auer's former work (Schmid, 1974, Auer et al., 1983) in the areas of (political) system theory) and cybernetics (von Bertalanffy, 1973, Wiener, 1971) which is much about policy congruence and complementarities. Ethics, especially questions of equality, equity and justice, which are strong components of Schmid's work,[14] play a large role in the TLM approach.

A common root for both flexicurity and TLM is also research on labour market policies, both active and passive. More specifically, the global perception of 'transitions' in and around the labour market as a system implies insisting on the interdependency between broad activity spheres such as education, job search, domestic and benevolent tasks and retirement. The perspective has recently been grounded on a micro approach: social risk management (Schmid, 2006b), focusing on the different 'framing' of risk perception by actors.

The TLM approach takes into account the domestic sphere as a major component of the system of interdependent transitions. The connection with the sociological approach of 'life course' (Anxo and Erhel, 2006) is straightforward. All this underlines the stronger emphasis put on equality, and on gender equality, as a central goal and on the long-term consequences of transitions.

Regionally, we saw that the concept of flexibility has much to do with the US labour market and with a comparison of US and European labour markets. Flexicurity and the TLM have their regional origin in the analysis of the labour markets of 'old' member states of the EU, and a critical assessment of their success and failures (Auer and Gazier, 2006). This analysis has been extended to include transition economies, most of which are now member states of the EU (Cazes and Nesporova, 2003 and 2005).

Capabilities

The fourth of the reform agendas or thoughts – capabilities – is less anchored in labour market studies but goes far beyond into development theory and has therefore a developing country focus, although the concept claims universal application as can be seen in Human Development Indicators that are also relevant for developed countries.

The capabilities approach has a stronger link to ethics than the other approaches and puts equality of access to resources and capacities to use them according to physical and cultural conditions at the centre. Capacities to use substantive freedom for achieving welfare states (status) are at the core of this doctrine (Sen 1985, Nussbaum, 2000). Martha Nussbaum (2000) has shown what kind of capabilities are at stake (e.g. life, health, affiliation, control over one's environment, etc.). The Human Development Indicators following from ideas of Armatya Sen (Sen, 1982) relate to three main areas: wealth (per capita income in US Purchasing Power Parities), health (life expectancy) and education (enrolment and literacy rate).

In the other approaches labour market variables (employment rates, unemployment rates for all or for specific groups (e.g. women)) are the main outcomes of both regulations and policies, although objectives of fairness, equality and other more ethical dimensions, eventually even happiness, are at stake. In Sen's approach also outcomes are broader: the aim is human development.

Clearly employment and income play a role, but not the dominant one, although recently the role of employment for poverty reduction and capacity building and usage has been underlined. But the question of capabilities as effective freedom *used* for human development is important for both the flexicurity and the TLM approach. The 'flexibility only' approach would probably assert that flexibility is linked to freedom as it is about choices and would in any case result in better allocation of productive resources and bring about more wealth. This automatic outcome would be denied by all other reform agendas, which see a role for policies.

PERFORMANCES, CLUSTERS AND AGENDAS: A FIRST APPRAISAL

Are these reform agendas, which to some extent have also created their indicators and measurements, successful in attaining envisaged goals? What follows is a very preliminary and crude exercise of measuring some achievements of the reform agendas. This is more of a think piece than a thorough reflection of achievements. We will try to identify key indicators which can be associated more or less directly to the outcomes and means selected by each approach, and to test their relevance. Such an attempt, while being certainly limited, allows checking assumptions made in the different reform agendas.

We will process in two steps: first, we will perform a statistical analysis, which deliberately clusters countries according to their degree of flexibility in the labour markets and looks at socioeconomic variables, which are here considered as outcomes of different degrees of labour market flexibility. Second, we will try to enlarge our discussion and to assess the relevance of our four agendas.

A Simple Cluster Analysis

Reform agenda 1 (flexibility)
If we check the assertion that more flexible labour markets produce better outcomes than regulated labour markets and cluster EU15 countries according to their degree of labour market flexibility and compare the

outcomes for these clusters, the following patterns emerge (see also Appendix, Table 2.1 'Economic, labour market and social performance').[15] Countries with flexible labour market regulations (as witnessed by lower tenure, lower disparity of tenure classes, lower EPL for regular jobs), produce better outcomes in productivity levels and growth, have higher employment rates than the two other more regulated clusters (the difference is less pronounced for full-time equivalent employment rates though) and have a lower share of temporary but a much higher share of part-time jobs. They show also the lowest unemployment rates and lowest youth and long-term unemployment rates.

They show relatively high (lower than group A, but higher than group B) income dispersion and have a high share of people in risk of household income poverty but do well both on the Human Development Index (HDI) and Gender Development Index (GDI) rank and show high transition rates from temporary to permanent and from low to higher wage jobs. They spend much more on labour market policy than the two other clusters but less on social protection benefits.

At face value being flexible seems to give many of the advantages that the doctrine predicts. However, there is an important divide in the flexible countries: there are countries that are flexible without many institutions and policies and there are others that are in fact the classical countries organised along flexicurity principles in that cluster.

Reform agenda 2 (flexicurity)

Outcomes of this cluster (including Denmark and the Netherlands) are as follows: the cluster has the highest hourly productivity level (while productivity growth lag behind) and by far the highest employment rates both in uncorrected and in Full Time Equivalents terms. It features also the lowest unemployment rates (total and in particular for youth and for the long-term unemployed). Flexicurity countries show also the lowest income dispersion (Gini) and the lowest risk of poverty rates. They have about the same HDI and GDI ranks as the two countries classified under 'flexibility', UK and Ireland, and have about the same transition rates from temporary to permanent jobs and only slightly fewer transitions from low wage to higher wages. However, they also have a markedly lower incidence of low pay than the flexibility countries.

An indication that these differences are related to the institutions on the labour market is their markedly higher spending on labour market policy and on social benefits in general.

Reform agenda 3 (transitional labour markets)

There is no clear-cut pattern as it would need an array of statistics to map, for example, all successful transitions (between school and work, maternity, paternity, parental, training leaves and employment, etc.) for the three clusters; a proxy for the performance of this cluster are the transition rates from temporary to permanent jobs and from low to higher wage, but they are also very crude and should for example be corrected by a level indicator such as incidence of temporary jobs or low pay. A full set of variables to construct country typologies and meaningful clusters for successful TLM countries has still to be recorded.

Reform agenda 4 (capabilities)

HDI and GDI are the main indicators used for country comparison in the human development reports and suggest measuring success in human development. However, as the labour market is not the focus, but rather institutional features such as health (longevity), education and GDP per capita, capabilities is not really an agenda that considers work and employment and decent work and is therefore quite distinct from flexicurity and TLM approaches. However, the simple analysis reaches its limits: as capabilities is in reality no labour market reform agenda, any correlation with the flexibility variables could be random and would in any case need additional explanations; true, the HDI and GDI ranks are better for the flexibility and flexicurity countries than for the other clusters, although the most 'regulated' cluster does better than the second less regulated cluster.

A More General Discussion

We considered three distinctive labour market reform agendas (flexibility, flexicurity, TLM) and a fourth 'agenda' (capabilities) whose goal is broader: human development. We also tried to link the agendas to some indicators and outcomes. The exercise remains partial but shows that flexicurity countries seem to be quite successful when a broad outcome pattern including inequality and poverty is considered. Flexicurity countries (and we can maybe heroically subsume TLM countries here) have a tighter regulatory framework than 'flexibility' countries (a sort of medium degree of legal regulation) and use more policy intervention, and have a well-developed social dialogue and collective bargaining, which permits to bargain compromises between flexibility and security, and this institutional setting seemingly contributes to good outcomes.

Flexibility countries do well in terms of productivity and also labour market performance, but less well in income distribution and the risk of poverty. Their good stance in the HDI and GDI (equivalent and even slightly better in comparison to flexicurity countries) requires explanation.

This very crude analysis seems at least to indicate that embarking on a reform agenda called flexicurity and TLM seems promising, but there are many caveats in clustering as well as outcomes, which induce us to be prudent: there are certainly many ways to happiness and workers in some countries might live well with stricter employment regulations than others. Integrating variables for taking into account internal flexibility, the degree of coverage by collective bargaining etc., would also be required for a full picture. Further work on clustering shows that if such additional variables are introduced, countries change positions. However, Denmark and the Netherlands are relatively stable across all clustering attempts and always end up in the flexicurity box, albeit at a distance (on clustering see also European Commission, 2006 and 2007b).

There is also the question of causality: is good performance caused by flexicurity or can these countries organise their labour markets in a flexicurity fashion, because they have good results? This cannot be proven at this level of analysis and one can only confirm that in some countries the congruence between the employment and labour market system and the economic and social system seems to be better than in others. At the beginning of this chapter we referred to critical voices with regard to flexicurity. In empirical terms there seem to be less negative externalities as for example in the pure flexibility approach. While it might not be feasible politically to introduce a Danish or Dutch system in other countries, it could help to develop home-grown versions compatible with a specific country context.

CONCLUSION

Three main conclusions can be drawn from this tentative analysis.

First, the success of flexicurity as a buzzword and a policy agenda seems related to its intermediate stance between adaptation to market pressures and capabilities development, and to the bargaining perspective it offers: even if firms need security (and workers some forms of flexibility), the main proposal is to exchange in a negotiated way some selected increases in flexibility for firms and some selected increases of security for workers. Of course, its inclusion as a key component of the 'soft law' adopted by the European Employment Strategy adds a specific dimension, located between discourse and implementation.

Second, the positioning of flexicurity among labour market policies and reform agendas gives it quite a good rank. Performing better than labour market flexibility alone, and not in contradiction with the capabilities approach, flexicurity policies (in a wide sense including TLM approaches) can be seen as an asset. In analogy to the financial systems (that need some flexibility, with too much being disastrous as we see today with the financial market upheaval) which calls for regulation rather than deregulation, the labour market only needs marginal flexibility to adjust, but this must be balanced with regulations and policies that ensure worker security.

Third, the question of the nature and limits of flexicurity can be addressed by considering the various and more or less competing/diverging/converging agendas. First, we can observe that all the priorities identified above meet most policymakers' concerns: adaptation to global market competition, social policies and education and health policies are important too, as well as freedom enhancement. The difference between the agendas is the way they combine, put in hierarchical order and ponder each priority. Exploring and clarifying these various possible combinations is a possible research field.

Finally, the connections to existing theories seem to be pluralistic, not at all exclusive. Not one, but sometimes several theories (e.g. the existence of moral hazard, efficiency wages, economic efficiency and social justice in a Pareto, Rawls or Dworkin sense, a theory of basic needs, etc.) at quite different levels of theoretical development, contribute to the line of arguments and indicators which underlie these agendas. Exploring these connections and the congruence and incongruence between these theories and the concrete policy proposals of the agendas might be a promising field of research and would show whether Calmfors' intuition that major trade-offs are 'swept under the carpet' is correct. In a similar vein research could be undertaken to examine whether or not indicators, which are sometimes numerous and sophisticated, and in other cases are few and simple, are adequate measurements of the theories and policies that form the base of the agendas.

APPENDIX

Table 2A.1 Economic, labour market and social performance

Economic, labour market and social performance (Data for 2000–06 average, unless otherwise specified)	Belgium France Greece Italy Luxembourg Portugal	Austria Finland Germany Spain Sweden	Denmark Ireland The Netherlands United Kingdom (C+ = DK and NL)	
Country groupings	A	B	C	C+
Average tenure	12.3	10.6	9.4	9.7
Ratio -1year/+10years of tenure**	1:3.9	1:2.3	1:1.4	1:1.4
Employment Protection Strictness, regular jobs (2003)	2.5*	2.5	1.8	2.3
Productivity level (GDP per hour worked, constant 1990 US$ at PPP)	27.2 US$	27.2 US$	30.3 US$	30.4 US$
At risk of poverty (-60% median income) BEFORE and AFTER social transfers Inequality and (Gini index)	24.4 16.5 30.7	24.7 13.1 26.4	28.2 15.2 28.9	25.9 11.2 25.5
Human development index (2005)	0.934	0.948	0.952	0.951
Gender-related development index (2005)	0.928	0.942	0.945	0.948
Employment rates for 15–64	61.6	67.2	71.9	74.9
Employment rates for 15–24	29.6	43.3	58.1	65.3
Employment rates for 55–64	35.7	45.9	51.5	51.1
Employment rates women	51.7	60.9	64.5	68.2
Share of temporary jobs	11.8	17.3	8.6	12.0
Share of part-time jobs	12.4	16.9	26.5	32.5
Transition rates temp-perm Transition rates low-pay – higher pay	37.5 37.2	27.4 33.7	41.0 34.0	40.6 32.8
Total unemployment rate	7.4	7.6	4.4	4.1
Youth unemployment rate	23.2	16.4	8.5	7.2
Long-term unemployment rate	3.5	2.5	1.2	1.1
LMP Spending per 1% of unemployment	0,29	0,37	0,61	0,97

Note: * Excluding Austria and Luxembourg due to missing data ; ** Data for 2002.

NOTES

1. These common principles are 'catch-all' notions offering many policy options, thereby satisfying more or less all relevant stakeholders.
2. We do not deny of course the existence and importance of the strict criteria of the growth and stability pact as well as 'hard' European legislation in social and labour law.
3. Guideline 21 of the Integrated Guidelines for growth and jobs for the period 2005–2008: 'Promote flexibility combined with employment security and reduce labour market segmentation, having due regard to the role of social partners.' See also the current Guideline 7 of the Europe 2020 Integrated Guidelines for economic and employment policies of the Member States and of the Union.
4. The fourth strategic objective, labour standards, applies without saying.
5. The DG Employment, responsible for the EES, integrates social protection, however there is overlap with the work of other DGs like Development and Cooperation (AIDCO) or Education and Culture (EAC) as well as the Economic and Finance Affairs Committee (ECOFIN).
6. Although dominance of a 'doctrine' is difficult to establish: for example one of the proponents of what many would call the leading doctrine, economic liberalism, Nobel prize winner (for his contribution to microeconomic methods together with McFadden) James Heckman criticises an alleged 'prevailing view' of 'institutionalists' like Freeman or Abraham and Houseman who contend that labour market regulations are not the culprits for high unemployment (Heckman and Pagès, 2000). This example shows that a sort of reciprocity exists in defining doctrines as dominant.
7. The ILO's constitution from 1919 asserts that 'labour is not a commodity'.
8. See Berg and Cazes, 2007.
9. The unweighted rank of all 15 European countries was 96 in 2008; the average rank was pushed up by Denmark and the UK.
10. As in Wilthagen (2005 and 2007), and partially also in the TLM and the capabilities approach.
11. This more 'fatalist' view is implicit in Auer (since 2003) and others, although scepticism as to the changes in the labour market due to globalisation remains (Auer and Cazes, 2003).
12. When suggesting directing attention to the least well off (or those most difficult to place in the labour market).
13. The relationship with labour law needs special mention, as laws regulating hiring and firing in particular are important for all approaches.
14. See, for example, Schmid, 2006a.
15. A big caveat applies: country clustering, even if sophisticated and using for example factor analysis (principal components) is always subject to errors or implausible attributions. For example, here Sweden is clustered together with countries like Greece and Italy, only because Sweden has relatively stable employment relationships and high EPL. In outcomes it differs from other countries in its cluster, which have also tight regulations, but much lower employment rates, especially for women.

REFERENCES

Anxo, D. and C. Erhel (2006), 'Irreversibility of time, reversibility of choices? The life-course foundations of the Transitional Labour Market Approach', *Cahiers de la Maison des Sciences Economiques* 2006.58, Paris: Centre d'Economie de la Sorbonne.

Auer, P., B. Penth and P. Tergeist (1983), *Arbeitspolitische Reformen in Industriestaaten: Ein internationaler Vergleich*, Frankfurt/New York: Campus Verlag.

Auer, P. and S. Cazes (eds) (2003), *Employment Stability in an Age of Flexibility*, Geneva: ILO.

Auer, P. and B. Gazier (2006), *L'introuvable Sécurité de L'emploi*, Paris: Flammarion.

Berg, J. and S. Cazes (2007), 'The Doing Business Indicators: Measurement Issues and Political Implications', Economic and Labour Market Paper 2007/6, Geneva: ILO.

Calmfors, L. (2007), 'Flexicurity – An Answer or a Question?', European Policy Analysis 6, Stockholm: Swedish Institute for European Policy Studies (SIEPS).

Cazes, S. and A. Nešporová (2003), *Labour markets in transition: Balancing flexibility & security in Central and Eastern Europe*, Geneva: ILO.

Cazes, S. and A. Nešporová (2007), *Flexicurity: A Relevant Approach in Central and Eastern Europe*, Geneva: ILO.

Dworkin, R. (2000), *Sovereign Virtue: The Theory and Practice of Equality*, Cambridge, MA: Harvard University Press.

Esping-Anderson, G. (1990), *The Three Worlds of Welfare Capitalism*, Cambridge: Polity.

European Commission (2006), *Employment in Europe 2006*, Luxembourg: Office for Official Publications of the European Communities.

European Commission (2007a), Communication 'Towards Common Principles of Flexicurity: More and better jobs through flexibility and security', Brussels, COM(2007) 359 final.

European Commission (2007b), *Employment in Europe 2007*, Luxembourg: Office for Official Publications of the European Communities.

Gazier, B. (2008), 'Flexicurité et Marchés Transitionnels du Travail: Esquisse d'une réflexion normative', *Travail et Emploi*, **113**, 117–128.

Gazier, B. and J. Gautié (2008), 'The Transitional Labour Markets Approach: Theory, History and Future Research Agenda', paper presented at the Conference 'Transitional Labour Markets: Past, Present and Future', Carry-le-Rouet, 16 and 17 June 2008.

Heckman, J. and C. Pagès (2000), 'The cost of job security regulation: Evidence from Latin America', NBER Working Paper No. 7773, Cambridge, MA: National Bureau of Economic Research.

International Labour Organization (1999), *Decent Work*, Geneva: ILO.

International Monetary Fund (2003), 'Unemployment and labor market institutions: Why reforms pay off', *World Economic Outlook 2003*, Chapter 4, Washington: IMF, pp.129–150.

Jobert, B. and P. Muller (1987), *L'Etat en action: Politiques publiques et corporatismes*, Paris: Presses Universitaires de France.

Jørgensen, H. and P.K. Madsen (eds) (2007), *Flexicurity and Beyond: Finding a New Agenda for the European Social Model*, Copenhagen: DJØF Publishing.

Madsen, P.K. (2003), '"Flexicurity" through labour market policies and institutions in Denmark', in P. Auer and S. Cazes (eds) (2003) *Employment Stability in an Age of Flexibility*, Geneva: ILO, pp.59–105.

Muller, P. (2005), 'Esquisse d'une théorie du changement dans l'action publique: Structures, acteurs et cadre cognitif', *Revue Française de Science Politique*, **55**(1), 155–187.

Nussbaum, M. (2000), *Women and Human Development*, Cambridge: Cambridge University Press.

Schmid, G. (1974), *Funktionsanalyse und politische Theorie*, Düsseldorf: Düsseldorf: Bertelsmann Universitätsverlag.

Schmid, G. (1975), *Steuerungssysteme des Arbeitsmarktes – Vergleich von Frankreich, Großbritannien, Schweden, DDR und Sowjetunion mit der Bundesrepublik Deutschland*, Göttingen: Verlag Otto Schwartz.

Schmid, G. (1980), *Strukturierte Arbeitslosigkeit und Arbeitsmarktpolitik*, Königstein im Taunus: Athenäum Verlag.

Schmid, G. (2006a), 'Arbeitsmarktpolitik: Zwischen ökonomischen und sozialen Anforderungen', talk delivered at the Forum '60 Jahre WSI: Wirtschafts- und Sozialforschung im Spannungsfeld zwischen Wissenschaft, Politik und Gewerkschaften' on 7 December 2006, available at www.guentherschmid.eu/pdf/vortraege/berlin-06.pdf (accessed 15 August 2011).

Schmid, G. (2006b), 'Social risk management through transitional labour markets', *Socio-Economic Review*, **4**(1), 1–33.

Schmid, G. (2008), *Full Employment in Europe: Managing Labour Market Transitions and Risks*, Cheltenham, UK: Edward Elgar.

Schmid, G. and B. Gazier (eds) (2002), *The Dynamics of Full Employment: Social Integration through Transitional Labour Markets*, Cheltenham, UK: Edward Elgar.

Sen, A. (1982), *Choices, Welfare and Measurement*, Oxford: Basil Blackwell

Sen, A. (1985), *Commodities and Capabilities*, Amsterdam: North Holland.

Von Bertalanffy, L. (1973), *General system theory. Foundations, development, applications*, London: Penguin.

Wiener, N. (1961), *Cybernetics: or the Control and Communication in the Animal and the Machine*, 2nd revised edition, Boston: MIT Press.

Wilthagen, T. (2005), 'Striking a balance? Flexibility and security in European labour markets', in T. Bredgaard and F. Larsen (eds) *Employment Policy from Different Angles*, Copenhagen: DJØF Publishing, pp.253–267.

Wilthagen, T. (Rapporteur) (2007), 'Flexicurity Pathways: Turning Hurdles into Stepping Stones', Report of the European Expert Group on Flexicurity, Brussels, June.

Wilthagen, T. and F. Tros (2004), 'The concept of "Flexicurity": a new approach to regulating employment and labour markets', *Transfer*, **10**(2), 166–186.

World Bank (2003 to present), Doing Business Report Series: Annual Reports, Washington, DC: World Bank.

3. Transitional labour markets and flexicurity: managing social risks over the life course

Günther Schmid

DOES A EUROPEAN FLEXICURITY CONSENSUS EMERGE?

When the idea of balancing flexibility and security was introduced by the first Kok Report (Kok et al., 2004) into the employment policy debate at the end of 2003, 'flexicurity' was still considered as an oxymoron, which means something that is a contradiction in itself.[1] Only a few years later, in its 2006 Employment Report, the European Commission appealed to the strategy of flexicurity in the following way:

> A consensus is ... emerging ... that countries should adopt institutional configurations in the labour market that better combine the requirements of flexibility and security – in other words 'flexicurity'. This implies that, in an environment where workers experience more frequent transitions between employment and non-employment, and between different kinds of employment, policies need to put in place the right conditions for individuals to successfully manage these transitions, thereby ensuring sustainable integration and progress of individuals in the labour market. (European Commission, 2006, p. 111)

Related to the 'right conditions', the Commission submitted a Green Paper in November 2006 asking member states and social partners to take a position on 14 questions on modernising labour law. This process was supported by a task force on flexicurity which delivered its report in 2007. On the basis of this report, the Commission announced four components of flexicurity in July 2007: (1) flexible and reliable contractual arrangements, (2) comprehensive lifelong learning strategies, (3) effective active labour market policies, and (4) sustainable social protection systems. After a lengthy debate, the European Council eventually decided on eight common principles of flexicurity in December 2007 (European Commission, 2007).

These principles already contain a good deal of compromise between the various schools of flexicurity (Auer, 2007), and within these principles one can easily detect some key elements of the transitional labour market concept (Rogowski, 2008). In brief, the eight principles emphasise (1) good work through new forms of flexibility and security; (2) a deliberate combination of the four flexicurity components; (3) a tailored approach according to the member states' specific circumstances; (4) overcoming segmentation through stepping stones and through managing transitions both in work and between jobs; (5) internal as well as external flexicurity; (6) gender equality in the broader sense of reconciling work, family and private life; (7) the crucial importance of the social dialogue in implementing flexicurity, which means – in transitional labour market terms – negotiated flexibility and security; and, finally, (8) fair distribution of costs and benefits, which means – in the wording of social risk management – the fair sharing of risks in critical transitions over the life course.

However, the ongoing debate shows that the concept of flexicurity is far from unitary. Despite a common rhetoric, country-specific connotations exist, and there is the danger that the concept becomes instrumental for various and even contradicting political interests.[2] Furthermore, as the current economic crisis demonstrates, flexicurity strategies have to be coordinated with effective monetary and fiscal policies. The theory of transitional labour markets (from now on TLM) aims at providing a consistent analytical framework to give flexicurity – embedded in a proper macro-institutional context – a clear direction. The first step of such a framework is to clarify the meaning of flexicurity from an analytical point of view.

WAYS IN WHICH TO 'MARRY' FLEXIBILITY AND SECURITY

The confusion stems especially from the complexity of the interrelationship between flexibility and security. At least four elements for each dimension can be distinguished: external or internal numerical flexibility and internal or external functional flexibility on the one hand, and job security, employment security, income security and option security on the other hand.[3] The link between these eight dimensions is more complicated than is usually considered (Table 3.1).

The flexibility-security nexus is not always a trade-off. The employer's flexibility gain does not necessarily mean a loss of security for employees; and the employee's security gain does not necessarily mean a loss of flexibility for employers. Employers also have an interest in security, for instance in the loyalty and reliability of workers. Employees, vice versa, also have an interest in flexibility, for instance in working-time flexibility to combine family, life and work, or in job changes to gain new experiences, to extend social networks and to indulge changing preferences.

Table 3.1 The flexibility–security nexus

	Security			
Flexibility	Job security	Employment security	Income security	Option security
External numerical	to	to / vt / vs	to / vt / vs	to
Internal numerical	vt	vt	(to) / vt	to / vt
Internal functional	vt	vt	to / vt	(to) / vt
External functional	vt	to / vt / vs	to / vt	to / vt

Note: to = trade-off; vt = virtuous cycle; vs = vicious cycle.

Take, for instance, the first column of the flexicurity matrix, the nexus between job security and various forms of flexibility. There is clearly a trade-off between job security and external numerical flexibility: the more freedom employers have to hire and fire, the lower the job security is for individual employees and vice versa. If, however, employees trade in internal flexibility (for example, accepting working time variability and wage flexibility) against job security, flexibility and security may turn into a virtuous cycle.

Job security can also induce employees to be loyal to the employer, to invest in firm-specific human capital, to co-operate and to pass over tacit knowledge to other employees because they do not have to fear internal competition. All this increases internal functional flexibility. An example of external functional flexibility would be the opportunity of employers to use high-quality job services provided by temp-agency workers. The reason is that temp-agencies can pool the risk of fluctuating demand for such services and thereby provide security for the internal workforce of individual employers as well as job security for skilled workers in their own organisa-tion. In other words, the flexicurity labour market will increasingly be characterised by hybrid employment relationships combining the advantages of internal and external labour markets.

Regarding the link between external numerical flexibility and employment security, hire and fire does not necessarily affect employment security. If the labour market provides plenty of job opportunities, for instance through high job turnover combined with effective demand management, then flexibility and employment security can go hand in hand.

The nexus, however, can also be deadly vicious. Apart from rising fluctuation costs, hire and fire policies can lead to an overall feeling of employment insecurity. This feeling may lead, in turn, to exaggerated savings of employees, thereby lowering consumption and effective demand on the one hand, and on the other hand – as the case of East Germany has drastically shown – employment insecurity also leads to postponing family planning, thereby lowering the birth rate. In addition, employment insecurity also reduces the investment in human capital, thereby leading to a decline in highly skilled labour supply and eventually ending in a vicious circle of flexibility and security.

These examples point out that the flexibility-security nexus should not be considered as a menu à la carte (Gazier, 2007). Whether relationships between the different types of flexibility and security turn out to be trade-offs, virtuous or vicious cycles depend on the coherent design of labour market policy, especially the complementarity of institutions at the micro-, meso- and macro-level (Hall and Soskice, 2001). The Danish 'Golden Triangle', for instance, compensates the high risk of job insecurity with generous income security, and active labour market policies greatly contribute to employment security.[4] Sweden is a good case of balancing option security and functional flexibility. Universal public child-care provisions and generous parental leave schemes enhance employment options for men and women, whereas comprehensive education and training opportunities at all ages ensure adaptability to labour market changes.

Figure 3.1 shows flexibility as the vertical axis and security as the horizontal axis in a continuum from the negative to the positive. This makes four possible combinatory relationships: two kinds of trade-offs, one in which the increase in flexibility goes at the expense of security, and one in which greater security goes at the expense of flexibility. And there are two complementarities: a virtuous cycle, in which flexibility and security re-enforce each other in a positive direction, and a vicious cycle, in which flexibility and security re-enforce each other in a negative direction.

As in real marriages, most people probably like to have the best of all worlds, i.e. the virtuous cycle. However, as was shown at the beginning, conflicts or trade-offs turn up as well and vicious cycles loom large in real life. Each country will have to find its own ideal balance between flexibility

Transforming European employment policy

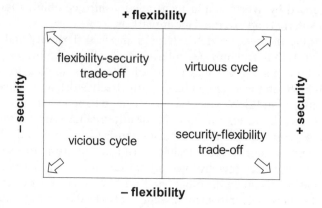

Figure 3.1 Combinations of flexibility and security

and security. At the European level, one can only formulate some general guidelines. These guidelines can be divided into four strategies: protected flexibility (1), negotiated flexibility (2), negotiated security (3) and minimum standards (4), and all four strategies can be differentiated according to the level of policies – whether they work at the micro, meso or macro level of political activities (Figure 3.2).

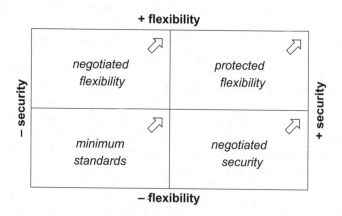

Figure 3.2 Strategies for managing the balance between flexibility and security

Regarding the first priority, protected flexibility would be the proper way to foster a virtuous cycle between flexibility and security. In general, this strategy compensates risk-taking by additional securities or monetary incentives.

a)   From the macro perspective, the exchange of job security for high income security to foster job mobility would be one possibility to set the virtuous cycle of 'flexicurity' in motion. In a knowledge- and service-based economy, especially in an economy with overwhelmingly small and medium-sized firms and network-like work organisation, the competitive pressure of globalisation requires more and more external flexibility. If one further assumes that higher job turnover affects especially low- and medium-skilled people, the combination of generous income security with employment security through active labour market policy seems to be a promising strategy. This is exactly the flexicurity model of the Danes. Another way, the Dutch way, would be life course saving accounts for covering income risks related to flexible employment contracts. The provision of efficient placement services, education or training services and transferable social securities are further cases of protected flexibility at this level.

At the labour demand end, temporarily dispensing employers from the payment of contributions to social security would be a possibility to compensate for the high risks of employers recruiting young people looking for their first job, as for instance the Portuguese government recently did successfully.[5] Moreover, the neglect of macroeconomic policy also leads to a lack of functional equivalents of labour market flexicurity on the demand side. Cheap consumer credits, tax-subsidised learning accounts, inequality insurance and real estate price insurance would be examples for flexicurity on the demand side (Shiller, 2003).[6]

b)   At the meso level, collective agreements going beyond wages and covering also training funds and training leaves could foster a symbiotic relationship between flexibility and security.

c)   At the micro level, civil servants can be regarded as the prototype for 'flexicurity'. This provocation can only be justified in referring to the original concept and not to the often denigrated practice of today. In the classical model the state did not guarantee job security to its high-level civil servants. As an employer the state provided only employment security in exchange of the acceptance to take over all kinds of jobs in the range of the servants' ability, including the obligation of regional mobility without any limits. I will not recommend re-establishing this model. The institution of the 'civil servant', however, reminds us that employment security even with the same employer does not exclude contractual arrangements that enhance all kinds of internal and external flexibility. This is probably the reason why we find almost no change in the development of so-called job tenure. There is even evidence that long job tenure – in fact the better expression would be employment tenure – up to a certain limit seems to foster productivity (Auer, 2007).

Second, the proper strategy to turn the flexibility-security trade-off into a win-win situation would be 'negotiated flexibility'.

a)   At the macro level, centralised wage formation through collective bargaining without interference of the state is the prototype for negotiated flexibility. However, one could imagine an innovative extension of this model: the social partners could negotiate an anti-cyclical wage flexibility scheme by putting – in case of an economic upswing – parts of the wages into a training fund which could then be used to finance continuous vocational education and training in the cyclical downturn; the state would jump in as co-financing partner by providing tax incentives for such funds.

b)   Good practice at the meso level are collective agreements with opening clauses at the firm level that under certain conditions allow wage flexibility in exchange of employment protection, so-called concession bargaining. Such negotiated flexibility can also be understood as a way to create procedural justice which – as we know from the new behavioural economics (e.g., Fehr and Falk, 2002) and empirical research – is so important for the acceptance of wage flexibility, especially in case of downward wage adjustment.

c)   An example for good practice at the micro level would be the legal right to working time reduction under the condition that employees accept the interest of employers in negotiating the implementation of this right. The Netherlands and Germany have introduced such conditional rights.

Third, the proper strategy to turn the trade-off between increasing security and decreasing flexibility into a win-win situation is 'negotiated security'.

a)   At the macro level, the so-called 'soft jobs' and 'flexible jobs' in Denmark are a good example. These types of jobs provide employment security for handicapped, disabled, hard-to-place people in exchange of the acceptance to change jobs or taking over jobs with lower responsibilities and corresponding lower wages. In addition, flexibility is enhanced through competitive bidding of public resources and negotiated out-contracting with municipalities or other organisations providing these types of jobs.

b)   At the meso level, one could imagine collective agreements about flexible pension entitlements backed up by pension law that allow building up virtual time accounts (virtual contributions) that compensate for discontinuities during the life course.

c)   At the micro level, entitlements to career leaves (option security) in exchange for negotiated functional flexibility within the firm would be good practice. Another example are so-called activation contracts between authorised case managers and the unemployed in which the unemployed – before signing the agreement – have the opportunity to negotiate the conditions; also opening clauses for re-negotiation would be good practice.

Fourth, the proper strategy to overcome vicious cycles would be 'minimum standard regulation' at national or European level.

a)   At the macro level, national minimum wages (NMW) to avoid cut-throat competition is a highly-contested example. To turn this into good practice, it is necessary to include the social partners in the setting, differentiation and continuous adjustment of minimum wages. Although there is no reasonable argument for a unique EU minimum wage, the development of common rules for such a process should be considered. The institutionalisation of the Low Pay Commission (LPC) for setting and monitoring the British NMW is a good practice example. Evidence of about 10 years' experience shows that the NMW raised the real and relative wage of low paid workers (equity) without adverse employment consequences (efficiency) (Metcalf, 2008). Due to the high risk of social exclusion through low skills, the issue of minimum standards for education at national or EU level may be even more urgent than considering standards for minimum wages.

b)   At the meso level, European standards for running temp-agencies – especially by establishing the equal treatment principle – would be a precondition that these intermediate institutions can play a larger role in preventing downward spirals of flexibility and security through their capacity of risk pooling.

c)   At the micro level, universal social rights beyond employment – for example rights to training, parental leaves, career leaves and giving workers voice at the firm level – can overcome the prisoners' dilemma individual employers and employees are facing in case of non-cooperative games. This dilemma is the result of time incongruence, which means the fact that such rights usually induce higher short-term costs than benefits but higher long-term returns than costs. The universality of these rights could avoid opportunistic behaviour in favour of short-term solutions.

To sum up, whether relationships between the different types of flexibility and security turn out to be trade-offs or virtuous cycles or vicious cycles depends on the coherent design of labour market policy, especially the complementarity of institutions at the micro, meso and macro levels. The Danish 'Golden Triangle', for instance, compensates the high risk of job insecurity with generous income security, and active labour market policies greatly contribute to employment security. Sweden is a good case of balancing option security and functional flexibility. Universal public child-care provisions and generous parental leave schemes in Sweden enhance employment options for men and women, whereas comprehensive educa-tion and training opportunities at all ages ensure adaptability to labour market changes.

The most important point of this exercise, however, is that the complexity of the flexibility-security nexus allows countries to choose different combinatory regimes (Klammer, 2007). This conclusion has been con-firmed by many other successful EU member states since the existence of the Lisbon strategy. However, the concept of TLM claims that a 'deliberate combination' of the four flexicurity components – flexible and reliable contractual arrangements, comprehensive lifelong learning strategies, effective active labour market policies and modern social protection systems – means to follow consistent normative and analytical principles. The next section deliberates on the normative principles.

THE THEORY OF TRANSITIONAL LABOUR MARKETS

As a normative concept, TLMs envisage a new stage of active labour market policy which focuses on social risks over the life course. The core idea is to empower individuals to take over more risks over the life course, not only through making work pay but also through making transitions pay. Four principles underlie this theory.

The first principle is *justice as fairness*. Concerning the goals of policy intervention, the concept of TLM is opposed to the utilitarian assumption of maximising the happiness for all. TLM theory rather emphasises the difference principle by John Rawls (2001), according to which inequality is only justified if the position of the least advantaged is also improved. We have to turn around Tolstoy's famous introductory statement in his novel *Anna Karenina*: 'Each unhappy family is unhappy in its own way.' There are many ways to happiness, but the reasons for unhappiness are few. Reducing unhappiness, especially caused by long-term unemployment and poverty, is something that we can achieve. Maximising happiness is a moving and often futile target as the booming happiness research shows (Layard, 2005, Offer, 2006).

The second principle is *justice as solidarity*. TLM theory follows Ronald Dworkin (2000), who discovered an important blind spot in John Rawls' theory of justice. The strategy of maximising welfare for the most disadvantaged is ethically insensitive. People are and have to be concerned about the responsibility for their choices. Rights and obligations have to be balanced. Demanding more individual responsibility, however, requires endowing all individuals with equal opportunities. It also requires *ex ante* solidarity in the sense of periodically redistributing resources over the life course in favour of equal opportunities since market forces regularly distort distributive justice.

The third principle is *justice as agency*. Following the Nobel Prize winner Amartya Sen (2001) and in its footsteps Salais and Villeneuve (2004), TLM theory assumes great differences in the individual ability to utilise resources for a fulfilling personal life course. Labour market policy, therefore, has to concentrate on capabilities, which include not only individualised endowments of resources but also a supportive economic, social and political infrastructure. Institutional capacity-building, therefore, is of utmost importance for a sustainable development.

The fourth principle is *justice as inclusion*. TLM theory assumes an increasing interdependency of individual, regional and national economic actors. Globalisation (including Europeanisation) of labour markets in particular requires a spatial expansion of the principle of social inclusion, in other words, an expansion of risk-sharing communities beyond ethnic, regional and national boundaries (Ferrera, 2005). The reason is that open and opening market economies produce winners and losers in an asymmetrical way.[7]

As an analytical concept, TLMs emphasise the dynamics of labour markets. They focus on flows between different employment relationships rather than on stocks, and they focus on transitions over the life course rather than on one-way job-to-job changes. They distinguish especially between integrative maintenance and exclusionary transition sequences or job careers. They have stimulated a rich set of empirical research studies on life course mobility which cannot be presented here.[8]

TLMs, however, also emphasise transitions within employment relationships. The often quoted fact that international research finds no remarkable downward trend in job tenure and no remarkable increase in job-to-job transitions is completely in line with the concept of TLMs (Auer and Cazes, 2003). The reason is that many transitions can be performed within stable employment relationships, for instance the shift from full-time to part-time work due to parental leave, or the combination of part-time work with off-the-job training, or internal job rotation.

Such flexibility within a continuing employment relationship explains, for instance, the fact that the nominal employment rate in Sweden is about 74 per cent, whereas the effective employment rate – which means the rate of employed people who actually work in a week – amounts to around 64 per cent. This observation might even be turned into a normative statement: the more transitions there are within an employment relationship that are allowed or demanded, the higher the employment rate must be to keep the 'machinery' of economic prosperity running. The Lisbon objective of a 70 per cent employment rate, therefore, might even be too modest in the long run.

The main challenge, however, is the imbalance between integrative maintenance and exclusionary transitions. In fact, the current dynamics of transitions tends to lead to new forms of labour market segmentation. Many people get stuck in exclusionary transitions, especially in low-skilled jobs or in – often precarious – non-standard employment relationships. The following graph of non-standard employment in the EU member states gives only an impression of this challenge. The figures represent aggregate non-standard employment rates which comprise all jobs in part-time work, temporary work or own self-employment (Figure 3.3).

The comparison of the EU member states reveals three messages: first, non-standard employment rates vary enormously between the 24 EU member states represented in Figure 3.3[9] ranging from about 7 per cent in Estonia and 43 per cent in the Netherlands in 2008. Through differentiation by gender, the picture – not shown here – becomes more telling. Both the level (EU average of about 15 per cent for men, 21 per cent for women in 2008) as well as the dynamics (EU average of about 2 percentage point change from 1998 to 2008 for men, about 4.5 percentage point change for women) hint to the fact that non-standard employment mainly affects women.

As the clustering according to employment systems shows, the so-called social democratic systems (including the champion Netherlands, as a hybrid system) as well as the 'liberal' systems are on the top; the family-centred continental-conservative systems as well as the Mediterranean systems are in the middle; and all of the transition countries (the new member states) – with the exception of Poland[10] – are at the bottom. The aggregate non-standard employment rate correlates positively – not shown here – both with labour force participation and with economic prosperity in terms of GDP per capita.[11] This pattern allows the conclusion that high contractual variety of employment relationships seems to be a prerequisite for higher prosperity in economic terms.

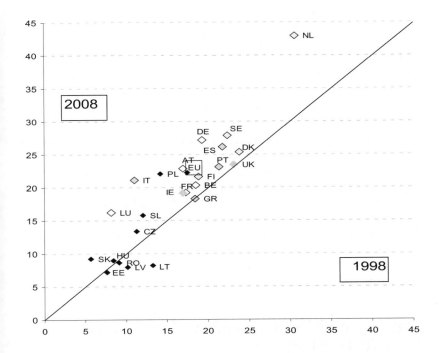

Sources: Eurostat, Labour Force Survey; own calculations; the 'aggregate' non-standard employment rate measures the number of people in part-time, fixed-term and own self-employment as percent of the working-age population (15–65) by controlling for possible overlaps (e.g., part-time work might be related with fixed-term contracts as well as with open-ended contracts; own self-employment might be part-time as well as full-time).

Figure 3.3 Aggregate non-standard employment rates in Europe, 1998 and 2008

Second, as the clustering above the steady-state diagonal – the implicit time axis – demonstrates, non-standard employment increased in almost all EU member states, especially in the Netherlands, Germany and Italy. On the other hand, it is remarkable that most of the transition countries not only cluster together in the left corner of the figure, but some of these countries, especially Latvia, Lithuania and Romania, experienced even a decline in the aggregate non-standard employment rate. The most likely explanation for this feature is, first, that work in the informal economy is a functional equivalent of formal non-standard employment; and, second, that part-time work (the most important component of formal non-standard employment) does not provide enough income for women in transition countries engaged in formal labour market work.

Third, the fact that 'social democratic' as well as 'liberal' systems rank high in terms of non-standard employment can be taken as circumstantial evidence that non-standard jobs are related to very different regulatory frameworks. Whereas the Dutch or Danish non-standard employees are well covered by employment and income security arrangements, this cannot be said, for instance, for their counterparts in Britain. Further, not all of these jobs are precarious or exclusionary. They can serve as stepping stones or as intermediary jobs within a meaningful work life career. Nevertheless, even in countries with high security standards, non-standard jobs often involve higher risk of exclusion than standard jobs.

This increasing contractual variety of employment relationships is the empirical starting point of TLM theory. Against this backdrop, the aim of TLMs is, metaphorically speaking, to provide 'social bridges' that compensate for the higher risks of this increasing contractual variety and to ensure that non-standard jobs become 'stepping stones' to sustainable job-careers. In order to establish such institutional arrangements, it is therefore helpful to think in terms of social risk management, which will now be explained and illustrated with some examples.

EMPLOYMENT STRATEGIES FOLLOWING THE THEORY OF TLMS

TLMs concentrate on five critical events over the life course: transitions from education to employment, transitions from one job to another, transitions between employment and unemployment, transitions between private household activities and gainful work, and eventually transitions from employment to retirement.

Each of these transitions is associated with specific risks: first, the risk of too little or eroding human capital or income capacity over the life course; second, the risk of income volatility due to fluctuating demand and job-to-job transitions or even the risk of working poverty due to low wages; third, the risk of restricted income capacities due to social obligations such as child care or elderly care; fourth, the risk of income insecurity due to unemployment; fifth, the risk of reduced or zero income capacity due to disability, chronic illness or old age.

The theory of TLMs assumes that specific risks also require specific securities. According to the principle of requisite variety (Ashby, 1979), the higher the variety of risks the higher the variety of social securities should be. It also rests on modern behavioural economics, notably on prospect theory (Kahneman and Tversky, 2000), which does not assume consistent rational behaviour but asymmetric risk perceptions. Loss aversion tends to be greater than risk-taking for gains. People tend to be myopic when related to high risks with low probabilities, but far-sighted when related to low risks with high probabilities. As a consequence, many people tend to insure themselves, for instance, against possible disruption of their travel plans but not against the possibility of long-term vocational disability; they are also less willing to save for any education or training that may be necessary in the future than to save for a new and maybe prestigious car. Social protection systems, therefore, often follow a logic that is too simple or that is different from that required by life course risks. In the following, we present some of these systematic misfits and possible remedies.

We thereby distinguish three strategies of social risk management: the prevention or the mitigation of risks and the coping with risks. Prevention directly tackles the causes of risks and should therefore be given priority. However, uncertainty looms large and thus makes prevention impossible. Prevention can also be prohibitively expensive or restrict flexible adjustment. Mitigation and coping strategies, therefore, have to complement prevention.

First, according to the principles of TLMs, it does not make sense to protect people against the risk of too little or of eroding human capital through high- and long-term unemployment benefits. On the contrary, such generous benefits would damage more than resolve the underlying problem. Equally, in-work benefits for unemployed youth would not make sense, since they would perpetuate the lack of human or social capital. Prevention is the main solution here. To prevent youth unemployment, social risk management must start in the kindergarten, in pre-schools and primary schools. Not only should equal opportunities in elementary and secondary education be adapted to a knowledge society, but also elementary social skills for communication and learning abilities have to be ensured.

As mitigation strategy, it is of the utmost importance that the state ensures a training place or a job after six months of unemployment at the latest. All firms must share the risk of the lack of human capital and contribute at least financially to vocational training if they are not able or willing to offer the training themselves.

Sufficient education and vocational training are a crucial element of active securities over the life course. It is also a precondition for taking on more individual responsibility than in the traditional welfare state. To cope with this risk, active labour market policy, therefore, should ensure for everybody a second or third investment chance over the life course.

Sweden provided the best example in this respect. Between 1997 and 2002, the Swedish government invested 350 million euros yearly for low-skilled people – independent of whether they were unemployed or employed – in order to lift their knowledge to a level appropriate to the knowledge economy (Albrecht et al., 2005). This allowed about 100,000 people to get continuous vocational education and training in addition to the normal stock of trainees, which roughly corresponds to 2.5 per cent of the working age population.

Second, income volatility over the life course is often caused by externally induced job changes or externally enforced short-time work. Income volatility, however, can also be caused more and more by endogenous changes such as changing job preferences, family relocation or even the wish to take a sabbatical. Working poverty results if wages are so low that the wage income falls below a decent minimum income despite full-time work. A basic income guarantee, especially in old age, is a powerful preventative strategy to ensure income security for people with a discontinuous life course and related income volatility. The Netherlands and the Nordic countries offer good examples in this respect. Minimum wages also prevent working poverty, to some extent, through three channels: first, by protecting a basic level of decent wages, second by avoiding cut-throat competition and third by stimulating continuous investment in competitive workplaces.

Long-term saving or lifelong learning accounts are proper strategies to mitigate and cope with volatile income risks. Since the resulting flexibility or mobility through such saving schemes creates positive external effects, the state could step in as a co-financing institution by providing tax incentives.

The Dutch life course saving plan (Wotschack, 2006) and the Belgian career break system (Román, 2006) are good practices that could be adopted by other EU member states. However, care has to be taken with respect to some flaws in the present design of these schemes. Young adults, especially, are usually in a life course phase in which they are not able to build up enough savings. Education and care credits might be arranged to cope with the risk of low earning and saving capabilities.

Third, if people's income capacity is restricted, for instance due to family obligations, this risk has to be compensated by income supplements or in-kind benefits. The best and most powerful preventative measures are the public provision, or at least public financing, of day-care facilities. In-work benefits, including tax credits, are a proper instrument of risk mitigation, especially for low income earners. As a coping strategy, full-time or part-time leave from work due to social obligations should be compensated like wage replacements in case of involuntary unemployment.

Concerning good practice, some EU member states, for example Sweden and Denmark, have already arranged such schemes. The Grand Coalition in Germany introduced in 2007 wage-related parental benefits compensating for about 58 per cent of wages up to 14 months, two of which have to be taken up by men. Due to the high individual costs of child care, but also due to the high benefits of child care for the whole of society, and, last but not least, for reasons of gender mainstreaming, the wage replacement could even be more generous for low- and medium-income earners. Since children and frail grandparents often need care that cannot be planned in advance, wage replacement for some days per year should be available. Sweden, for instance, acknowledges this need through a contingent of up to 60 days per year at a wage replacement of 80 per cent.

Fourth, the proper response to the risk of income insecurity (caused by unemployment, for instance, through cyclical demand variations or through redundancy dismissals) is to provide for generous income security. It is of the utmost importance to consider income protection in this case not as a passive measure but as active security.

First of all, however, preventative measures through job creation and continuous vocational education and training have first priority. Without thriving job dynamics and without employability that fits the requirements of the knowledge economy (Rodrigues, 2002), income protection would indeed turn into a passive measure. The best income security measure for the involuntarily unemployed is the creation of new competitive jobs through a sound macroeconomic policy.

If the risk, however, has occurred, the proper mitigating strategy is to compensate the income loss through generous unemployment benefits. A generous wage replacement allows the unemployed person to search for a new job that corresponds to his or her capabilities without the fear of getting trapped into a career of poverty. Generous wage replacement helps to maintain a worker's qualifications and competence. It also improves the efficiency of job matching. High matching efficiency through unemployment insurance is, for instance, reflected in longer job tenures after the rematch of insured unemployed persons compared with uninsured unemployed persons. In its recent Employment Outlook, even the OECD discovered by econometric work that reducing the generosity of unemployment benefits may induce some unemployed persons to leave unemployment more quickly, but it also significantly reduces productivity.

Appropriate coping measures are intensive job search and case-oriented job placement services. Again, such services are an investment and not wasteful consumption. Many EU member states still underinvest in such services during the first months of unemployment. However, long-term or even unlimited wage-related unemployment benefits do not make sense for this risk category. Apart from inducing moral hazard, they would not help the long-term unemployed – far from it.

Good practice in combining mitigation and coping measures in the management of redundancies is shown by the Austrian work foundations

(*Arbeitsstiftungen*) and the new Finnish measure 'Change Security' (*Muutosturva*). The Austrian practice is to set up a work foundation which functions as a kind of transition agency. These transition agencies ensure an integrated approach in terms of organising and financing. The funding comes from four sources: first, the foundation's capital is given by the firm, thus granting it its independence as long as it is needed. Second, the redundant workers themselves make a contribution by depositing 50 per cent of their redundancy payments into the foundation. Third, workers remaining in their positions pay the foundation a small proportion of their monthly wages as a solidarity contribution. Fourth, the public employment service guarantees the payment of unemployment benefits up to four years, which covers the majority of the costs. The foundation ensures an early start to reintegration and organises a wide range of individualised services that are helpful when workers are seeking new jobs in the regional labour market. These characteristics lead to a very important consequence: firms that cause redundancies take over responsibility in a limited sense and workers that engage in retraining and placement activities are volunteers and get a strong start instead of suffering from the stigma of being redundant. Evaluations report reintegration success of up to 95 per cent.

The Finnish 'Change Security' programme was put in place in 2005 to address, in particular, large-scale redundancies. It aims at an early start to active measures in situations of mass dismissals and company closure through co-operation between different regional stakeholders. It includes the right of the employees to individual programmes or re-employment or re-education, free time for job searching and counselling while still on the job and higher levels of benefits in the transition period. It includes an obligation for employers to inform the employees and officials in time, and to make plans for re-employment together with the employees and the local public employment office. First-hand experiences with this new programme report positive results and emphasise, in particular, the new levels of co-operation in labour market affairs between the key stakeholders.

Fifth, it would be misplaced to protect the risk of reduced or zero income capacity due to disability or old age through long-term unemployment benefits. The use of unemployment insurance for early retirement was one of the greatest mistakes of several EU member states during the 1990s. This risk needs to be managed by other measures.

Active labour market policy – if it deserves its name – should concentrate on prevention, since the causes of diminishing income capacities are well known. Income capacity, therefore, should and could be re-established through regular individual work assessments and corresponding training measures. Much can also be done through workplace adjustment. In other words, not only do workers have to be made fit for the market, but also the market has to be made fit for the workers – a slogan aptly coined by Bernard Gazier (2007).

The risk of reduced income capacity can also be mitigated through partial compensation of the related income loss. Such wage insurance would be an essential and innovative element of transforming conventional unemployment insurance into employment insurance. Workers who are mature adults, especially, need such insurance, since they face large income losses if they become unemployed and subsequently re-employed. This need is also nourished by the fact that internal labour markets that provide implicit wage insurance are becoming eroded. Furthermore, the escape to early retirement as an income insurance device is no longer an option. Wage insurance would increase workers' willingness to take on lower-paid jobs, especially when it is combined with training vouchers to make the new jobs sustainable and to improve their chances of climbing up the career ladder again.

Last but not least, individualised rehabilitation is still a much underutilised measure to cope with the risk of diminishing income capacity. Another possibility is the creation of transitional jobs, as is the case in most Scandinavian countries, especially in the form of the Danish 'flexjobs', or jobs created by various forms of social enterprises, as is the case, for instance, in Sweden and the Netherlands.[12] Good practice is especially to be found in the comprehensive approach of active ageing in Finland, which succeeded in increasing the employment rate of elderly persons by 18 percentage points within eight years (Hartlapp and Schmid, 2008).

CONCLUSIONS: FROM ACTIVATION TO WORK-LIFE ORIENTATION[13]

To sum up, modern labour markets, first of all, are characterised by an increasing variety of employment relationships. This variety reflects new modes of production due to new technologies, new forms of work organisation due to increasing competition and international labour division, and new work-life risks related to social and demographic changes. Taking all these features together, modern labour markets seem to need both more flexibility and new securities. The European employment strategy adopted the slogan of flexicurity as an answer to these new challenges.

Second, flexicurity, however, is not and cannot be a unitary concept. The eight common principles of flexicurity for EU member states, now formulated by the European Council, are helpful in preventing an arbitrary usage or even political instrumentalisation of the term. They rightly emphasise that EU member states have to find their own deliberate combination of flexible and reliable contractual arrangements, comprehensive lifelong learning strategies, effective active labour market policies, and sustainable social protection systems.

Third, there is a lack of criteria for assessing equitable *and* efficient combinations of flexicurity arrangements. The call for a balance of flexibility and security is empty without such criteria. The concept of transitional labour markets provides a normative and analytical framework to develop such criteria based on a life course orientation. From such a perspective, one has to ask: why should income security only be related to the income risks of jobless people? Why should security not be provided for income risks related to critical transitions over the life course? Why should insurance not cover the income risks related to transitions between family work and gainful employment, between dependent work and self-employment, from high-paid to low-paid jobs, between full-time and part-time work, from work to gradual retirement?

From such a perspective, managing the balance of flexibility and security over the life course requires a wider set of opportunities than just 'making work pay'. It requires institutional arrangements that are also 'making transitions pay'. Such arrangements contain at least three new institutional ingredients: first, new social rights that go beyond employment, for instance the right to training leaves, care leave, intermediate working time reduction or even long-term sabbaticals; second, new forms of governance, especially arrangements that break with the traditional division between labour market and social policy (Supiot, 2001). This requires intelligent network models of co-operation and co-financing beyond labour market agents; third, an extension of the social insurance principle to income risks beyond unemployment, which means to income risks also related to critical transitions over the life course.

Fourth, a way in which to extend the social insurance principle to a broader set of life course risks than unemployment would be to establish a system of work-life insurance. Such a system would build on three pillars: first, a universal minimum income guarantee that ensures a life without persistent poverty; second, the extension of unemployment insurance to employment insurance; third, private or collectively negotiated insurance accounts targeted especially to life course risks such as lifelong learning accounts, time-saving accounts or care-leave systems. Governments could join such ventures at various levels through tax subsidies, standard setting and co-financing partners.

Fifth, the system of employment insurance would serve three functions: generous income protection for a restricted period of time in involuntary unemployment; employment security through active labour market policy that is not only confined to offering jobs and placing individuals in work but that also supports follow-up measures to transform mere workfare measures into stepping stones to sustainable work; and finally better inclusion of non-standard workers in labour law and social security systems. One innovative element of employment insurance is the concept of wage insurance. Such insurance would cover, to some extent, the loss of wage income when changes of employment become necessary due to structural change, for instance trade adjustment, or due to the loss of individual productivity, for instance through attrition of work and income capacities. Acceptance of intermediate downward mobility should be rewarded by active labour market policy aimed to re-establish upward mobility.

Sixth, it must be kept in mind that stakeholders often have conflicting interests that cannot be explained away. The problem of divergent interests can only be solved through negotiation as a device of information gathering, communication and building compromises. The revitalisation of the social dialogue, in other words, negotiated flexicurity at all levels – firm, branch, nation and Europe – is therefore of the utmost importance for putting more flesh on the bones of the European employment strategy. Negotiated flexicurity, however, may lead to new insider-outsider cleavages, since organised interests may set compromises on the costs of less well-organised interests. Care, therefore, has to be taken to avoid externalisation of social costs by setting minimum standards and fair rules of negotiation. The government at various levels may also jump in as co-financing partner to overcome the prisoner's dilemma in which rational actors choose a suboptimal equilibrium.

Seventh, as the successful countries demonstrate, flexicurity has to be embedded in sound macro-economic and macro social policy. Without sustainable job creation dynamics, all employability and stepping-stone strategies are in danger of ending in a cul-de-sac or of displacing other categories of workers. Because Europeanisation, in particular the Euro-zone, increases interdependencies, co-ordinated efforts to stimulate sustainable economic growth are required, especially through investments in a better European economic and social infrastructure. The extension of the European Social Fund to a European Employment Insurance Fund, or at least a complementation of the European Social Fund by a focused European Knowledge Lift Fund, would make the European Social Model more visible and tangible.

NOTES

1. As many other social inventions, the term has been coined by the Dutch around the mid-nineties; for its history see Wilthagen (1998).
2. See the unsurpassed and lucid epistemological reflections by Barbier (2007, 2008).
3. For a slightly different categorisation see Wilthagen and Tros (2004).
4. The best references for the Danish model are Bredgaard and Larson (2005) and Madsen (2006).
5. This dispense (23.75 per cent of the wages) for a maximum period of 36 months also holds for long-term unemployed; more than 80,000 were covered in 2006 (Ministério, 2007).
6. Even if it had to be put in the US context, of special interest and in the vein of Dworkin's concept of distributive justice is Shiller's proposal of an inequality insurance. 'The idea…is that the government should set by legislation the level of income inequality, in most cases probably initially roughly equal to the level of inequality today, and create a tax system that prevents inequality from getting worse. The idea is that if income inequality begins to get worse, then taxes automatically become more progressive as a correction. The tax changes would be automatic because the tax would be framed as enforcing a measure of inequality rather than specifying tax rates. I am calling the program *insurance*, quite loosely, to frame the program in the public mind as the risk management vehicle that it is, and to highlight that it will not wrest from anyone from the standpoint of today. Inequality insurance is not a Robin Hood plot to take money from the rich and give it to the poor. Like other risk management devices it focuses only on protecting all of us from future risks' (149). That system would ultimately pay negative taxes to people of the lowest income. There is a risk, because the economy is a very unpredictable allocator across people. Especially in the rich countries, inequality is increasing. Advanced technology often means that a smaller number of skilled people supply their services over a wider area, producing a 'winner-takes-all' effect, where only the best do well, and these lucky few command enormous incomes (Shiller, 2003, 149–164).
7. To give just one telling example: thanks to mass production in hog farming (killing the small hog farming), pork prices dropped by about one-fifth in the United States between 1970 and 2004, providing annual savings of about $29 per US consumer. With the opening of borders, the US giant Smithfield storms into Eastern Europe with the same intent and comparable effects on a global scale. In Romania, the number of hog farmers has declined by 90 per cent – to 52,100 in 2007 from 477,030 in 2003. In their place, the company employs or contracts with about 900 people and buys grain from about 100 farmers (International Herald Tribune, 6 May 2009).
8. See, among others, O'Reilly et al. (2000), Schömann and O'Connell (2002), Schmid (2002a, 2002b), Schmid and Gazier (2002), Mosley et al. (2002), Gazier (2003), Gangl (2003); Muffels and Luijkx (2006), Román (2006), Schmid (2006), Howe (2007) and various contributions in five recently published rich volumes on flexicurity and transitional labour markets by Jørgensen and Madsen (2007), de Koning (2007), Lassnigg et al. (2007), Muffels (2008) and Rogowski (2008).
9. For lack of reliable data or comparability, Bulgaria, Cyprus and Malta are excluded.
10. Although Poland's employment rate is low like in most of the transition countries, its share of temporary work is very high. Fixed-term employment rocketed from 514,000 (1998) to 3,207,000 (2008), whereas total employment stagnated. The reason probably is the lax regulation of temporary work which allowed fixed-term chain contracts without any limit until 2003. Only in 2004, Poland introduced stricter regulation, except in the seasonal and temp-agency sector. In fact, the height of fixed-term contracts was in 2007, and the number of temporary workers declined slightly in 2008.

11. Luxembourg, as an exceptional small insular country, has been excluded in this correlation as an outlier; through commuting from neighbour countries, total employment in Luxembourg is higher than its working age population.
12. The target group of the Danish 'flexjobs' consists of persons with a permanently reduced work-ability who are not entitled to pre-pensions. The employer receives a wage subsidy amounting to one-third, one-half or two-thirds of the minimum wage depending on the extent to which the work-ability of the person is reduced. The person in a 'flexjob' receives wage according to the collective agreement. The number of persons in such jobs rocketed recently to the level of 40,000, which would correspond in Germany to the level of 600,000, 1.5 per cent of the active labour force. As of January 2006, the Swedish 'plusjob' is an enhanced form of employment subsidy made available to 20,000 long-term unemployed men and women, targeted at quality-improving work in the public sector in order to minimise displacement effects. The employer receives a subsidy of 100 per cent of the wage cost up to a specific ceiling.
13. This conclusion summarises not only the chapter but also parts of my book, Schmid 2008.

REFERENCES

Albrecht, J., G.J. van den Berg and S. Vroman (2005), 'The Knowledge Lift: The Swedish Adult Education Program That Aimed to Eliminate Low Worker Skill Levels', IZA DP No. 1503, Bonn.
Ashby, W.R. (1979), *An introduction to cybernetics*, London: Methuen.
Auer, P. (2007), 'In search of optimal labour market institutions', in H. Jørgensen and P.K. Madsen (eds) *Flexicurity and Beyond: Finding a New Agenda for the European Social Model*, Copenhagen: DJØF Publishing, pp.67–98.
Auer, P. and S. Cazes (eds) (2003), *Employment Stability in an Age of Flexibility*, Geneva: ILO.
Barbier, J.-C. (2007), 'From political strategy to analytical research and back to politics, a sociological approach of "flexicurity"', in H. Jørgensen and P.K. Madsen (eds) *Flexicurity and Beyond: Finding a New Agenda for the European Social Model*, Copenhagen: DJØF Publishing, pp.155–188.
Barbier, J.-C. (2008), 'There is more to job quality than "precariousness": a comparative epistemological analysis of the "flexibility and security" debate in Europe', in Ruud Muffels (ed.) *Flexibility and Employment Security in Europe: Labour Markets in Transition*, Cheltenham, UK and Northampton, MA, USA: Edward Elgar, pp.31–50.
Bredgaard, T. and F. Larsen (eds) (2005), *Employment Policies from Different Angles*, Copenhagen: DJØF Publishing.
de Koning, J. (ed.) (2007), *Evaluating Active Labour Market Policy: Measures, Public Private Partnerships and Benchmarking*, Cheltenham, UK: Edward Elgar.
Dworkin, R. (2000), *Sovereign Virtue: The Theory and Practice of Equality*, Cambridge, MA: Harvard University Press.
European Commission (2006), *Employment in Europe 2006: Recent Trends and Prospects*, Luxembourg: Office for Official Publications of the European Communities.
European Commission (2007), *Council Conclusions Towards Common Principles of Flexicurity*, Brussels: European Council, COM(2007) 359 final.
Fehr, E. and A. Falk (2002), 'Reciprocal fairness, cooperation and limits to competition', in Edward Fullbrook (ed.) *Intersubjectivity in Economics*, London: Routledge, pp.28–42.

Ferrera, M. (ed.) (2005), *The Boundaries of Welfare: European Integration and the New Spatial Politics of Solidarity*, Oxford: Oxford University Press.

Gangl, M. (2003), *Unemployment dynamics in the United States and West Germany: Economic restructuring, institutions, and labor market processes*, Heidelberg, New York: Physica/Springer.

Gazier, B. (2002), 'Transitional Labour Markets: From Positive Analysis to Policy Proposals', in G. Schmid and B. Gazier (eds) *The Dynamics of Full Employment: Social Integration through Transitional Labour Markets*, Cheltenham, UK: Edward Elgar, pp.196–232.

Gazier, B. (2003), *'Tous Sublimes' – Vers un Nouveau Plein-Emploi*, Paris: Flammarion.

Gazier, B. (2007), '"Making Transitions Pay": The "Transitional Labour Market's" Approach to "Flexicurity"', in H. Jørgensen and P.K. Madsen (eds) *Flexicurity and Beyond: Finding a New Agenda for the European Social Model*, Copenhagen: DJØF Publishing, pp.99–130.

Hall, P.A. and D. Soskice (eds) (2001), *Varieties of Capitalism: The Institutional Foundations of Comparative Advantages*, Oxford: Oxford University Press.

Hartlapp, M. and G. Schmid (2008), 'Labour Market Policy for "Active Ageing" in Europe: Expanding the Options for Retirement Transitions', *Journal of Social Policy*, **37**(3), 409–431.

Howe, B. (2007), *Weighing Up Australian Values: Balancing Transitions and Risks to Work and Family in Modern Australia*, Sydney: University of New South Wales Press.

Jørgensen, H. and P.K. Madsen (eds) (2007), *Flexicurity and Beyond: Finding a New Agenda for the European Social Model*, Copenhagen: DJØF Publishing.

Kahneman, D. and A. Tversky (eds) (2000), *Choices, Values and Frames*, Cambridge, MA: Cambridge University Press.

Klammer, U. (2007), 'Flexicurity and the life-course: labour market integration over the life-course in different European welfare state regimes', in H. Jørgensen and P.K. Madsen (eds) *Flexicurity and Beyond: Finding a New Agenda for the Euro-pean Social Model*, Copenhagen: DJØF Publishing, pp.307–334.

Kok, W. and C. Dell'Aringa, F.D. Lopez, A. Ekström, M.J. Rodrigues, C. Pissarides, A. Roux, G. Schmid (2004), 'Jobs, Jobs, Jobs: Creating More Employment in Europe', Report of the Employment Task Force Chaired by Wim Kok, Luxembourg: Office for Official Publications of the European Communities.

Lassnigg, L., H. Burzlaff, M.A.D. Rodriguez and M. Larssen (eds) (2007), *Lifelong Learning: Building Bridges through Transitional Labour Markets*, Apeldoorn-Antwerpen: Het Spinhuis.

Layard, R. (2005), *The New Happiness*, London: Penguin Press.

Leschke, J., G. Schmid and D. Griga (2007), 'On the marriage of flexibility and security: lessons from the Hartz reforms in Germany', in H. Jørgensen and P.K. Madsen (eds) *Flexicurity and Beyond: Finding a New Agenda for the European Social Model*, Copenhagen: DJØF Publishing, 335–364.

Madsen, P.K. (2006), 'How can it possibly fly? The paradox of a dynamic labour market', in J.L. Campbell, J.A. Hall and O.K. Pedersen (eds) *National Identity and the Varieties of Capitalism: The Danish Experience*, Montreal: McGill-Queen's University Press, pp.321–355.

Metcalf, D. (2008), 'Why has the British national minimum wage had little or no impact on employment?', *The Journal of Industrial Relations*, **50**(3), 498–512.

Ministério do Trabalho e da Solidariedade Social (2007), *Labour and Solidarity: An Overview*, Depósito Legal 261639/07, Lisbon.

Mosley, H., J. O'Reilly and K. Schöman (eds) (2002), *Labour Markets, Gender and Institutional Change: Essays in Honour of Günther Schmid*, Cheltenham, UK: Edward Elgar.

Muffels, R. and R. Luijkx (2006), 'Globalization and male job mobility in European welfare states', in H. Blossfeld, M. Mills and F. Bernardi (eds) *Globalization, Uncertainty and Men's Careers*, Cheltenham, UK: Edward Elgar, pp.38–72.

Muffels, R.J.A. (ed.) (2008), *Flexibility and Employment Security in Europe: Labour Markets in Transition*, Cheltenham, UK and Northampton, MA, USA: Edward Elgar

Offer, A. (2006), *The Challenge of Affluence: Self-Control and Well-Being in the United States and Britain Since 1950*, Oxford: Oxford University Press.

O'Reilly, J., I. Cebrián and M. Lallement (eds) (2000), *Working-Time Changes: Social Integration through Transitional Labour Markets*, Cheltenham, UK: Edward Elgar.

Rawls, J. (2001) *Justice as Fairness: A Restatement*, Cambridge, MA: The Belknap Press of Harvard University Press (edited by E. Kelly).

Rodrigues, M.J. (ed.) (2002), *The New Knowledge Economy in Europe: A Strategy for International Competitiveness and Social Cohesion*, Cheltenham, UK: Edward Elgar

Rogowski, R. (ed.) (2008), *The European Social Model and Transitional Labour Markets: Law and Policy*, Aldershot: Ashgate.

Román, A.A. (2006), *Deviating from the Standard: Effects on Labor Continuity and Career Patterns*, PhD thesis, Amsterdam: Dutch University Press.

Salais, R. and R. Villeneuve (eds) (2004), *Europe and the Politics of Capabilities*, Cambridge, MA: Cambridge University Press.

Schmid, G. (2002a), *Wege in eine neue Vollbeschäftigung. Übergangsarbeitsmärkte und aktivierende Arbeitsmarktpolitik*, Frankfurt a.M.: Campus.

Schmid, G. (2002b), 'Transitional labour markets and the European Social Model: towards a new employment pact', in G. Schmid and B. Gazier (eds) *The Dynamics of Full Employment: Social Integration through Transitional Labour Markets*, Cheltenham, UK: Edward Elgar, pp.393–435.

Schmid, G. (2006), 'Social risk management through transitional labour markets', *Socio-Economic Review*, **4**(1), 1–37.

Schmid, G. (2008), *Full Employment in Europe: Managing Labour Market Transitions and Risks*, Cheltenham, UK: Edward Elgar.

Schmid, G. and B. Gazier (eds) (2002), *The Dynamics of Full Employment: Social Integration through Transitional Labour Markets*, Cheltenham, UK and Northampton, MA: Edward Elgar.

Schömann, K. and P.J. O'Connell (eds) (2002), *Education, Training and Employment Dynamics: Transitional Labour Markets in the European Union*, Cheltenham, UK: Edward Elgar.

Sen, A. (2001), *Development as Freedom*, New York: Alfred A. Knopf.

Shiller, R.J. (2003), *The New Financial Order: Risk in the 21st Century*, Princeton: Princeton University Press.

Supiot, A. (Rapporteur) (2001), *Beyond Employment: Changes in Work and the Future of Labour Law in Europe*, Oxford: Oxford University Press.

Wilthagen, T. (1998), 'Flexicurity: A New Paradigm for Labour Market Policy Reform?', WZB Discussion Paper FS I 98-202, Berlin: Social Science Research Centre Berlin (WZB).
Wilthagen, T. and F. Tros (2004), 'The Concept of "Flexicurity": A New Approach to Regulating Employment and Labour Markets', *Transfer*, **10**(2), 166–186.
Wotschack, P. (2006), 'Lebenslaufpolitik in den Niederlanden. Gesetzliche Optionen zum Ansparen längerer Freistellungen', Discussion Paper SP I 2006-115, Berlin: Wissen-schaftszentrum Berlin für Sozialforschung.

4. Privatisation of placement services in light of the transitional labour market approach

Petra Kaps and Holger Schütz

INTRODUCTION

Contracting out placement services to private agencies has become widespread in many countries. Examples that have gained both experience as well as created much debate can be found in Australia, Great Britain and the Netherlands (see de Koning, 2007). An alternative approach of public–private governance of placement services are vouchers, which has fewer international proponents in job placement policies. In Germany, both approaches were supported by the so-called Hartz reforms in 2003: contracting out to support the public employment service in placement acitivities was intensified and placement vouchers became a large-scale labour market policy instrument.

While advocates of privatisation measures of placement services are in favour of either contracting out (Bruttel, 2005) or of a voucher system (Berthold and von Berchem, 2005), it is by no means clear which kind of public–private mixes are in fact best suited for the provision of placement and counselling services (see de Koning, 2007). However, there is growing evidence that the effects of privatisation are far less positive than often claimed. This chapter discusses the prospects and limits of privatisation for labour market policy by drawing on evaluation of experiences with privatisation in four countries: Germany, Australia, the Netherlands and the United Kingdom. Furthermore, it addresses governance issues raised by changing modes of public–private cooperation on placement services and labour market policy.

The conceptual framework is provided by the transitional labour markets (TLM) approach. The TLM approach is interested in mitigating old and new risks[1] of individuals in their employment careers over the life course. Risky junctions occur at the transitions from school to work, between employment and unemployment (and vice versa), between different jobs, between employment and non-employment and between employment and retirement. In terms of labour market regulation and policies the governance of TLM in the 21st century raises two sets of questions: firstly, how should and can the rights and responsibilities of individuals and private and public societal actors engaged in labour market risk policies be usefully conceived in normative terms and thereby equity/equality and efficiency be reconciled? Secondly, which policies and socio-political configurations of actors and inter-organisational arrangements might provide 'good governance' of labour market risks?

This chapter focuses on the second question but also touches upon the first one to some extent. It is interested in estimating the potential of different public–private mixes in placement services for the reduction of unemployment and re-employment risks as well as promotion effects for the employability of individuals (and firms). The criteria for this evaluation are drawn from the TLM approach (Schmid, 2002: 239f):

1. Increasing individual autonomy through empowerment and extended rights;
2. Promoting solidarity by reliable and accepted social security schemes;
3. Improving effectiveness of services through specialised agents and organisations in co-ordinated competition and partnership arrangements;
4. Improving efficiency through management tools like controlling, benchmarking as well as rigorous evaluation.

With respect to governance modes of different public–private mixes, this chapter discusses whether contracting out and vouchers are adequate tools for the provision of effective and efficient job placement services. A key assumption of the TLM approach in this context is that governance and outcomes of policy measures and organisations turn out to be efficient if appropriate risk-sharing and win-win constellations of the actors and political stakeholders are installed. For the goal dimensions of autonomy and solidarity it can be asked whether freedom of choice, responsiveness and equal opportunities are promoted by the instruments in question.

The central argument of this chapter is that, given the complex functional pre-requisites and regulatory requirements of quasi-markets, the potential of contracting out public job placement services to private agencies as a means of increasing efficiency is limited.

THEORETICAL ASPECTS

Contracting out and vouchers are two modes of functional privatisation (Schuppert, 1995: 767). Both represent institutional arrangements by which for-profit and non-profit private and privatised former public agencies compete for publicly financed service delivery. Those types of arrangements are referred to as quasi-markets in institutional economics (Le Grand and Bartlett, 1993: 10).

The term 'contracting out' refers to the commissioning of private providers by public authorities to deliver services for consumers/clients, with providers being chosen in a competitive public tendering process and thereby creating an ex-ante competition. The public sector remains responsible for financing and ensuring that the functions are performed, but is no longer performing them itself.

The economic theory of contracting out argues that outsourcing to private agents increases effectiveness and efficiency of services previously delivered by public agencies because of market competition. However, these quasi-markets have to be created and regulated by the public principal to commit private service providers to public goals. This is to be attained by setting financial incentives, by monitoring performance and by the threat of imposing penalties or not renewing contracts.

As ensuring institutions, public authorities can finance the private delivery of public services alternatively by means of a 'voucher system', the public part being to distribute the vouchers to beneficiaries, to redeem the vouchers and monitor the performance of the private service providers. As with contracting out, the voucher system is intended to improve effectiveness of service because of competition. But in contrast to contracting out it seeks to enhance competition not by tendering but by giving beneficiaries as consumers the freedom to choose between private placement organisations (Ensor, 2003; Morley-Fletcher, 2002).

Whether efficiency and effectiveness can be improved in comparison to public service delivery depends on the existence of regulation protecting the functioning of quasi-markets and promoting service quality. Quasi-markets require the guarantee of low market barriers, a clear separation of principal and agent, intelligent incentive structures and pricing mechanisms, choice, maximal transparency, minimal transaction costs, providers thinking in economic categories and control (Le Grand and Bartlett, 1993; Struyven, 2004; Zwinkels et al., 2004). At the same time, in managing contract-based competition models, various goal conflicts need to be reconciled (Struyven, 2005).

Furthermore, quality assurance in personal services is far more demanding to achieve than in services that can be easily standardised. In the case of the latter (typical examples: cleaning services, refuse collection), efficiency has repeatedly been increased through contracting out. However, spinning off the production of highly specific goods and services can produce sunk costs. Completely outsourcing a function to private agents can in the medium term diminish public-sector expertise and know-how, making public authorities more dependent on private providers (Miranda and Lerner, 1995). There is therefore much to be said in favour of the public sector maintaining specific competencies of its own in order to retain standards for comparison and reserve capacities when outsourcing general interest functions (Niskanen, 1971). Moreover, where personal services are delivered by private for-profit actors, there is always a risk of 'creaming' to maximise profits.

CONTRACTING OUT AND VOUCHERS IN GERMAN PLACEMENT SERVICES

Until 2008,[2] three measures were used by the German public employment service with respect to private placement services:

1.   Various placement services for unemployed persons were contracted out to private profit or non-profit agencies (*commissioning the delivery of placement services*, § 37 Social Code III, introduced in 1998)[3]
2.   *Integration measures* for groups of unemployed needing intensive placement support were contracted out to private profit or non-profit agencies (§ 421i Social Code III, introduced in 2003);[4] and
3.   The *placement voucher* was introduced for unemployed persons which allows them to engage a private agency to place them into employment (§ 421g Social Code III, introduced in 2002).[5]

In 2005 about 425,500 people were assigned to commissioned placement services, a figure that rose to 443,700 in 2008. However, while about 35,900 people participated in integration measures in 2005, this figure declined to only 8,000 in 2008. The number of placement vouchers issued can only be estimated, but the figure is likely to have been between 400,000 and 500,000 per year, with 50,300 people who found a new job by using them in 2005. In 2008, about 67,400 vouchers were cashed in.

An important step towards reorganising the control of labour market services via contracting out was taken in early 2004: purchasing was shifted from local employment offices to regional purchasing centres of the Federal Employment Agency (REZs) (Gülker and Kaps, 2006). This reform step was primarily intended to reduce the cost of integration services, to establish transparency and to release staff for placement activities. For this purpose, services were standardised and put out for tender. In 2006, REZs purchased employment service capacities for about 1 million participants with a budget of about €2.1 billion.

Impact Analysis of Privatised Placement Services

In the following selected findings of the WZB/infas (2006) evaluation of the Hartz reforms are presented with a focus on the placement instruments.[6] The WZB/infas (2006) evaluation is essentially a multi-dimensional implementation study and an econometric impact analysis with control group design. The results presented draw on the segment of the evelution study dealing with unemployment insurance (Social Code III).[7]

What the impact analysis shows is that contracted agencies were no better in integrating the unemployed than the public agencies. Private contractors of the two instruments were not able to place their clients significantly faster into the labour market compared with the Public Employment Service (see Table 4.1).

The voucher achieved a better placement rate than the employment service, but only for the year 2005. This gross effect, however, is diminishing when deadweight and abuse effects of about the same size are taken into account.[8] Thus vouchers can hardly be said to improve placement efficiency to any major degree. The voucher system produced very poor results during the first three years of implementation. The modified version in use since 2005[9] showed better results for the short-term unemployed. This modified voucher system was the only tool to offer a larger group of short-term unemployed reliably positive gross and net effects.

Implementation Analysis of Privatised Placement Services

The governance framework for the three placement instruments varies considerably, as Table 4.2 shows. However, the implementation analysis detected for all the three instruments serious functional problems of the quasi-market structures.

Table 4.1 Impact of private placement services on labour market integration of participants/users

	Treatment	Non-treatment	Difference	p-Value	Treatment	Non-treatment	Difference	p-value
	2004				2005[3]			
Commissioning to deliver placement services (§ 37)								
Average Treatment Effect (ATT)	0.045	0.040	0.0059	0.67	0.053	0.060	-0.0074	0.55
Accumulated ATT	0.176	0.154			0.210	0.237		
Average months of unemployment since treatment	3.67	3.71	-0.04	0.68	3.68	3.61	0.07	0.53
Average months of employment after treatment	10.58	16.00	-5.42	0.01	9.12	9.65	-0.53	0.56
	2004				2005[3]			
Integration measures (§ 421i)								
Average Treatment Effect (ATT)	0.041	0.045	-0.004	0.49	0.050	0.052	-0.002	0.78
Accumulated ATT	0.523	0.627			0.488	0.052		
Average months of unemployment since treatment	16.50	15.94	-0.56	0.48	10.81	10.60	-0.21	0.66
Average months of employment after treatment	13.90	12.57	1.33	0.21	9.82	9.02	0.80	0.28

Placement voucher (§ 421g)	2003/2004				2005[3]			
Average Treatment Effect (ATT)	0.041	0.040	0.0006	0.93	0.095	0.066	0.0290	0.00
Accumulated ATT	0.146	0.157			0.364	0.258		
Average months of unemployment since treatment	3.71	3.73	−0.02	0.99	3.39	3.57	−0.18	0.00
Average months of employment after treatment[1]	10.43[2]	10.86[2]	−0.45	0.38[2]	9.59	10.20	−0.61	0.23

Notes:
[1] Relative to voucher holders who used their vouchers.
[2] Figure for 2004.
[3] Figures refer only to Social Code III area.

Source: WZB/infas 2006, own presentation.

Market structure

The market is open to new bidders. But since smaller agencies generally have fewer resources for managing complex tendering procedures than bigger organisations, high transaction costs of the tendering process and frequent changes of the tendering procedure may translate into actual entry barriers for small companies.

The voucher system initially promoted private job placement without any market access obstacles. Since the beginning of 2005 providers must have a licence to cash in vouchers, but this is cheap and easy to obtain from the trade supervisory office. The licence does not impose compulsory compliance to quality standards in the sector. Transaction costs for the use of vouchers are relatively low.

Incentives

The contracting-out process promoted very strong price competition and created strong incentives for price dumping. Both instruments used outcome-related payments to promote successful private service delivery. For integration measures, the bonus-malus-system imposed high repayments on providers if they fail to fill their integration quota. There is no systematic relation between the remuneration structure and placement difficulties of the jobseekers transferred to the agents so far. Market price building has been restricted due to highly complex and frequent changes in conditions for payment.

Prices for the contracted placement services have been significantly lower than the fixed voucher fee that is defined by regulation. Equal fees for all jobseekers under the voucher system as well as 'no cure no pay'-contracts have encouraged strong selection effects to the detriment of the unemployed with little chance in the market. Participant survey data show that providers working with vouchers reject jobseekers with relatively poor regional or sector-specific market prospects. In the early years, windfall profits and considerable abuse became evident. These negative effects were curbed by modification of the voucher, especially by later payment of the first rate. Nevertheless, incentives for deadweight persist.

Transparency, monitoring and transaction costs

Complex and often changing criteria for decisions, changes in the timing of tendering, as well as changes in the content of tools have reduced the transparency of tendering procedures. Neither the results of tendering nor the impact of contracts have been monitored systematically. Short contract terms and frequent calls for tender mean that providers often change and transaction costs are high. The performance of the voucher system has not

Table 4.2 Regulation of contracted out placement measures and placement vouchers

	Commissioning to deliver placement services	Integration measures	Placement voucher
Size of lot (in participants)	50–2000	20–100	Individual voucher
Incentive structure of the contracts	No cure no pay: Success fee or No cure less pay: fixed amount plus success fee as bonus	No cure less pay: fixed amount plus bonus-malus-system	No cure no pay
Duration of contracts	3–12 months	6–12 months	3 months, prolongable
Content specifications for service	None until 2005 Concepts evaluated since 2006	Concepts evaluated in search for innovation	None
Performance target of contracts	Defined integration rate	Defined integration rate	Individual placement
Quality specifications as basis for rating submissions	None until 2006 Conceptual manuals since 2006	Conceptual manuals	–
Price competition	Very strong	Strong	Very low (fixed price)
Risk for agents	No cure no pay: very high No cure less pay: high	Very high (because of malus)	Medium (because of choice)
Assessment and choice during procurement procedure	Until 2005 lowest price, no quality concerns; Since 2006 best offer as weighted sum for quality aspects divided by price; minimum standard expected	Best offer as weighted sum for quality aspects divided by price; minimum standard expected	No regulation, no permission
Choice for clients	No	No	Yes
Choice for agents	No	No	Yes

been monitored at all. Since 2005, there are not even data available on the number of issued vouchers.

Quality

No conceptual manuals on re-integrating the jobseekers were required to be submitted when bidding for the delivery of placement services, and the quality aspects of the services provided were neglected until 2006. In the case of integration measures, conceptions had to be submitted but the price-quality ratio of the bid was biased towards price.

With an eye on de-bureaucratisation, legislation has transferred quality assurance for the voucher system to the professional federations of private placement services. The sector itself has not yet managed to find comprehensive solutions to the quality problems. In spite of adopted minimum quality standards, business without due respect for these standards cannot be excluded. The fragmented sector organisations have so far failed to agree on procedures for advancing quality assurance. The market remains opaque.

Moreover, problems with competitive tendering or vouchers are accompanied by local implementation problems in three dimensions.

Choice

Jobseekers and private employment agencies have no options with respect to contracting out, as the public employment service allocates the participants. By contrast, the voucher gives jobseekers freedom of choice, but it does not contribute much to promoting competition between placement agencies since transparency in this quasi-market is missing. For less competent jobseekers, in particular, it can be difficult to find a suitable placement organisation.

Transaction costs

There have been repeated conflicts between public employment agencies and private service providers about what placements are to be recognised and paid for, because, while participants are assigned to outside services, the Federal Employment Agency still included them in their placement activities.

Monitoring

There is a lack of monitoring tools permitting appropriate supervision of agencies in the performance of their tasks. The Local Employment Agencies therefore have to invest considerable resources in clarifying quality problems with private agencies, resources they would urgently need for their own placement activities. In cases of fundamental breach of a contract they have to initiate an escalation procedure with the REZ being responsible for demanding service delivery and terminating contracts if necessary.

Some of these operative problems were reduced during various rounds of tendering or re-regulation of the voucher. Despite some changes for the better, the lack of ex-post competition in service quality, the absence of systematic monitoring, the avoidance of selection effects and the transparency of the incentive scheme remain major procedural problems.

In sum, the Regional Purchasing Centre contract management did not succeed in stimulating fair competition and providing incentives for quality competition. As the tendering procedures are still to be improved in the course of organisational learning, it remains an open question which governance procedure – vouchers or contracting out – has more potential of increasing performance and productive efficiency, if at all.

CONTRACTING OUT PLACEMENT SERVICES IN AUSTRALIA, THE UNITED KINGDOM AND THE NETHERLANDS

A look at Australia, the United Kingdom and the Netherlands shows that in other countries, too, contracting out and voucher procedures are no panacea for job placement. The privatisation of job placement is farthest advanced in Australia. All placement counselling and integration services are handed to private agencies. In the Netherlands and Britain, counselling services have been retained by the public sector, while integration services have been privatised.

Australia

In Australia, new structures for labour market services were introduced in 1998 to ensure the optimum dovetailing of the hitherto separate functional areas of labour market policy (Department of Employment and Workplace Relations, DEWR),[10] job placement (Commonwealth Employment Services, CES), and for the disbursement of tax-financed social benefits.[11] Centrelink, a government organisation with about 400 offices, has since been responsible for registering the unemployed, disbursing social benefits, for the profiling and ensuing assignment of jobseekers to special placement and integration programmes of private for-profit- and non-profit organisations, for maintaining the nationwide job information system and for sanctioning applicants where need be.

The Department develops and finances programmes to advise, assist, and place jobseekers, which operate on a contracting out basis.[12] Quality assurance is tackled by means of so-called 'Star Ratings', a performance measure which is used for allocating business share. Three-year contract terms favour quality development and assurance, and transparency is ensured by regular publication of the ratings. Jobseekers eligible for measures can themselves select a service provider, but are then bound to this provider.

Evaluation of the Australian model has hitherto ranged from neutral to critical. Although some efficiency gains in the sense of cost reduction are in evidence, they were achieved at the cost of creaming and parking and weak integration quality (Finn, 2009; Struyven and Steurs, 2005; Carney, 2005; Productivity Commission, 2002). There are no reliable studies on the net integration effects of contracting out in the Job Network. Adjustments have had to be made in every round of tendering to compensate for moral hazard and the externalisation of costs by providers:

a)   Pure job placement was put out to tender on a price competitive basis. Providers subsequently had difficulty delivering services at the prices bid, so fixed prices were introduced.

b)   The minimum prices for the Intensive Support programme stifled price competition, resulting in fixed prices. However, 'parking' and less training remained particular problems for the most needy clientele. Individual Jobseeker Accounts were introduced to prevent such neglect.

c)   The number of bidders decreased over three successive rounds of tendering. In the fourth round, market access was denied to new providers. Now existing contracts are being thoroughly sifted to identify those that can be terminated to open the market to new agencies again.

In sum, the main contract management problems lie in establishing and maintaining competitive quasi-market structures, achieving productive efficiency, and regulating incentives to avoid disadvantaging difficult target groups. Furthermore, the question of guaranteeing responsiveness appears not to be a subject of discussion.

In the Australian system, continuous adjustment to counter persistent malfunctioning is required. Having opted for the full privatisation of job placement, the system must repeatedly update arrangements for coping with moral hazard among providers. Fixed prices are used to counter any decline in prices and hence in quality. If no providers in a region are willing to accept Department terms, the price is raised until someone is found. In addition, the 'Star Ratings' monitoring system needs diligent efforts to safeguard transparency and outcome control.

Since there is no 'residual' public placement system, the public sector buffer function can be ensured only through higher funding for private service providers. This precludes comparative impact evaluation of private and public job placement. Since no comparison to a public service delivery is possible, it cannot be said whether the system generates efficient placement structures.

The Netherlands

The current institutional structure of job placement in the Netherlands is based on the reforms introduced by the Work and Income (Reorganisation) Act (*Wet Structur Uitvoeringsorganisatie Werk en Inkomen*, SUWI) of 2001, which reorganised the legal framework for job placement, unemployment and invalidity insurance, as well as social assistance (Struyven and Steurs, 2003; Knuth et al., 2004). The SUWI legislation created a complex, legally binding system of contract management. The educational centres attached to the old employment service were privatised and the employment service itself split up between five organisations, shedding 1,500 of 9,000 jobs in the process.

The 131 Dutch Centres for Work and Income (CWI) not only handle applications for unemployment benefit but are also the central address for registering and profiling jobseekers and placing applicants with good market prospects. People who face placement obstacles, in contrast, are assigned to the Social Insurance Institute (UWV) if they have insurance entitlements or to municipalities for social assistance recipients and the non-insured. The UWV and municipalities outsource actual job placement services to private agencies by means of competitive tendering.

UWV became the sole implementing agency for social insurance of employees (there had previously been five implementing organisations). This organisation thus makes support payments but is also responsible for placement-service contract management for its clientele. The UWV has a free hand in awarding 10 per cent of all measures.

Dutch municipalities retained responsibility for implementing social assistance and were also entrusted with labour-market re-integration and case management for employable social assistance recipients. Since 2004 they have been given full responsibility for the re-integration of the long-term unemployed (Inspectie Werk en Inkomen, 2006).

Since the SUWI Act, local authorities have had to put out at least 70 per cent of placement and integration services to tender for private providers.

Dissatisfied with the performance of private service providers, municipalities have recently managed to regain the right to deliver job placement services themselves from 2006 (SEO, 2006; Sol, 2005).

Dutch experience with competitive tendering for re-integration measures is also no unadulterated success story. The first years showed only weak market development, and evaluations of placement outcomes were lacking (de Koning, 2004). Such impact evaluations are unfortunately also lacking for the more recent period (see also Verveen et al., 2006: 33).

Many deficiencies in tendering practice remain virulent, for example bureaucratic implementation arrangements, heightening conflict between the goals of transparent accountability and efficiency, as well as moral hazard problems (Sol, 2005: 167). Moreover, there is clear evidence of strong social selection effects among re-integration firms, attributable at least partly to the incentives of the competitive tendering system (see SEO, 2006; van Berkel and van der Aa, 2005; Struyven and Steurs, 2005; Zwinkels et al., 2004: ch. 3).

However, there is a trend towards greater quality competition and less intensive price competition, towards differentiated, target-group specific tendering procedures, greater transparency, better fit of the purchased products and greater choice through individual integration agreements. At the same time, strong competition continues between providers, curbing quality development and discouraging investment, and which, by imposing a higher proportion of fixed-term employment, is also to the disadvantage of contract provider staff (Verveen et al., 2006: 14–17).

A research report points out that competitive tendering tends to become less important in the Netherlands (SEO, 2006: 50). Instead, there has been an increase in individual integration agreements (IRO) based on the choice of an integration firm by the unemployment benefit recipient. Under this system, no tendering takes place. So far, the shares of gross inflows into UWV measured by IROs is between approximately 20 per cent (disabled persons) and 33 per cent (persons with unemployment benefits).

In the Netherlands there seems to be a trend towards considering market control via competitive tendering as one of many means to an end rather than an end in itself, as was the case when privatisation began. Practitioners and observers have lost many illusions about the potentials of contract management. Market competition is seen as only one factor in the delivery of labour-market services. Government organisations and many types of cooperative grouping are beginning to play a more important role in implementing labour market policy (RWI, 2006: 11–15).

United Kingdom

The system of public employment services in the United Kingdom comprises the Jobcentre Plus (JCP) with its network of sites, set up in 2001 by merging the Employment Service (hitherto competent for job placement) with parts of the Benefits Agency (Schütz, 2005; Knuth et al., 2004; Zwinkels et al, 2004). Jobcentre Plus is an agency of the Department for Work and Pensions (DWP), responsible for employment and labour market policy. JCP local sites are responsible for registering and placing jobseekers as well as for activating them via fortnightly work-focused interviews.

Long-term unemployed are transferred by JCP to private providers within the highly differentiated target-group programmes of the so-called New Deal, which are designed as measures for intensified integration support. The services of third parties were procured by regional JCP offices by means of competitive tendering. Long contract terms of three years have been usual (Knuth et al., 2004: 24).

In initially six structurally weak regions, the Department launched a model project to contract out so-called Employment Zones (EZ), completely transferring responsibility for integrating long-term unemployed jobseekers into the labour market to private companies. In 2004, this strategy was extended to a total of 15 regions. In six Employment Zones, competition was enhanced by commissioning several providers. In these regions, the long-term unemployed were assigned to local contract providers on a random basis. This system gave jobseekers no freedom of choice. Moreover, private providers could externalise costs by giving less intensive support to difficult-to-place jobseekers. If Employment Zone providers could not place jobseekers into work within six months, they passed them back to the public Jobcentre Plus during the early stage of the programme. In the later stage, jobseekers were again assigned to the private agency in that case. Once jobseekers had been placed by the provider, the public employment service was again responsible for them in the event of subsequent unemployment. The short-term unemployed in Employment Zone regions – like 95 per cent of all the jobless in Britain – were served by the public Jobcentre Plus.

There are two impact analyses of Employment Zones (Hasluck et al., 2003; Hales et al., 2003). The study by Hasluck et al. is particularly often cited as showing the strong impact of Employment Zones on integration (see also Finn, 2005: 241–247). To be exact, however, the two studies mentioned provide no clear evidence for any positive effects of participating in an EZ programme compared to JCP-regions with New Deal (Davies, 2008; Finn, 2009).

One finding by Hasluck et al. (2003: 67) is the negative effect of EZ programme participation on unemployment duration between 2000 and 2001 compared with long-term unemployed from the same region who had not participated in EZs. Hasluck and colleagues interpret this as a success of the Employment Zone assuming an activating effect on the unemployed who did not wish to apply to a private provider. They also report a lock-in effect, resulting in participants finding work later than non-participants. In the absence of micro data, the study is confined to a regional comparison. This alone throws a more favourable light on Employment Zones, owing, however, to higher integration rates for long-term unemployed who were *not* EZ participants, as shown earlier. Moreover, the study by Hasluck et al. also failed to produce any evidence of efficiency gains in the system as a whole and provides no evaluation of cost-effectiveness.

The study by Hales et al. (2003) examines Employment Zones on the basis of interviews with jobseekers in EZ regions and in comparable regions without such programmes, conducted 11 and 20 months after entry into the programmes. In a nutshell, this study shows only very weak evidence for improved employment prospects as a result of EZ treatment as such. Again, the small positive effects of Employment Zones are due not to participation but to non-participation in EZ programmes in the region. Non-participants occupied most of the sustainable jobs.

More recent results from impact analyses are relatively scarce. A literature review on EZ evaluation studies adds some insights from an internal DWP paper (Griffith and Durkin, 2007: 25f), in addition to presenting the results of Hales et al. (2003) and Hasluck et al. (2003). The authors argue that EZs were more effective in placement and short-term employment, but encountered significantly higher costs than comparative New Deals. EZs' better results were due to highly incentivised funding combined with their operational and financial flexibilities.

In 2009, as a consequence of a recent report (in Britain known as the 'Freud Report'), an enhanced Jobseekers Regime of the JCP and Flexible New Deal have been introduced with a four-stage process for jobseekers. JCP is delivering the first three stages (Self-managed, Directed and Supported Jobsearch). The fourth stage, the Flexible New Deal, is contracted out to so-called Prime Providers for each district, similar to the EZ programme, to reduce transaction costs for the public tendering.[13] Prime providers can subcontract smaller providers, thereby transferring the risk of outcome-related payment structures to them. Discussions on incentives and payment structures are going on despite the general re-regulation.

DISCUSSION

The aim of this chapter is to assess, from the perspective of the TLM approach, the performance potentials of the quasi-market arrangements, contracts and vouchers. Evaluation results for these arrangements from four countries are not very convincing in terms of impact and governance performance. Rigorous impact evaluations are still missing for the Dutch and Australian cases; the British and German impact evaluations do not provide strong evidence for superior performance of contracted-out placement services. Concise efficiency analyses for the instruments of the four countries are missing, too.

In particular, the German impact analysis showed hardly any positive effects arising from the tools for contracting out job placement services. Overall, participants had slightly less chance of being integrated into the general labour market than the control group. Private contractors, operating with the tools under study, managed to find work for easy-to-place target groups in good labour market situations.

Only in the case of the placement voucher does the impact analysis suggest that private agencies could place people into work more successfully than public employment service. However, the extent of deadweight losses in connection with placement vouchers is high and therefore overall effectiveness remains unclear. The voucher also provoked strong creaming. Furthermore, given the fixed price for the voucher, the price formation mechanism was invalidated. There is thus no way to ascertain whether integration services were provided at an optimum price. All the countries mentioned have difficulties maintaining good quality services at reasonable prices through competitive mechanisms.

In conclusion, the reference criteria of the TLM approach (autonomy, solidarity, effectiveness through coordinated competition and partnership arrangements, efficiency through benchmarking and evaluation) have not been sufficiently pursued and attained through the placement services that were contracted out.

None of the contract-management tools give clients choice options and could thereby increase autonomy. Only the German placement voucher and its Dutch equivalent, the individual integration agreement (IRO), satisfy the responsiveness or autonomy criteria partly as there is some autonomy for voucher holders. However, information limits of individuals about providers' quality persist and in the end not the jobseeker but the provider decides whom to work for. And only jobseekers registered by the social insurance system are entitled to get the German voucher.

All tools had problems ensuring equality of opportunity for participants. Jobseekers who have difficulties meeting market conditions have fewer prospects of active integration into placement services in both the German placement voucher system as well as the contract-based systems.

Turning to governance issues, firstly, the tools in question were clearly intended to intensify uncoordinated competition either between public and private job placement agencies (as in Germany and Britain) or competition between private for-profit and non-profit placement agencies (as in Australia and the Netherlands). And a fully privatised market structure as in Australia is no guarantee for coordinated competition at all.

Secondly, governance of quasi-markets by contracting out and vouchers has so far displayed a number of implementation and regulation deficits. The problems of contracted-out services lie in both the procurement process and local implementation. Short-term cost advantages, a weakening rather than strengthening of market structures through exaggerated competition or new market access barriers, opportunistic behaviour (moral hazard) on the part of private providers, the disadvantaging of target groups and lacking responsiveness are common effects. Pay cuts for private provider staff, worsening overall working conditions and a lack of investment are other typical consequences of price competition in order to gain contracts for the delivery of labour-market services.

The empirical findings clearly support the theoretically convincing claim that well-functioning contract management is highly demanding. Contract management is likely to fail if its incentive system is not continuously ameliorated. Independent institutions for market regulation are a necessary condition for this.

What could be viable institutional options for placement services promoting the goals of TLM? A number of alternatives are available.

Raising the Performance Potentials of Local Public Employment Services

There are at least two important roads to raise overall performance capacities of the PES (where it exists): the first is promoting public–public competition and benchmarking across local PES units, the second is increasing decentralised competencies of the local units.

Looking at the first option, it has to be said that this is fairly standard practice. Performance comparison based on outputs, outcomes and benchmarking are nowadays commonplace in many European countries. Probably best known is the lean Swiss approach of comparing local PES performance by four impact indicators, controlled for regional factors not influenced by the local PES (Hilbert, 2007). These systems become increasingly strong tools to promote performance orientation, even though they suffer often from management and implementation deficits and failure. However, if bringing control of quantitative results and dialogue-based evaluation and learning into better and relatively stable balance, there is still a high potential for performance management and benchmarking.

The second option has long been neglected and deserves more attention: a significant increase of the local discretion of the public employment agencies could improve the overall efficiency of placement services at least in those countries where PES headquarter centralism turns out to be a serious problem as in Germany. This goal could be attained with a number of different measures.

With regard to contracting out, there is a simple solution of lowering the share of compulsory central or regional tendering. Local PESs may still be obliged to purchase a certain percentage of their labour market measures through centralised tenders, but would get an enlarged share for free procurement managed by themselves if they want it. This resembles the options of Dutch municipalities as to whether they refer to tendering or free placing.

Another solution to increase local PES competencies would be the introduction of an unregulated, free 'experimental fund' for local PES agencies as an alternative to pre-determined, regulated placement tools. Agencies would receive a discretionary budget that could be activated at short notice and by which third parties could be specifically commissioned to deliver special services.

An even more radical approach that might be implemented as a very interesting pilot project is the exemption of local PES agencies from binding central and regional regulations; in addition to their funds the local units would receive only generally defined goals and targets from central sources. They would have the right to complete self-management of policies, processes and organisational tasks. This radical decentralised PES model would also be appropriate for a performance competition with Private placement agencies: both competitors would then be endowed with equal starting conditions and scope.

Supplementing Delivery Systems with Alternative Public–Private Arrangements

Transparency and easy access to information are necessary conditions to enable and empower citizens to choose, which in turn promotes quality competition between service providers. Professional associations can be made responsible for quality assurance of their members but are not necessarily suited or willing to provide maximum transparency for advice-seeking individuals. Independent, community-based information and consultation centres at local districts or even neighbourhoods might take on this task to support the needed information flows. This might be based, for instance, on co-funding from PES, private employment agencies or their associations, employers and municipalities. The partners involved would need to be willing to provide as much information as possible about the service agencies. Local community centres of this type would collect feedback information from clients' experiences with placement service providers to be used as one source for quality management of these services (also conceivable as an ombudsman function). In other words, a local partnership approach could be a partial solution for the deficiencies of contract and voucher systems in terms of market transparency, quality control, choice and coordinated competition.

However, the emergence or institutionalisation of well-functioning local social partnerships is contingent, i.e. there is neither an unequivocal guaranteed 'how-to-do-it-right' strategy nor any failsafe enforcement mechanism. Furthermore, reconciling market orientation with citizen values is also not without its tensions (Evers et al., 2002).

In a broader perspective, organisational forms of PPP might also be conceivable as an alternative or at least as a supplement to contract management or the quasi-market voucher system:

- concession models respectively franchising models, especially for implementation at regional level, or;
- models of public–private placement companies with pooled financing.

Concession models, generally speaking, are long-term contracts endowing an agency with the rights to design, produce, maintain and purchase a certain service or product. They enable long-term trust relationships with few partners and lower transaction costs, trust being a performance resource that is, as a rule, missing in the contracting model. On the other hand, concession models are potentially prone to market failure because of mono- and oligopolies as well as corruption. By contrast, short-term performance-based contracts are better equipped to maintain a competitive environment, but produce even higher control costs. To bring about and maintain at the same time competition and trust-based co-operative service delivery structures remains one of the unresolved challenges.

Franchising models of service delivery could be an interesting option in countries where regional competition between different units is to be promoted. One key idea of a franchising system is the organisational division between the system leader and the system satellites: the system leader is responsible for continuous concept development and monitors the implementation of this concept through the franchise agents. The franchise agents, in turn, produce and purchase the products of the system's concept in own financing and process responsibility but stick to the standards of the general framework. Financial compensation and grants schemes provide mutual incentives and risk sharing for optimal performances. Competition between the franchise agencies and information feedback loops to the system leader are used to transfer good practices and to bring about learning and system innovation.

Transferring the franchising approach to placement and labour market policies, it is possible to think of regional authorities providing a specific system concept for service delivery which is implemented by their local 'satellites' which could be either public or private. Performance and institutional competition would take place both across the regions as well as within the regions between the local agencies.

At local level, public employment services could be conceived of as profit centres that have to take their own decisions about the budget shares for personnel, infrastructure and policy measures on the grounds of global budget allocations from their regions. Eventual savings should be made transferable into successive budget years to be used for new investments. The local agencies might also be enabled to demand fees for specialised high-quality services, for example assisting employers in hiring employees. They might also be free to raise additional funds for placement activities within local partnerships. So far, there are no examples for qualified franchising systems in labour market policies but maybe the time is ripe to test them, even if it requires a change of legislation in some countries.

A completely different approach to the public–private mix issue is enlarging the variety of placement service providers. One option would be a new generation of public–private placement companies pooling resources from private and public stakeholders. Such a placement company would neither resemble the traditional 'employment company' (*Beschäftigungsgesellschaften*) with its strong focus on implementation of job creation measures beyond the regular labour markets. Nor would it be the same as out-placement companies of dismissed workers or the Austrian work foundations. Rather the approach would follow the idea of demand-led 'in-placement foundations' (Schmid, 2002: 292) or companies in which jobseekers are prepared and trained for jobs or job applications for specific firms with respective demand. Instead of being just a foundation of one particular firm, a placement company of this type might pool voluntary funds and grants from regional employers, raise short-term and longer-term qualification and recruiting needs of the regional firms, and provide training and placement for a whole region and not just one or a small number of employers. Employers could then profit by getting 'tailor-made' applicants, but in turn they should also bind themselves to recruit some harder-to-place candidates besides the tailor-made ones.

To sum up, improving public employment services through decentralisation and benchmarking, increasing involvement of civic communities and organisations in public and public–private employment agencies and local partnerships, as well as competitive regional franchising PPPs and placement companies represent alternatives to market-type instruments such as performance contracting and vouchers. Almost none of these alternatives outlined has been seriously implemented yet. Many of these solutions provide new patterns for public–private risk sharing, include new actors and actor coalitions, and promote empowerment and positive activation through new forms of information and accountability systems. These components correspond well with the TLM goals of preventing social exclusion, reducing labour market inequalities and raising effectiveness and efficiency of labour market policy institutions.

NOTES

1. Among the new risks are in particular higher uncertainty and the risks of job instability, income volatility even for people with higher education, 'compressed working careers' as well as diminishing earning capacities over the life course (Schmid, 2008).
2. Due to a general realignment of labour market policy instruments, the two contracting out measures have been merged with aptitude tests, training and other measures to a new instrument called measure for activation and job integration since 2009. This new measure is contracted out to private agencies with a bonus-malus-incentive structure.
3. The PES decides on the use of this instrument. If a person's unemployment exceeds six months, she or he is legally entitled to be assigned to a private agency for support. The service offered may include profiling, job application training, case management or the entire placement procedure. The analysis here is confined to full service in order to be able to evaluate the impact of the private agency. The full service can also best be compared with the other two placement tools.
4. Integration measures are used for unemployed persons with special needs and requiring intensive support. Agencies are free to decide on content and means for the flexible and innovative re-integration of clients into the labour market.
5. After six weeks of unemployment, people are entitled to a placement voucher to obtain individual support from a private agency. The voucher is worth €2,000 and is valid for three months. It can be renewed if success is not forthcoming.
6. This evaluation was a joint research project of WZB and infas Bonn. The final report is available at www.wzb.eu/ars/ab/pdf/hartz_endbericht/endbericht_komplett.pdf (accessed 15 August 2011). Doris Hess and Reiner Gilberg (infas) were responsible for the impact analysis and Petra Kaps and Silke Gülker (WZB) for the implementation analysis. Part of the data for this chapter is drawn from this project. For further details see Kaps (2009).
7. In 2005 a considerable regime change took place including a clear separation of unemployment insurance (Social Code III) from the new means-tested basic income support (Social Code II). Whereas responsibility for the insurance tier rests with the Public

Employment Service, income support is granted either by local authorities or by a mixed system involving PES and local authorities.

8. The deadweight effects cannot be precisely quantified. However, some 8 per cent of respondents exchanging vouchers admitted that potential employers had informed them beforehand about the voucher. It is to be assumed that these applicants were requested to fetch the voucher from the public employment office before hiring.

9. The most important change: during the first years half of the placement fee was paid at the very first day of employment. Since 2005 it has been paid only after six weeks of employment.

10. Due to the new Government since 2008 is has been reorganised to Department of Education, Employment and Workplace Relations (DEEWR).

11. There is no unemployment insurance in Australia.

12. For details of recent changes of contracting out by the Employment Pathway system, see Finn (2009).

13. As of September 2009, several Employment Zones contracts have been moved to Flexible New Deal contracts.

REFERENCES

Berthold, N. and S. von Berchem (2005), *Arbeitsmarktpolitik in Deutschland. Seit Jahrzehnten in der Sackgasse*, Berlin: Stiftung Marktwirtschaft.

Bredgaard, T. and F. Larsen (eds) (2005), *Employment Policy from Different Angels*, Copenhagen: DJØF Publishing.

Bruttel, O. (2005), 'Contracting-out and Governance Mechanisms in the Public Employment Service', WZB-Discussion Paper SP I 05-109, Berlin: Wissenschaftszentrum Berlin für Sozialforschung.

Carney, T. (2005), 'Lessons From Australia's Fully Privatised Labour Exchange Reform (Job Network): From "rights" to "management"?', *Zeitschrift für ausländisches und internationales Arbeits- und Sozialrecht*, **19**(1), 77–105.

Davies, S. (2008), 'Contracting out employment services to the third and private sector: a critique', *Critical Social Policy*, **28**(2), 136–164.

de Koning, J. (2004), *The Reform of the Dutch Public Employment Service*, Rotterdam: SEOR, Erasmus University Rotterdam.

de Koning, J. (ed.) (2007), *The Evaluation of Active Labour Market Policies: Measures, Public Private Partnerships and Benchmarking*, Cheltenham, UK: Edward Elgar.

Ensor, T. (2003), 'Consumer-led Demand Side Financing for Health and Education: An International Review', available at http://www.whoban.org/dsf_international_review.pdf (accessed 10 May 2008).

Evers, A., U. Rauch and U. Stitz (2002), *Von öffentlichen Einrichtungen zu sozialen Unternehmen: Hybride Organisationsformen im Bereich sozialer Dienstleistungen*, Berlin: edition sigma.

Finn, D. (2005), '"Contracting Out" and Contestability: Modernising the British Public Employment Service', in Thomas Bredgaard and Flemming Larsen (eds) *Employment Policy from Different Angels*, Copenhagen: DJØF Publishing, 233–249.

Finn, D. (2009), 'Differential pricing in contracted out employment programmes: Review of international evidence', Department for Work and Pensions: Research Report No 564.

Griffith, R. and S. Durkin (2007), 'Synthesising the evidence on Employment Zones', Department for Work and Pensions: Research Report No 449.

Gülker, S. and P. Kaps (2006), 'Effizienzsteigerung der Arbeitsvermittlung durch Contracting-Out? Eine Prozessanalyse zur öffentlich-privaten Kooperation bei vermittlungsnahen Dienstleistungen', *Zeitschrift für Sozialreform*, **52**(1), 29–52.

Hales, J., R. Taylor, W. Mandy and M. Miller (2003), *Evaluation of Employment Zones: Report on a Cohort Survey of Long-Term Unemployed People in the Zones and a Matched Set of Comparison Areas*, London/Sheffield: National Centre for Social Research.

Hasluck, C., P. Elias and A. Green (2003), *The Wider Labour Market Impact of Employment Zones*, Warwick: Institute for Employment Research.

Hilbert, C. (2007), 'Implementation of performance measurement in public employment services in Switzerland', in J. de Koning (ed.) *The Evaluation of Active Labour Market Policies: Measures, Public Private Partnerships and Benchmarking*, Cheltenham, UK: Edward Elgar, pp.330–356.

Inspectie Werk en Inkomen (2006), 'Aanbesteden van re-integratieopdrachten door gemeenten: Verkennende studie', Den Haag.

Kaps, P. (2009), 'Marketization of placement services as a double recommodification of labour', in F. Larsen and R. van Berkel (eds) *The New Governance and Implementation of Labour Market Policies*, Copenhagen: DJØF Publishing, pp.95–113.

Knuth, M., O. Schweer and S. Siemes (2004), *Drei Menüs – und kein Rezept? Dienstleistungen am Arbeitsmarkt in Großbritannien, in den Niederlanden und in Dänemark*, Bonn: Friedrich-Ebert-Stiftung.

Le Grand, J. and W. Bartlett (1993), *Quasi-Markets and Social Policy*, London: Macmillan.

Miranda, R. and A. Lerner (1995), 'Bureaucracy, Organizational Redundancy, and the Privatization of Public Services', *Public Administration Review*, **55**(2), 193–200.

Morley-Fletcher, E. (2002), 'Vouchers and Personal Welfare Accounts', Paper for the 9th BIEN International Congress, Geneva, available at http://www.basicincome.org/bien/pdf/2002Morley-Fletcher.pdf (accessed 10 May 2008).

Niskanen, W.A. (1971), *Bureaucracy and Representative Government*, Chicago and New York: Aldine Atherton.

Productivity Commission (2002), Independent review of the job network, Inquiry Report 21, Melbourne: Productivity Commission.

RWI (2006), *De route naar resultaat: Reintegratiemarktanalyse 2006*, Raad voor Werk en Inkomen.

Schmid, G. (2002), *Wege in eine neue Vollbeschäftigung:Übergangsarbeitsmärkte und aktivierende Arbeitsmarktpolitik*, Frankfurt and New York: Campus.

Schmid, G. (2008), *Full Employment in Europe. Managing Labour Market Transitions and Risks*, Cheltenham, UK and Northhampton, MA, US: Edward Elgar.

Schuppert, G.F. (1995), 'Rückzug des Staates? Zur Rolle des Staates zwischen Legitimationskrise und politischer Neubestimmung', *Die Öffentliche Verwaltung*, **48**(18), 761–770.

Schütz, H. (2005), 'Reformprozesse und Controlling öffentlicher Beschäftigungsdienste: Großbritannien, die Niederlande und Deutschland im Vergleich', in H.

Schütz and H. Mosley (eds) *Arbeitsagenturen auf dem Prüfstand – Leistungsvergleich und Reformpraxis der Arbeitsvermittlung*, Modernisierung des öffentlichen Sektors, Sonderband 24, Berlin: edition sigma, pp.241–269.

Schütz, H. and H. Mosley (eds) (2005), *Arbeitsagenturen auf dem Prüfstand – Leistungsvergleich und Reformpraxis der Arbeitsvermittlung*, Modernisierung des öffentlichen Sektors, Sonderband 24, Berlin: edition sigma.

SEO (2006), *Werkt de reintegratiemarkt? Onderzoek naar de marktwerking op de reintegratiemarkt*, Eindrapport in opdracht van het Ministerie van Sociale Zaken en Werkgelegenheid, Amsterdam.

Sol, E. (2005), 'Contracting out of Public Employment Systems from a Governance Perspective', in T. Bredgaard and F. Larsen (eds) *Employment Policy from Different Angels*, Copenhagen: DJØF Publishing, pp.155–173.

Struyven, L. (2004), 'Design choices in market competition for Employment Services for the long-term unemployed', OECD Social, Employment and Migration Working-Papers No. 21. Paris: OECD.

Struyven, L. (2005), 'The New Institutional Logic of Public Employment Services', in T. Bredgaard and F. Larsen (eds) *Employment Policy from Different Angels*, Copenhagen: DJØF Publishing, pp.175–190.

Struyven, L. and G. Steurs (2003), 'Towards a Quasi-Market in Reintegration Services: First Assessment of the Dutch Experience', *Australian Journal of Labour Economics*, **6**(2), 331–355.

Struyven, L. and G. Steurs (2005), 'Design and redesign of a quasi-market for the reintegration of jobseekers: empirical evidence from Australia and the Netherlands', *Journal of European Social Policy*, **3**(15), 211–229.

van Berkel, R. and P. van der Aa (2005), 'The marketization of activation services: a modern panacea? Some lessons from the Dutch experience', *Journal of European Social Policy*, **15**(4), 329–343.

Verveen, E., S. Bunt, C. Bos and M. van der Aalst (2006), 'Ontwikkelingen op de reintegratiemarkt. Ervaringen van opdrachtgevers en opdrachtnemers', study by Research voor Beleid commissioned by Raad voor Werk en Inkomen Den Haag.

WZB/infas (several authors) (2006), Evaluation der Maßnahmen zur Umsetzung der Vorschläge der Hartz-Kommission. Modul 1a: Neuausrichtung der Vermittlungsprozesse, Final Report 2006, Berlin, Bonn.

Zwinkels, W., J. van Genabeek and I. Groot (2004), 'Buitenlandse ervaringen met de aanbesteding', study by SEO and TNO Arbeid, commissioned by Raad voor Werk en Inkomen, Den Haag.

5. Working-time options over the life course: challenges and company practices

Philip Wotschack

INTRODUCTION

For a number of reasons life course oriented approaches have a specific significance for organising working-time. Among these reasons are current demographic changes and profound transformations in the system of gainful employment and employment biographies. The aim of life course oriented approaches is to create new and better ways for employees to adapt their working time to their changing needs over the life course, in particular to have time for providing care and nursing, and for recreation and further education. This chapter uses empirical examples of long-term or working-life time accounts to examine whether and under which conditions these approaches are actually implemented in company practice. It also outlines new risks and challenges raised by the recent economic crisis. First, current demands regarding the organisation of working time are outlined and new approaches to life course oriented working-time policy are presented. The opportunities and restrictions associated with individual options for the organisation of the working lifetime are then discussed on the basis of recent research results on the distribution and utilisation of working-life time accounts. The results indicate that there are significant barriers to and difficulties with the implementation of working-life time accounts. They underline the need for an integrated approach to life course oriented working-time organisation that links individual working-time options with working-time reductions and active employment policy at both the company and collective-bargaining and statutory levels.

THE TRANSFORMATION OF EMPLOYMENT BIOGRAPHIES: NEW DEMANDS ON WORKING-TIME ORGANISATION

The structure of gainful employment and the employment biographies of workers are changing. One significant characteristic of this trend is the increase in risks and in the necessity for action with respect to the way that workers shape their lives (see Anxo et al., 2008; Ester et al., 2008; Schmid, 2008; Groot and Breedveld, 2004; Naegele et al., 2010).

Periods of unemployment and company or occupational crises have become the new normality for many workers – a situation that has been further exacerbated by the current economic crisis (European Commission, 2009). The prospects of enjoying uninterrupted employment biographies, long-term employment with a single employer and career trajectories within one company are increasingly limited nowadays (Heinz, 2005; Schmid and Protsch, 2009) and are even less likely as the crisis persists. The share of temporary, precarious and unstable forms of employment has increased. Already, at the beginning of the crisis, around 3 million workers were in precarious employment relationships in Germany (Giesecke and Wotschack, 2009). According to a representative survey carried out by *Sozialforschungsstelle Dortmund* at the end of 2005, almost every third German enterprise had reacted to falling orders by laying off temporary employees. There is thus substantial evidence that the weakened economic climate is leading enterprises to cut back on so-called non-core workers. There is a particular need for supportive measures to maintain and/or improve the labour market chances and employability of the groups at risk of job loss, for example through the enhancement of skill potentials with a view to creating access to new employment opportunities (European Commission, 2008; Moraal, 2007).

The access of enterprises to human capital has grown overall. High workloads increase the risk of premature unemployability or occupational invalidity and restrict the duration of workers' potential tenure in the employment system (Green, 2007; European Commission, 2009). The flexibilisation and lengthening of working hours in recent years have shifted the temporal parameters to a prioritisation of employment (Seifert, 2004). This jeopardises both the reconciliation of gainful employment with other areas of life, especially those involving family and care obligations, and the long-term maintenance of health (Plantenga and Remery, 2006; Fagan, 2004; Wotschack et al., 2007). At the same time, short innovation cycles and new strategies of work organisation and personnel management pose new and constantly changing demands on employees with respect to job specifications and skill requirements and presuppose their investment in continuous further training (see Bosch et al., 2010; Mayer and Solga, 2008; Solga, 2008; Adecco Institute, 2009).

As a consequence of an increase in female employment and family-friendly employment arrangements, the traditional male life course – based on a tripartite division into a training, employment and retirement phase – is losing significance. Similarly the alleged female counterpart in the form of a division into training phase, employment phase and family phase is also losing ground. Furthermore, as the population ages, care demands on families are increasing (Den Dulk and Van Doorne-Huiskes, 2008). Frequent overlaps and (recurring) transitions between phases of training, employment, childcare, nursing care, unemployment, different employers and vocational reorientation are increasingly becoming the norm. The time burden in the mid-phase of life is exacting on workers with family and care responsibilities, which can lead – especially for women, but increasingly also for men – to severe problems in managing the work-life balance (Fagan, 2004; Cousins and Tang, 2004; Plantenga and Remery, 2006; O'Reilly et al., 2000; O'Reilly, 2003).

Rapid demographic change – caused by low birth rates alongside growing life expectancy – and the associated social and economic risks have set into motion a political debate on reform calling for longer employment durations and an increase in the labour force potential of society (see European Commission, 2005 and 2008). Important interim goals identified along this path are improved possibilities for both men and women to reconcile the occupational and non-occupational demands facing them in life. The keywords here are 'easing' of dense time burdens in mid-life, redistribution of employment and care work between women and men, and lifelong learning approaches within the context of in-company further training.

The changes outlined here are straining the confines of many of the existing institutional arrangements at statutory, collective agreement and company level. New solutions are required (Anxo et al., 2008: 83; Ester et al., 2008; Schmid, 2008; Schmid and Gazier, 2002), in particular new approaches to the organisation of working time that seek to reorganise working time over the course of workers' employment biographies (Klammer, 2008; Anxo and Boulin, 2006; Den Dulk, 2001). The next section discusses such approaches with a focus on the concept of life course oriented working-time organisation.

LIFE COURSE ORIENTED APPROACHES TO WORKING-TIME ORGANISATION

The concept of life course oriented working-time organisation concerns arrangements that enable better adaptation of individual working time to the changing demands of the different spheres of life over the life course. In Germany, the 7th Family Report of the German Federal Ministry for Family Affairs, Senior Citizens, Women and Youth stressed the concept of 'optional periods' (*Optionszeiten*) to describe an approach that would enable workers to take time out during their working life for family duties ('care periods'), for preventive or reintegrative training measures ('educational periods') and for civil engagement ('social periods') (BMFSFJ, 2006).

A main prerequisite for such options (their implementation via the concept of optional periods will not be discussed further here[1]) is the possibility of periodic reductions (at least) in the volume of working time over the course of working life in accordance with individual family, educational or health-related needs. Such options must also take into account the unpredictability and complexity of these needs, for example as a result of changing interests and life situations, personal or occupational crises, or the unexpected need to provide care or nursing (Den Dulk and Van Doorne-Huiskes, 2008; Anxo and Boulin, 2006; Naegele et al., 2003).

The extent to which such options are actually available in practice for employees depends first and foremost on in-company working-time arrangements, which cannot, in turn, be seen in isolation from individual company's working-time organisation, performance policy, remuneration structure and corporate culture. In the current debate on working time, it is possible to identify three basic approaches to achieving better adjustment of the volume of working time to specific temporal needs over the life course (for further details, see Anxo et al., 2006a, 2006b and 2008).

First, we find approaches that enable a reduction of gainful employment on the occurrence of events that have been defined in advance or when a worker arrives at a particular age threshold. Examples are maternity leave, parental leave, nursing-care leave, semi-retirement and regulations on (early) retirement. These can be termed 'life-phase oriented' working-time options because they are linked to the occurrence of particular events such as the birth of a child or the worker's arrival at statutory retirement age.

Such approaches are distinguished, second, from optional models that allow employees to react individually and flexibly to their concrete time needs and time interests over the life course, for example by means of leave and part-time options, working-time accounts and working-life time models. These approaches can be called 'life course oriented' working-time options, because they are formally subject to the decisions of the individual worker, but not necessarily bound to the occurrence of predefined life phases or events.

A third variant, which has not been at the forefront of political debate in recent years, but may certainly become significant again in the context of the current economic crisis, seeks collective reduction of weekly working hours (see, e.g., Spitzley's 2005 proposal regarding 'short full-time'). Unlike the life-phase oriented model outlined above, this approach could represent the basis for better reconciliation overall between the different areas of life.

Optional models of life-course oriented working-time organisation are currently receiving particular consideration in the public debate. For Germany this is evidenced, for example, by the above mentioned concept of 'optional periods' described in the 7th Family Report, and most recently by a number of 'demographic collective agreements' signed by German trade unions. For the last few years, enterprises, too – using concepts of 'demographically conscious personnel management' (see Bertelsmann Stiftung, 2008) and 'life-cycle oriented personnel work' (IW, 2006) – have increasingly been anticipating the risks and problems associated with demographic change as represented by ageing workforces, the generally diminishing labour force potential and the growing need for skilled labour (see, e.g., the Kienbaum study 'Personalentwicklung 2008'). In this context, working-time organisation is named as a major field for action, in addition to reconciliation of work and family life, lifelong learning, personnel development, management of age and ageing and health management (see IW, 2006; Econsense, 2006; Adecco Institute, 2009). In recent years, many enterprises have launched projects in the areas of demographically conscious and life-cycle oriented personnel work (see Bertelsmann Stiftung, 2008; Wotschack and Hildebrandt, 2008). As regards the area of working-time organisation, models have been introduced in particular that appear suited to reconciling enterprises' need for flexibility with individual organisational options for employees. In this respect, enterprises, the state and the bargaining partners are especially examining long-term or working-life time accounts as a potential new instrument of life-course oriented labour policy. The question that thus arises is how this instrument affects company practice and whether and under which conditions it actually does justice to the goals of life-course oriented working-time organisation.

INDIVIDUAL OPTIONS FOR ORGANISING WORKING TIME OVER THE LIFE COURSE: WORKING-LIFE TIME ACCOUNTS IN COMPANY PRACTICE

The utilisation of working-life time accounts and their potential for the life organisation of workers was the leading question behind our empirical research project 'Working-life time accounts and biographical life organisation' carried out from 2006 to 2008 at the Social Science Research Centre Berlin (WZB)[2] (for details, see Hildebrandt et al., 2009; Wotschack and Hildebrandt, 2008). The study was based on a representative company survey, detailed interviews with decision-makers and experts in leading companies, and standardised employee questionnaires and in-depth interviews with workers. The most important results of our study with respect to the importance of working-life time accounts in the context of life course oriented working-time organisation will be outlined in the following. They evidence fundamental barriers to and difficulties with the implementation of life course oriented working-time options, which provide insights as to required improvements and extensions to working-life time models – also in reference to the current economic crisis.

Working-life time accounts are defined in the following as all working-time accounts with a balancing period of over one year. In autumn 2005, 7 per cent of the German companies offered their employees working-life time accounts, while among large enterprises with more than 500 employees, every fourth company already had such accounts (Wotschack and Hildebrandt, 2008). The basic functioning of a working-life time account is simple: employees can deposit overtime hours, other time components (such as residual holiday leave) or due remuneration in a time account over the course of many years and then withdraw these deposits at a later point in time for prolonged periods of leave, for example for holidays lasting several months, or for childcare, further training or early retirement. The advantage for enterprises is greater scope for flexibility. In periods of high demand, they can use overtime work by their employees without having to compensate these extra hours directly – i.e., immediately – through remuneration or free time or by means of supplements or bonuses. Every hour worked above and beyond contractually agreed weekly working hours can be deposited in the working-life time account. The enterprise thus has a working-time instrument at its disposal that enables at the same time better reconciliation of work and family life over the employees' employment biography and better management of time periods for lifelong learning in the context of in-plant further training.

Working-life time accounts can be of great benefit to employees especially in the family phase of life, when the presence of children increases the household's need for time and money in equal measure. They allow workers to withdraw time from the account and work less during certain periods without having to forfeit their income. The same applies to other goals, such as further training and study, voluntary activities, early or gradual retirement, and lengthy time-out periods for recuperation and relaxation. The availability of such time options over the course of life can contribute not only to increasing employees' satisfaction and the quality of their work and life in general; they also offer the possibility of compensating for overtime hours at least in the long term and using the time gained for maintaining health and employability and achieving more successful reconciliation of gainful employment with other areas of life.

Low Distribution and Low Utilisation

The results of the project on the actual utilisation of working-life time accounts are rather sobering, however. Working-life time accounts are rarely found in small and medium-sized enterprises. In those companies where working-life time accounts are made available, their designated purposes are often limited. In large enterprises, especially, these accounts are mainly used for dealing with the transition into retirement (see Table 5.1).

Table 5.1 Distribution of uses for working-life time accounts, by company size (multiple responses possible) – in %

	All companies	*1–9 employees*	*10–49 employees*	*50–249 employees*	*250+ employees*
Further training	17	17	12	27	50
Sabbatical	6	2	9	17	27
Family time	27	17	39	42	26
Temporary part-time	30	17	45	47	28
Semi-retirement	7	6	1	23	69
Early retirement	6	6	1	20	54
Other	64	64	70	51	34

Note: Only companies with working-life time accounts: n=204.

Source: WZB evaluation of a representative company survey carried out by Sozialforschungsstelle Dortmund (2005).

In addition, in most companies, adjustment to fluctuations in orders plays an important role in this context. When working-life time accounts are organised in this way, little time credit can be accumulated for later use for training, family life, care-giving or recuperation. This can be demonstrated by a simple model calculation: if every year two hours a week are deposited in the working-life time account, it would take around 22 years – given 220 working days a year – before leave amounting to one year would become possible. The way that this time credit is then used, either preventively so as to achieve a better balance between the different areas of life or for further training, or remedially for early exit from working life, must be given careful consideration. Workers would hardly find it possible to do both.

Surprisingly, few employees in companies with working-life time accounts tend to actually use the accounts, and if they do, then they do so by and large modestly. Among the workers surveyed in a large service company (with over 10,000 employees), only every fourth employee took advantage of this possibility. This general impression is supported by the results from almost all the companies surveyed. Likewise among the workers questioned in a medium-large industrial company (with fewer than 10,000 employees), at the time of the survey only every fourth was in favour of extending the existing working-time accounts into the form of a working-life time account.

A major problem that emerges is that the working-life time account is used significantly less by employees who work in the operative or blue-collar sector (see Figure 5.1), who have low skills and income, who have precarious employment relationships and who have to cope with challenging non-work demands outside their occupation.

Thus, those employees who are faced particularly often with problems of reconcilability and health deterioration and have considerable need for further training are the very ones who have the least credit in their working-life time accounts. In short, the working-life time account is available less often to those employees for whom it is meant to represent a particularly important instrument within the framework of life course oriented working-time organisation. What are the reasons for this?

Reasons for Low Distribution and Low Utilisation

Our study identified five barriers to use that represent a severe impediment to widespread adoption and successful application of working-life time accounts within the context of life course oriented working-time organisation.

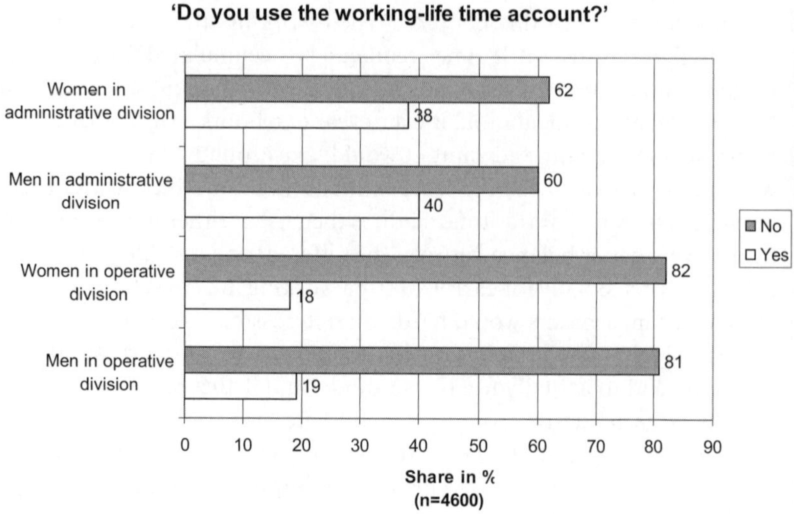

'Do you use the working-life time account?'

		Share in % (n=4600)

Women in administrative division: 62 / 38
Men in administrative division: 60 / 40
Women in operative division: 82 / 18
Men in operative division: 81 / 19

Legend: ■ No □ Yes

Sources: Wotschack et al., 2008: WZB evaluation of a survey among employees in a large service enterprise.

Figure 5.1 Utilisation of working-life time accounts, by gender and corporate division

Limited temporal and financial resources

The maintenance of the daily work-life balance leaves workers little scope for the working-life time account. Most employees – regardless of gender, company position and life phase – attach high priority to an appropriate balance between work and non-work activities (see Figure 5.2). Many workers from low-skilled and low-income groups, who depend on remuneration for overtime hours, and many workers with small children or care-giving duties, have little time left for accumulating hours in their working-life time account.

Inadequate integration with and support from personnel policy

In company practice, working-life time accounts are often used as an 'alternative solution' to state-funded semi-retirement or premature exit from working life. Employees rarely receive explicit encouragement to make individual use of working-life time accounts during their working lives. Indeed, employees who wish to withdraw time deposits often meet with reservations on the part of their superiors. One of the problems here is a lack of relevant training and experience on the part of managers. As a

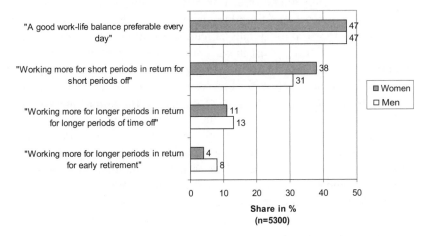

'Which personal time management do you prefer?'

Source: Wotschack et al., 2008: WZB evaluation of a survey among employees in a large service enterprise.

Figure 5.2 Preferred time management of male and female workers

result, employees often receive little assistance in the use of the working-life time account. We also found that there was no systematic link between the working-life time account and other areas of personnel policy in any of the companies we surveyed. Even companies with specific programmes in the areas of further training, health and reconcilability do not integrate these with the working-life time account.

Lack of long-term perspective

A working-life time account does not develop its full benefit until the medium or long term, when substantial time deposits have been accumulated. However, a long-term perspective is no longer a matter of course for a growing share of workers. Temporary employment contracts, precarious career paths and the threat of job loss make the likelihood of remaining at length with a single company seem uncertain. Almost all the enterprises we surveyed have made substantial redundancies in recent years, which has created great insecurity among the employees. Of the service employees we questioned, only every second worker reported a sense of job security, and only every fourth envisaged good career prospects for him or herself. If a worker's future in a company is uncertain, then the sense and purpose of a working-life time account also becomes doubtful.

Problems with insolvency protection and transferability
In the case of premature termination of the employment relationship, the working-life time account is said to 'break down'. This usually means that the credit in the account should be reimbursed monetarily. However, this option does not always exist in current practice, which increases the risk that the credit will be forfeited. According to a representative survey carried out by the German Institute for Employment Research (IAB), in 2006 only one-third of enterprises had protected their working-life time accounts against insolvency (Fischer et al., 2007). Protection against insolvency is much more widespread in German companies with a works council, according to a works council survey carried out by the WSI in 2007. Insolvency protection is especially a problem in small and medium-sized companies and in those without a works council. While a new German ('Flexi II') law (on improving the parameters for the protection under social law of flexible working-time regulations) created the possibility to transfer credit to the new employer, there is still no guarantee that the new employer will actually take over the credit. These uncertainties render the working-life time account less attractive for many workers.

Impaired trust
An important variable that influences the acceptance of working-life time accounts in enterprises is the working-time and corporate culture of the enterprise itself. Workers who have experienced a balanced equilibrium between company and employee interests in the past, who trust the management and executive levels and who envisage security and career possibilities for themselves in the company are also more willing to use a working-life time account. By contrast, impaired relationships of trust in these areas have a negative effect on employees' willingness to adopt a new working-time instrument such as the working-life time account.

New Risks Posed by the Economic Crisis

All in all, the results of our study show that the potential of working-life time accounts to improve the balance between different areas of life over the employment biography or to increase participation in further training by employees has hardly been exploited to date. A particularly serious problem appears to be the instrument's high degree of selectivity, which leads to particularly low utilisation of working-life time accounts among employees in the blue-collar or operative sectors, among low-skilled and low-income groups, and among employees with care obligations. Moreover, employees in the group of so-called non-core workers, consisting of agency workers or workers on short-term contracts, are rarely entitled to a working-life time account.

In the current economic crisis, there is a growing risk that the goals of short- and medium-term safeguarding of employment will be sought at the expense of a preventive labour market policy geared towards the maintenance of employability and labour market availability. Preliminary evidence of this danger is found in recent studies. At the end of 2005 (i.e., prior to the current crisis), in a representative survey carried out by Sozialforschungsstelle Dortmund, almost two-thirds of the companies with working-life time accounts reported that they reacted to slack order periods by depleting time credits. In a recent ad-hoc survey of 1,700 German enterprises (between May and June 2009), almost a quarter of all companies (including those without working-life time accounts and those faced with declining demand) reported that they were reacting to the current crisis by using up time credits (IW Consult GmbH, 2009).

Similar to the instrument of short-time work, such consumption of overtime and time credits in order to bridge slack periods is associated with shifting costs onto employees, who use up their time credits in order to avoid a possible loss of income or of their job. The employees' medium- and long-term plans for the time credits, such as leave for family life, further training, early retirement or maintenance of a 'time buffer' for the event that a family member might suddenly require care, can be jeopardised by this practice. Such access by the company to the employees' working-life time accounts – even if it takes place in the interests of the employees – runs the risk of undermining trust in this instrument. The concrete design and regulation of the working-time account or working-life time account are vitally important here. Some large enterprises have separate account systems within the framework of working-life time accounts to ensure job security in the event of (long-term) falls in orders. There are also special, protected time accounts for in-company further training or for individual use. These solutions prevent the risk of the goal of job security standing in conflict with other goals. In the case of working-life time accounts, insolvency protection is another extremely important factor. Although insolvency protection is prescribed by law, in actual practice less than every third enterprise with working-life time accounts is insured against bankruptcy (Fischer et al., 2007). Thus, in times of crisis, especially, there is a substantial risk of employees losing their time credits as a result of company bankruptcy.

CONCLUSIONS: THE NEED FOR AN INTEGRATED APPROACH TO WORKING TIME POLICIES

Against the background of the problems outlined above, three conclusions may be drawn for a successful, life course oriented organisation of working time. These become particularly important in the context of the current economic crisis and relate to (1) the concrete configuration of working-life time models (instrumental level), (2) required extensions to purely optional models of life course oriented working-time organisation (company operational level) and (3) required supportive measures on the part of the bargaining partners and the state (state and sectoral operational level).

Specific Orientation and Design of Working-life Time Models

In order to make better use of the possibilities for implementing working-life time accounts within the framework of a life course oriented or demographically conscious personnel policy, it would make sense to distinguish between leave for further training, recuperation, family life and care-giving, and other purposes such as early retirement or job security that are increasing in significance due to the current crisis. Some enterprises (e.g., Airbus) already have separate account systems for company and employee purposes and for joint company–employee interests such as bridging slack periods. These have proven to be effective in practice.

A systematic link between the working-life time account and company policy on further training, health and the work-life balance would also make sense. In this way, periods of time for lifelong learning, family, care-giving and recuperation could be created for company labour policy. In order that credit withdrawals are actually made possible for these purposes, there are two essential prerequisites: on the one hand, binding regulations regarding entitlement to withdrawals and, on the other, specific training and advice for managers so that they are able to implement time withdrawals within the framework of the company's work organisation.

Finally, there is a clear need for specific, supportive measures for low-skilled and low-income groups and for employees with family and care duties, in order to also enable these groups to accumulate adequate time credits. At the same time, the access of so-called non-core workers (agency workers and workers on short-term contracts) to working-life time accounts should also be ensured. Not only is the job security of this group at particular risk, but the brief duration of their employment contracts also means that they are rarely able to build up benefit entitlements from unemployment insurance that would secure their livelihood. The accumulation of time credits in a working-life time account would enable them to bridge phases of unemployment and use the free time for further vocational training. Given that one of the main reasons for the low utilisation of working-life time accounts are the structural, temporal and financial restrictions faced by large groups of workers, a general increase in willingness to use them cannot be achieved only at the instrumental level. This is where company and sectoral policy on working time, remuneration and performance can play a role.

Linking Optional Instruments with Working-time Reductions

The three varieties of life course oriented working-time organisation described at the beginning of this chapter – optional, life-phase oriented and collective working-time reductions – are not by any means mutually exclusive. On the contrary, they depend on each other in many respects and associations between them can be very productive, for example by linking collective working-time reductions with working-life time accounts or leave models. Thus, individual working-time options targeted at temporary reductions in working time or leave over the life course can only produce a comprehensive effect if standard working hours and work requirements leave scope for leave or phases of part-time employment. In addition to working-time organisation, appropriate company performance policy and adequate staffing are thus also required. In particular, individual account models (such as long-term or working-life time accounts) based on deposits of overtime hours and due remuneration will only help to comprehensively reduce the time burden on employees if their collectively agreed or contractual working hours allow them to accumulate sufficient time credits without severely jeopardising the daily balance between gainful employment, partnership, family life, leisure time and recuperation. This possibility rises the more the collectively or contractually agreed volume of working time decreases; in other words, overtime hours begin at a lower threshold. Finally, a role is also played by employment policy, which has become particularly significant under the circumstances of the current crisis. In order to develop a broad and integrative effect that also boosts job security and active labour market policy, life course oriented working-time organisation must combine individual models of redistribution or restructuring of working time over the life course with a policy of collective redistribution of gainful employment and improved possibilities for participation in working life. An attempt to combine working-time reductions with the aims of employment security and the provision of time for further training was briefly evident in Germany's second economic recovery package (*Konjunk-turpaket II*). In this context, the federal government had initially (until 30 June 2009) extended eligibility for short-time working allowance from 12 to 18 months and at the same time provided incentives for further training measures. The Federal Employment Agency reimbursed employers for their entire social insurance contributions if the period of short-time work was used for further training. This incentive was withdrawn again under the new regulation from July 2009 onwards.

Support for Company Working-time Policy from the State and Collective Bargaining

Research to date indicates that there is inadequate dovetailing between supportive measures and regulations at company, collective bargaining and legislative level (see Wotschack and Hildebrandt, 2008; Klammer, 2008). So far there is no evidence of a consistent, multilevel policy in Germany for dealing with the risks related to demographic change. On the contrary, there is a trend towards over-reliance on company-based approaches to preventive labour policy through the withdrawal or insufficient involvement of government policy, for example with respect to older workers' transition into retirement (retirement at age 67 or the expiry of state-funded semi-retirement) and in the area of reconciliation between work and family life (the infrastructure for childcare). Specifically, the question here is how 'remedial' or 'integrative' (Bertelsmann Stiftung, 2008) instruments of working-time and skills policy, which are aimed at safeguarding employ-ability and the organisation of older workers' (aged 50 plus) transition into retirement, can be combined with 'pre-emptive' or 'preventive' approaches for younger workers while avoiding the danger of competition from or excessive demands on company labour policy. Potential negative conse-quences (evidenced by current research) range from a low commitment by companies to preventive labour policy to counterproductive measures in the shape of a higher burden on younger workers or a one-sided orientation of labour policy towards transition into retirement (see Wotschack and Hildebrandt, 2008). The long-term risk is the reproduction or, worse, the exacerbation of companies' difficulties due to demographic change; in other words, the opposite of a preventively disposed labour policy and life course oriented working-time organisation.

All in all, the success of a working-time policy that takes account of demographic change and has a preventive orientation will depend substan-tially on whether it will prove possible to overcome access barriers described earlier in the chapter and work towards a useful integration in working-time policy of optional, life-phase oriented and collective working-time reductions. The current crisis has further exacerbated the economic pressure. This increases the risk that economic cost-benefit calculations and rationalisation strategies to reduce personnel costs in the short term will become more prevalent and lend further weight to the barriers described here. In this situation, it becomes even more important to find ways to overcome them. Otherwise, restricted access to and unequal opportunities to make use of preventive labour policy instruments may further deepen existing social disparities in employment and career biographies.

NOTES

[1.] On this topic, see the further-reaching concept of 'guaranteed optionality' (see, e.g., Hinrichs, 1992), which explicitly envisages linking entitlement to individual working-time reductions.

[2.] The study was funded by the Hans-Böckler-Stiftung.

REFERENCES

Adecco Institute (2009), 'Demographic Fitness of Companies in Rough Economic Waters', Demographic Fitness Survey 2007, Adecco Institute White Paper, London.

Anxo, D. and J.-Y. Boulin (coordinators) for the European Foundation, and co-authors: I. Cebrián, C. Fagan, S. Keuzenkamp, U. Klammer, C. Klenner, G. Moreno and L. Toharia (2005), *Working Time Options over the Life Course: Changing Social Security Structures*, European Foundation for the Improvement of Living and Working Conditions. Luxembourg: Office for Official Publications of the European Communities.

Anxo, D., J.-Y. Boulin and C. Fagan (2006a), 'Decent working time in a life-course perspective', in J.-Y. Boulin, M. Lallement, J. Messenger and F. Michon (eds) *Decent Working Time: New Trends, New Issues*. Geneva: ILO, 93–122.

Anxo, D., J.-Y. Boulin, C. Fagan, I. Cebrián, S. Keuzenkamp, U. Klammer, Chr. Klenner, G. Moreno and L. Toharía (2006b), *Working Time Options over the Life Course: New Work Patterns and Company Strategies*, European Foundation for the Improvement of Living and Working Conditions, Luxembourg: Office for Official Publications of the European Communities.

Anxo, D. and J.-Y. Boulin (2006), 'The Organisation of Time over the Life Course', *European Societies*, **8**(2), 319–341.

Anxo, D., C. Erhel and J. Schippers (2008), *Labour Market Transitions and Time Adjustment over the Life Course*, Amsterdam: Dutch University Press.

Bertelsmann Stiftung and Bundesvereinigung der Deutschen Arbeitgeberverbände (eds) (2008), 'Demographiebewusstes Personalmanagement. Strategien und Beispiele für die betriebliche Praxis', study carried out by M. Morschhäuser, P. Ochs and A. Huber at ISO Saarbrücken, Gütersloh.

Beynon, H., D. Grimshaw, J. Rubery and K. Ward (2002), *Managing Employment Change: The New Realities of Work*, Oxford: Oxford University Press.

BMFSFJ (2006), '7. Familienbericht. Familie zwischen Flexibilität und Verlässlichkeit – Perspektiven für eine lebenslaufbezogene Familienpolitik', Berlin: BMFSFJ.

Bosch, G., S. Krone and D. Langer (eds) (2010), *Das Berufsbildungssystem in Deutschland. Aktuelle Entwicklungen und Standpunkte*, Wiesbaden: VS Verlag für Sozialwissenschaften.

Cousins, R.C. and N. Tang (2004), 'Working Time and Work and Family Conflict in the Netherlands, Sweden and the UK', *Work, Employment and Society*, **18**(3), 531–549.

Den Dulk, L. (2001), *Work-Family Arrangements in Organisations*, Amsterdam: Rozenberg publishers.

Den Dulk, L. and A. Van Doorne-Huiskes (2008), 'Life-Course Policies in the Netherlands: An Answer to Work-Care Dilemmas in an Aging Society', in S. Brandl, E. Hildebrandt and P. Wotschack (eds) *Arbeitszeitpolitik im Lebensverlauf. Ambivalenzen und Gestaltungsoptionen in deutscher und europäischer Perspektive*, Düsseldorf: Edition der Hans-Böckler-Stiftung, pp.147–163.

Econsense (2006), 'Die demographische Herausforderung gestalten. Arbeitsdokument, November 2006', Berlin: Econsense – Forum Nachhaltige Entwicklung der Deutschen Wirtschaft e.V.

Ester, P., R. Muffels, J. Schippers and T. Wilthagen (eds) (2008), *Innovating European Labour Markets: Dynamics and Perspectives*, Cheltenham, UK and Northampton, MA, USA: Edward Elgar Publishing.

European Commission (2005), 'Confronting demographic change: A new solidarity between the generations', Green Paper, COM/2005/0094 final, Brussels.

European Commission (2008), *New Skills for New Jobs. Anticipating and Matching Labour Market and Skill Needs*, Luxembourg: Office for Official Publications of the European Communities.

European Commission (2009), 'Employment in Europe 2009. Employment, Social Affairs, and Equal Opportunities', Luxembourg: Office for Official Publications of the European Communities.

European Foundation for the Improvement of Living and Working Conditions (2006), *Employment Initiatives for an Ageing Workforce in the EU*, Luxembourg: Office for Official Publications of the European Communities.

Fagan, C. (2004), 'Gender and Working-time in Industrialized Countries: Practices and Preferences', in J.C. Messenger (ed.) *Working Time and Workers' Preferences in Industrialized Countries: Finding the Balance*, New York, Oxford: Routledge, pp.108–146.

Fischer, G., J. Wahse, V. Dahms, M. Frei, A. Riedmann and F. Janik (2007), 'Standortbedingungen und Beschäftigung in den Regionen West- und Ostdeutschlands', Ergebnisse des IAB-Betriebspanels 2006, IAB-Forschungsbericht 5/2007, Nürnberg: Institut für Arbeitsmarkt- und Berufsforschung der Bundesagentur für Arbeit.

Giesecke, J. and P. Wotschack (2009), 'Flexibilisierung in Zeiten der Krise: Verlierer sind junge und gering qualifizierte Beschäftigte', WZBrief Arbeit 01/2009, available at http://bibliothek.wzb.eu/wzbrief-arbeit/WZBriefArbeit012009_giesecke_wotschack.pdf (accessed 30 July 2009).

Green, F. (2007), *Demanding Work: The Paradox of Job Quality in the Affluent Economy*, Princeton: Princeton University Press.

Groot, L. and K. Breedveld (2004), 'Time over the Life Course: Preferences, Options and Life Course Policy', *Tijdschrift voor Arbeidsvraagstukken*, Special Issue, **20**(3) 288–302.

Groß, H. and M. Schwarz (2007), 'Betriebs- und Arbeitszeiten 2005', Ergebnisse einer repräsentativen Betriebsbefragung, Beiträge aus der Forschung, 153, Dortmund: Sozialforschungsstelle Dortmund (sfs).

Heinz, W.R. (2005), 'From Work Trajectories to Negotiated Careers. The Contingent Work Life Course', in J.T. Mortimer and M.J. Shanahan (eds) *Handbook of the Life Course*, New York: Springer Verlag.

Hildebrandt, E., P. Wotschack and A. Kirschbaum (2009), *Zeit auf der hohen Kante. Langzeitkonten in der betrieblichen Praxis und Lebensgestaltung von Beschäftigten*. Forschung aus der Hans-Böckler-Stiftung, Bd. 100, Berlin: Edition Sigma.

Hinrichs, K. (1992), 'Zur Zukunft der Arbeitszeitflexibilisierung: Arbeitnehmerpräferenzen, betriebliche Interessen und Beschäftigungswirkungen', *Soziale Welt*, **43**(2), 313–330.

IW (2006), 'Projektergebnisbericht: Lebenszyklusorientierte Personolitik – "Work-Life-Balance"-Modelle und "Demographietools" für die betriebliche Praxis', Studie des Instituts der deutschen Wirtschaft im Auftrag der DekaBank, Cologne.

IW Consult GmbH (2009), 'Ad-hoc-Umfrage "Momentane Situation" und zukünftige Einschätzung der deutschen Unternehmen im Hinblick auf die Ausbildungssituation und die Auswirkungen der Krise auf den Fachkräftebedarf', Ergebnisbericht der Institut der Deutschen Wirtschaft Köln Consult GmbH im Auftrag des BMfWT, Cologne.

Klammer, Ute (2008), 'Business cycle and life cycle – conflicting or complementary? Towards a life course policy integrating different interests and actors', in S. Brandl, E. Hildebrandt and P. Wotschack (eds) *Arbeitszeitpolitik im Lebensverlauf*, Düsseldorf: Edition der Hans-Böckler-Stiftung, pp.43–68.

Mayer, K.U. and H. Solga (eds) (2008), *Skill Formation – Interdisciplinary and Cross-National Perspectives*, New York: Cambridge University Press.

Moraal, D. (2007), *Continuing Vocational Training in Germany*, Bonn: Federal Institute for Vocational Training (BIBB).

Naegele, G., C. Barkholdt, B. De Vroom, J. Goul Anderson and K. Krämer (2003), 'A New Organisation of Time over Working Life – Results from a European Foundation Research Project', in G. Nagele (ed.) *Soziale Lebenslaufpolitik*, Wiesbaden: VS Verlag, pp.110–137.

O'Halloran, P.L. (2008), 'Gender Differences in Formal On-the-Job Training: Incidence, Duration, and Intensity', *Labour* **22**(4), 629–659.

O'Reilly, J. (ed.) (2003), *Regulating Working-Time Transitions in Europe*, Cheltenham, UK and Northampton, MA, USA: Edward Elgar Publishing.

O'Reilly, J., I. Cebrián and M. Lallement (2000), *Working-Time Changes: Social Integration through Transitional Labour Markets*, Cheltenham, UK and Northampton, MA, USA: Edward Elgar Publishing.

Plantenga, J. and C. Remery (2006), *Reconciliation of Work and Private Life: A Comparative Review of Thirty European Countries*, Luxembourg: Office for Official Publications of the European Communities.

Schmid, G. (2008), *Full Employment in Europe: Managing Labour Market Transitions and Risks*, Cheltenham, UK and Northampton, MA, USA: Edward Elgar Publishing.

Schmid, G. and B. Gazier (eds) (2002), *The Dynamics of Full Employment. Social Integration by Transitional Labour Markets*, Cheltenham, UK and Northampton, MA, USA: Edward Elgar Publishing.

Schmid, G. and P. Protsch (2009), 'Wandel der Erwerbsformen in Deutschland und Europa', Discussion Paper SP I 2009-505. Berlin: Wissenschaftszentrum Berlin für Sozialforschung.

Seifert, H. (2004), 'A Change of Model: From Uniform to Variable Distribution of Working Time', contribution to the 9th meeting of the International Symposium on Working Time in Paris.

Solga, H. (2008), 'Lack of training: The employment opportunities of low-skilled persons from a sociological and micro-economic perspective', in K.U. Mayer and H. Solga (eds) *Skill Formation: Interdisciplinary and Cross-National Perspectives.* New York: Cambridge University Press, pp.173–204.

Spitzley, H. (2005), '"Kurze Vollzeit" – eine Grundlage für gute Arbeit', *Gute Arbeit – Zeitschrift für Gesundheitsschutz und Arbeitsgestaltung 5/2005*, 21–23.

Wotschack, P., E. Hildebrandt and F. Scheier (2008), 'Langzeitkonten. Neue Chancen für die Gestaltung von Arbeitszeiten und Lebensläufen?' *WSI-Mitteilungen 11+12/2008*, 619-626.

Wotschack, P. and E. Hildebrandt (2008), 'Working-life time accounts in German companies: New opportunities for structuring working hours and careers?', in P. Ester, R. Muffels, J. Schippers and T. Wilthagen (eds) *Innovating European Labour Markets: Dynamics and Perspectives*, Cheltenham, UK and Northampton, MA, USA: Edward Elgar Publishing, pp.215–241.

Wotschack, P., J. Siegers, R. Wittek and B. Pouwels (2007), 'Labour Supply: The Effects of Employer Demand and Household Governance', in T. Van der Lippe and P. Peters (eds) *Competing Claims in Work and Family Life*, Cheltenham, UK and Northampton, MA, USA: Edward Elgar Publishing, pp.161–175.

Section 1.2

Promoting Capabilities

6. Making employees' pathways more secure: a critical examination of the company's responsibility

Bénédicte Zimmermann

Flexibility…is about successful moves ('transitions') during one's life course: from school to work, from one job to another, between unemployment or inactivity and work, and from work to retirement … It is about progress of workers into better jobs, 'upward mobility' and optimal development of talent.

(European Commission, 2007: 5)

In the 2007 Communication *Towards Common Principles of Flexicurity* cited above, the European Commission defined EU flexicurity policy as 'an integrated strategy to enhance, at the same time, flexibility and security in the labour market.' These Communication excerpts clearly indicate that flexicurity is not meant merely to combine flexibility and security but also to transform flexibility itself, turning it into a two-way process that will be equally beneficial to employers and employees and in which not only free enterprise but also freedom to work and develop at work become fundamental values and goals. To this end, the Commission identified four components as essential for any EU flexicurity policy: 1) 'Flexible and reliable contractual arrangements … through modern labour laws, collective agreements and work organisation'; 2) 'Comprehensive lifelong learning strategies to ensure the continual adaptability and employability of workers'; 3) 'Effective active labour market policies that help people cope with rapid change'; and 4) 'Modern social security systems that provide adequate income support, encourage employment and facilitate labour market mobility' (European Commission, 2007: 6).

These components are centred on employment and labour market policy, i.e., the legal and institutional dimensions of flexicurity; they leave aside the issue of fitting flexibility and security together in the work activity itself. A flexicurity policy that makes no mention of the company's role, specifically in connection with fostering employees' professional development, is condemned to asymmetry from the start, and its promise of achieving two-way flexibility can be no more than a pious hope. Empirical studies show, meanwhile, that in companies where employees *are* provided opportunities to develop occupationally, this works in favour of their security and flexibility alike on both internal and external labour markets. This chapter, based on two qualitative studies of employees' professional development in 13 French companies, conducted respectively in 2005 and 2009,[1] focuses on just this blind spot in European Union flexicurity policy: the 'black box' represented by the company.

First I define the concept of professional development and the conditions in which it may increase employee security and flexibility – the latter term being understood as freedom to work; i.e., to choose one activity over another and possibly to change activity. Capabilities are decisive here. While employability and skill development are crucial components of flexicurity policies, the notion of capability shifts emphasis toward people's agency, how much latitude they actually have for choosing and steering their professional pathways and the existence of collective supports that enable them to successfully realise their projects (Sen, 1993). In the second part I present the lessons from a case study, the Bigtrucks case. Bigtrucks is a company, which has a capability-friendly policy in at least four areas: employment conditions and work quality, training, work/life balance and voice (collective and self-expression). Considered in terms of these four dimensions, Bigtrucks' capability policy generates what I will call 'employee quality'. Co-produced by company and employee, employee quality is a source of security and flexibility for both. We may consider it as an important component of any flexicurity policy. It involves an integrative approach to social and economic development that presupposes regarding human beings not only as resources or economic capital but as persons, each with his or her own needs and desires for empowerment, cooperation, equity, sustainability and security – which I examine in the last part of the chapter according to the five dimensions of the human development approach.

CONCEIVING DEVELOPMENT IN TERMS OF CAPABILITY

Shortcomings of Employability and Skills Policies

European Union labour directives have made employability a cornerstone of national social protection reform.[2] This induces an increasing responsibility for individual workers, who are now each called upon to ensure their own employment security by making sure they keep their skills up to date.

In an employability logic, the absence of professional development and/or the causes of long-term unemployment are imputed to the individual worker, the understanding being that workers are 'free' to develop professionally and that it is therefore up to them to do so, without any attention being paid to the conditions in which such 'freedom' is actually exercised. Employability policies reduce freedom to its negative understanding – i.e., absence of any hindrances to action – whereas, as Amartya Sen has shown (1999), a positive sense of freedom (i.e., the ability/power to choose and act in a given situation) is what allows individuals to actually exercise responsibility.[3] Unless a person has a range of choice that includes at least two possible options, he or she cannot be said to exercise responsibility. The injunction to workers to take responsibility for making and keeping themselves employable – an injunction to be found in public policies and company management policies alike – requires us to carefully examine what latitude for action people actually have, what opportunities and means are available to them for developing their employability.

In France, employability is first and foremost a labour market policy category used in assessing and assisting job-seekers. Few companies feel accountable for ensuring their employees' employability (Corteel and Zimmermann, 2006 and 2007); in the companies' view, it is up to public institutions and workers themselves to ensure that future job applicants who come to them (the companies) are employable. In practical terms, employability is understood as workers' adaptability to company needs. This understanding goes together with short training periods (less than three months) aimed at adjusting unemployed persons' skills in the short term to the needs of a given company; such training is disconnected from any overall occupational plan or genuinely qualifying training (Dubar, 2008). Far from being a means of achieving the aim of making workers' pathways more secure, as is suggested by the theory, employability is in fact mainly used as a category of economic policy aiming at workers' adaptability. I would submit that this distortion is harmful not only to workers but also, over time, to companies.

The same observation applies to skill development within companies. In theory, skills development 'is about equipping people with the skills that will enable them to progress in their working lives, and help them find new employment' (European Commission, 2007: 6). In fact, empirical studies show that the point of reasoning in terms of skills, the *logique de compétences* as implemented in French companies, is above all to satisfy company demands for worker flexibility, versatility and adaptability. Roughly speaking, the *logique de compétences* aims at maximising individual autonomy at work. It is an answer to the economic imperative of reactivity and just-in-time adjustment, while remaining in most cases disconnected from individuals' choices, projects and the temporal and social dynamic of their pathways. Furthermore, whereas skills are considered personal attributes, which individuals are supposed to keep up to date, employees are not provided with the means of doing so (Zimmermann, 2004). In the company, the hierarchical superior is the one who decides who will get trained to do what and how. The individual's entitlement to training (*Droit Individuel à la Formation* or DIF) instituted in France in 2004 has not really changed this situation, contrary to what it seemed to promise.

Employee security does not lie exclusively in establishing ways of making transitions in the labour market;[4] it is also forged in and through work itself and the possibilities for professional development that work offers. This is my hypothesis here. It amounts to putting the generally eluded question of company responsibility for employees' professional development at the heart of the flexicurity debate. An unemployed person's employability largely depends on the employability of the employee he or she used to be. Both employability and skills are developed first and foremost in the course of work and occupational experience.[5] Most companies prefer not to take this fact into account, throwing back on to the labour market all would-be employees whom they deem unemployable without necessarily giving them a chance to develop occupationally and in some cases actually aggravating their 'unemployability' by confining them to non-quality work. The fact is that insecure employment is related not only to the job and its legal form (i.e., type of contract) but also to real working conditions, which can be a source of professional development or, on the contrary, vulnerability (Paugam, 2000). Far from being a matter of the worker's personal qualities alone, development and vulnerability are highly dependent on the capabilities the company makes available to its employees.

Companies are the main actors in matters of flexibility; they therefore have a decisive role to play in fitting together flexibility and security. Most of them, however, refuse to assume this role, a role that requires a professional development policy. Statistical sources show that whereas the proportion of trained employees in France has skyrocketed since 1977, the amount of training time provided by French companies has dwindled drastically and certification practices have collapsed (Bérêt, 2009: 72). Yet when companies do commit to their employees' professional development, they benefit from it, regardless of sector. The centre of gravity in employability policies must thus be shifted from the labour market to the workplace: professional development needs to be the shared responsibility of worker and company.

Professional Development

Skills and career designate different dimensions of professional development; both are related to the sphere of work. Professional development not only encompasses the two but exceeds them, transgressing the boundaries between work and other spheres of human activity, taking into account the interrelationships between these spheres at the individual level. In other words, professional development leads to apprehending people's development at work according not only to economic constraints but also to social, institutional and personal (i.e. family) constraints. Reincorporating work and economic activity into the entire set of human activities, re-examining relations between occupational and life trajectories – this is the programme that the capability approach calls upon us to adopt.

At the heart of Amartya Sen's work, development goes alongside freedom and capability. Apprehending development as 'a process of expanding substantive freedoms that people have' (Sen, 1999: 297) opens up original perspectives for reformulating the problematic of securing people's professional pathways.[6] Studies done in the 1930s by the Russian psychologist Lev S. Vygotski helpfully clarify the notion of development. For Vygotski, development involves not only factors internal to the person but also external ones. Going against internalist, determinist perspectives, he attributes a decisive role to the environment (Schneuwly, 2002), refuting any notion of predetermination and relativising the idea of pre-existing dispositions that need only be made to blossom. In other words, the meaning of development is not given *a priori*, nor is development unidirectional, linear or cyclical; it implies trials, ordeals and revolutions. These defining features lead to two fundamental conclusions: by including contingency, they break with simplistic functionalist or evolutionist models; and by emphasising relations between the person and his or her environment, they introduce the idea that development is socially constructed. Understood in this way, individual development is simultaneously an ever-singular transformation process and a relational process that takes place through contact with others and, more generally, the environment. In the broadest sense, the environment refers here to material, human, organisational, institutional, political and policy realities (apprehended at the level of company, territorial area or sector) as well as family ones. It is this meaning of development, as an interactive, eminently social practice, a process co-produced by the person and his or her environment, that underlies and informs the following analysis.

Capabilities as Ends and Means

With this clarification in mind, in what way does the capability approach enhance perspectives on professional development? The three dimensions commonly said to define capabilities lead to formulating development conjointly in terms of choice, potential for self-fulfillment, and power to achieve (De Munck, 2008). *Ability to choose* links development to people's freedom, reason and reflexivity; it raises the question of the extent and accessibility of opportunities. *Potential for self-fulfillment* points toward the values underlying development, the assumption being that individuals can manage to express what they have reason to value and make themselves heard when doing so. What people value may change from one individual to the other, it may change over time by relative weight of different spheres of life (family, work, citizen or associative commitments etc.) at different points in the same pathway. *Power to achieve* addresses development from the angle of accomplishment and available means to this end; the ability to convert opportunities and formal entitlements into genuine sources of development is decisive here.

I will locate professional development at the intersection of these three dimensions. Capabilities are both the ends and means of development. The distinction between 'opportunities-capabilities' and 'skills-capabilities' (Gasper, 2002: 446) allows us to specify the nature of these means. Capabilities are linked on the one hand to factors pertaining directly to the person (*skills*) and on the other to environmental data (*opportunities*). This distinction should be supplemented with a third factor: *entitlements and means* for action. Conceived in terms of these three dimensions, development covers personal aptitudes and dispositions, opportunities and means of action.

The capability approach identifies how ability to choose, potential for self-fulfilment, and power to achieve operate in the various areas that foster workers' professional development, namely training, work and the conditions in which it is realised, the balance between work and private life, the possibility for individual and collective expression (voice). Lifelong learning is often cited as *the* means of ensuring professional development. It is thus only one component among others. Whatever the quality of the training or education provided, it is not automatically a development factor. To be so, individual workers have to be able to orientate their training; that is, to be in a position to express their preferences and to have them prevail. And once such training has been taken, it has to lead to quality work in a quality job, and the work has to be compatible with the balance between occupational and personal life that the individual worker aspires to achieve. Conceived in terms of capabilities, professional development encompasses workers' personal development. Employees' capability to balance their work and private lives in a way that is consistent with their chosen priorities is thus an important dimension. This includes the freedom to say no to a career or an offer to assume increased responsibility at work without being stigmatised or relegated for doing so. Professional development integrates respect for the way people weigh and hierarchically order different commitments, including the choice not to put career first.

Being in a position to do quality work, train, achieve a balance between work life and private life, express one's preferences and have them prevail – it is at the intersection of these four capabilities that we may grasp the conditions of workers' development in the workplace. Voice capability plays a decisive role because above and beyond access to information and participation, it involves a valuation process (Dewey, 1991 [1939]); employees' voiced preferences are founded on just such valuation. Voice capability means that each worker is in a position to make known what he or she in his or her particular situation has reason to value in terms of work content and employment situation, training, and work life/personal life balance. Because the capability for voice implies both a valuation capability and the capability to make oneself heard, it transversally structures all other capabilities.

Thus conceived, professional development does not proceed out of any normative, predetermined definition but instead depends on the events and accidents that fashion individual pathways and assumes the value that given individuals attribute to those events. It refers as much to means that allow for freely opting to move in the course of one's work life, and for realising such moves (inside or outside the company, inside or outside the world of work), as it does to opportunities and individual aptitudes for moving from one position to another. Overall, we can think of professional development as the way in which capability for action is constructed over time at the intersection between personal aptitudes and dispositions, environmental conditions, and collective supports.[7]

'EMPLOYEE QUALITY' AS QUALITY CO-PRODUCED BY COMPANY AND WORKER

Bigtrucks, a company with 472 employees in the metallurgy industry sector that assembles trucks in its name, is the most capability-friendly company in our sample.[8] The vast majority of Bigtrucks' employees are 'operators' working on a non-robotic assembly line. The tightly compressed job pyramid at the company offers few opportunities to move up within the internal hierarchy. Nonetheless, there is clear evidence of professional development

in this company. It is achieved by way of employee participation programmes and a training policy that facilitates workers' movements on the
internal *and* external labour market.

The Bigtrucks' case clearly shows the impact of capabilities on professional
development (Zimmermann, 2010). Such development does not necessarily
give rise to an upward career, but rather what may be called *employee
quality*, locally recognised, valued and sought after. Bigtrucks' employees
enjoy a strong reputation among other employers and employees in the
local employment area. What I am calling Bigtrucks' employee quality is
produced by capabilities made available by the company in the areas of
work, training, employee participation and work/life balance. All members
of the company share in Bigtrucks' employee quality, which emphasises the
collective dimension of capabilities: before capabilities become individual
attributes, they arise from the conditions and possibilities made available by
the organisation. Because employee quality results from interaction
between a person and his or her work environment, all Bigtrucks' employees are *a priori* credited with having Bigtrucks' quality, regardless of their
work content, formal certification or classification.

Quality of Employment and Quality of Work

Employee quality is what Bigtrucks produces outside the normalised logic
of skills and career. Employee quality is a specific, hybrid product created
by means of professional development yet not susceptible to measurement
on any institutional scale. Employment status *and* working conditions are
important components of it. On the employment side, hiring procedures
(e.g., the fact that new hires are chosen from the factory's temporary worker
pool), work hours and schedules, wages and access to training contribute to
the quality of the employment relationship. Yet however decisive that
relationship is, it does not suffice to establish Bigtrucks' employee quality;
just as decisive is the quality of work, apprehended in terms of the concrete
conditions in which work is realised. Work quality is not merely a matter of
worker performance, it also depends on the conditions in which the work is
realised. It may be thought of as a shared good, co-produced by company
and employees – a collective good on which the interests of the different
parties converge. For the company it is a source of economic development,
while for the employees it helps make their professional pathways more
secure, just as quality employment conditions do. Whereas employment
quality is related to occupational security in the present, quality of work
concerns future security – preventively, through the capabilities it endows
people with. Bigtrucks' employees' reputation for quality exemplifies this.
Work quality is produced by a compromise between different concerns that

are in tension with each other: on the one hand, there is product reputation (the reputation of Bigtrucks' trucks) and the performance of the factory as a production group; on the other, working conditions for individuals, which are actually the conditions in which the collective performance is achieved: multitasking, working on a non-robotic assembly line, workpost rotation, delegation,[9] employee participation, etc.[10] Institutional rules (particularly labour law and entitlement to training) and organisation conventions (multitasking, delegation, participation) constitute supports for both company and employees in managing the tensions between the community of production taken as a whole and the individual worker. These supports can be likened to conversion factors that allow the conversion of available resources into quality work for the company and quality work conditions for the employee. They shed light on how the collective dimensions – apprehended at the level of institutions, labour relations, the factory or the work team – affect individuals' capabilities.

Training: A Means of Opening up Possibilities

Workers' capability to be trained, to develop and renew skills, is an important component of Bigtrucks' employee quality. Bigtrucks' employees' reputation for quality is related to training in two ways: training is 'a good in itself' in the sense of a goal deemed worthy of pursuing as such (Dodier, 2003: 19), but it is also a means of opening up possibilities and development potential. Training as a good in itself is measured in terms of volume, distribution and quality. Professional development is what such training makes possible in the way of later achievement. Rooted in the present as a good in itself, training is turned toward the future by the possibilities it opens up. Training, then, functions as a conversion factor, as illustrated by the case of Olivier, who signed up for a CIF (*Congé Individuel de Formation*: temporary leave to do a training programme) not so much to acquire new knowledge as to obtain the necessary qualification level for realising his own occupational plan, which is to move up from *opérateur* to *technicien* within the company (to do so, an employee needs to have a *baccalauréat* [high school]-level degree or qualification). While company training policies are usually evaluated exclusively in terms of training-as-a-good-in-itself, employee quality means that the degree to which training opens up possibilities and new employment prospects is just as important. It shifts attention from training to professional development likely to be generated by that training.

Bigtrucks contributes to professional development by offering access to a combination of different types of knowledge and know-how: knowledge and know-how specific to the company, knowledge and know-how specific to the automobile sector, and thirdly more general knowledge. The specificity of general knowledge is that it is readily transferable outside the company and even outside the sector. How this knowledge is acquired proves just as decisive as the knowledge itself. General knowledge is not only produced at Bigtrucks through individual formal training – in English, for example – but also through a variety of participative arrangements that foster on-the-job learning, initiative-taking and responsibility. The decisive characteristic of these arrangements with regard to professional development is that they integrate collective forms of producing knowledge, thereby promoting an active attitude and relation to knowledge and learning. Just as important as formal training in establishing the reputation for quality of the Bigtrucks' employee is the ongoing informal learning process at the company organised by the methods of participative management.

Work and Quality of Life

Work/life balance is a dimension of employee quality that is related at Bigtrucks to various features: pay, working hours (7.30–15.44) and health in the workplace: physical health (measures taken to prevent work accidents and muscular-skeletal disorders) and psychological health (measures for avoiding stress). Despite Bigtrucks' good reputation, some individual pathways bring to light a more uneven situation, where stress invades personal life not because of an excessively heavy workload but because the employee has been demoted or relegated ('put in the closet') – the supreme sanction in a world whose cardinal values are skill development and participative involvement. But with the exception of Roger, a union representative, employees do not mention this practice; they prefer to highlight quality of life in terms of reconciliation between work and private life, partly thanks to good working schedules, a point noted and valued by all.

Participation and Capability for Voice

The reputation for quality that Bigtrucks' employees enjoy outside the company involves relational skills and a sense of responsibility and cooperation within the company, features fostered by participative management. By opening up even a limited space for deliberation on work, participation captures individual workers' voice in a way that benefits the company. Recruitment officers at neighbouring companies note this feature favourably. Bigtrucks' workers themselves, by contrast, see participation as offering them an opportunity to help define how they want to work, even if it only concerns matters pre-circumscribed by management. Like training, participation may be thought of as both a good in itself and a conversion factor. As implemented at Bigtrucks,[11] it directly improves work quality and quality of life in the workplace while opening up prospects for the future, chances for mobility inside *and* outside the company. Damien, for example, hopes that his extended participative involvement will ultimately enable him to obtain promotion, as has happened for some of his colleagues. But such conversion is never guaranteed in advance; it remains in the form of potential and is in turn dependent on how participation interacts with other factors, legal or conventional (labour agreement regulations on employee classification for example), organisational (number of promotion slots), personal (aptitudes and skills) and relational (namely, relations with hierarchical superiors). Bigtrucks' workers' effective capability for professional development is produced through interaction among these various factors.

Interacting Conversion Factors

Freedom, as the capability to be and to do what one values, presupposes that a person is able to convert available opportunities and resources into valuable accomplishments. It implies that the different personal and environmental components that fashion his or her capability to act combine properly. Conversion factors help achieve this. But what gets converted varies; opportunities as well as resources of various types – economic, legal, organisational or personal – may get converted. Our study of approximately 20 workers' pathways at Bigtrucks brings to light how various and labile such conversion factors may be. As illustrated by training and participation, a given component can operate as a good in itself – i.e., an achievement one seeks to attain – or a conversion factor, depending on the situation. However, one single factor is seldom enough: capability results from interaction among different factors.

Consider the case of Olivier, 30. He joined Bigtrucks 12 years ago as a stockman with a CAP (*Certificat d'Aptitude Professionnelle*) professional certificate. In a few years he had advanced to the level of *pilote* (team leader assistant), but his low educational attainment level blocked any promotion in employee classification within the metallurgy sector. At the time of our interview, he was getting ready to start an eight-month training programme to become a *technicien* (taking CIF individual training leave to do so), which will qualify him to apply for a position as cluster leader if one opens up. His career development is being constructed at the intersection of various factors that allow the conversion of his personal aptitudes into achievements. Olivier's sense of commitment, his firm intention to move forward and his work performance (all personal factors) are not enough; as important are support from his hierarchical superior (a relational factor), being chosen for the company's *potential list*[12] and therefore supported by the company's human resources department (an organisational factor); lastly, being granted individual training leave, as this is what will allow his personal attributes to be converted into achievements (institutional and legal factor).

While the nature of such factors and their interactions vary from one case to another, we can nonetheless identify what factors structure professional development. Our study brings to light five sets:[13] *economic factors* (related to the world of production and the company's economic situation), *legal and conventional factors* (involving instituted labour regulations, employment and training arrangements, but also social protection and family-related policies), *organisational factors* (involving internal company organisation and governance), *social and relational factors* (ranging from instituted labour relations such as management-union dialogue to informal relations between a given employee and his or her superior and including union and ethnically based networks); lastly, *personal factors* (pertaining directly to the individual in question).

BOX 6.1 INTERACTING CONVERSION FACTORS

Economic
- product
- market
- company size and its economic and financial situation

Legal and conventional
- social protection and family law (legal and conventional arrangements)
- labour law, employment and training regulations (legal and conventional arrangements, including rules on employee classification)
- antitrust and competition law

Organisational
- material organisation of work and task distribution (multitask, workstation, etc.)
- hours and scheduling (work hours, clocking, pace, etc.)
- job pyramid
- the organisation's regulation modes (values, discipline, hierarchy, expert assessment, etc.)

- participation
- employee access to decision-making arenas, degree of decision-making process transparency
- diffusion and circulation of information

Social and relational
- shared culture and sense of belonging
- institutional labour supports (including union-management dialogue)
- networks and interpersonal relations

Personal
- formal qualification level
- occupational status and type of employment contract
- occupational skills
- performance, commitment to work, responsibility-taking
- relational skills
- self-esteem and self-confidence
- age
- gender
- state of health
- family situation
- ethnic background

Conversion factors may interact with each other in complementary or conflictual fashion. Depending on the situation, they affect capabilities either negatively or positively. This is exemplified by the case of women, of whom there are very few at Bigtrucks. Being female constitutes a negative conversion factor in this company. Rose, an operator, has not been promoted once in 13 years at the company whereas all of her male colleagues had moved up. The mere fact that an anti-discrimination law exists[14] is not enough to transform female gender from a source of negative discrimination into a source of positive discrimination. Formal rights are not enough to provide people with action capability; capability ultimately depends on the degree to which the law is applied, and on the factors that make it possible in a given situation to convert formal rights into effective ones.

HUMAN CAPITAL VERSUS HUMAN DEVELOPMENT

Professional development within companies is a complex process that occurs at the intersection of work organisation, management (including employment arrangements, training, participation, human resources policy) and personal features. Professional development as a power of becoming, projecting oneself into the future, depends on employees' power to be and do in the present. Bigtrucks has developed arrangements that to some degree combine company development with workers' development, but all of these arrangements are not equally accessible to all.

It is important to distinguish between professional development accessible to all, on the one hand, and career logic on the other. Professional development assumes at Bigtrucks its full meaning as the Bigtrucks' employees' reputation for quality. This collective label, distributed equally regardless of differences in gender, ethnic background, skills, employee classification or performance, is the most visible expression of Bigtrucks' capability policy. It is the key that opens up opportunities for mobility inside and outside the factory, and is therefore a guarantee of security for the future. In contrast to professional development, the notion of career at Bigtrucks is linked to a dedicated capability policy, accessible only to a small, elect circle. Whereas access to the employee quality label is governed by an equality principle founded on belonging to the factory work group, access to the limited circle represented by the *potential list* is supposed to be regulated by the merit principle. It is in the tension between these two principles of justice – the universalistic principle of equality and the discriminating principle of merit – that the space pertaining to capabilities at work is constructed at Bigtrucks. This gives rise to a possible scenario for capability development in the workplace, but that scenario remains incomplete, as suggested by what happens to women in the company.

However, analysing this possible scenario, its scope and limitations, still allows us to identify in more general terms the components of a company capability-friendly policy. Such a policy implies a shift from human capital theory to human development. According to Sen, the two can become complementary as soon as we conceive of development as a process of extending the range of choice of both companies *and* employees. This does imply a small revolution, however, in the way human beings are considered at the workplace.

Capability: An Integrative Approach to Economic and Social Development

Because the capability approach pleads in favour of integrating economic and social development, it calls for moving beyond the human capital theory and redeploying the issue of human beings at work. Following Marx, Sen recalls that 'human beings are not merely means of production, but also the end of the exercise' (Sen, 1999: 296). This is an essential difference between human capital theory, in which humans are confined to being mere resources or commodities ('human resources') and human development, in which they are thought of as ends in themselves. Whereas human capital theory associates professional development exclusively with increasing skills, a human development approach considers it as a process of extending possible choices and takes into account the values people are likely to refer to in choosing between the options available to them. This point opens up a crucial question: to what degree is an understanding of persons as ends in themselves reconcilable with the conception of the individual as a means consubstantial with capitalist economic activity? The five dimensions of development put forward in the 1996 global *Human Development Report* offers a synthesis of what is at stake in such a reconciliation. These dimensions are 'empowerment'; 'sustainability'; 'security'; 'cooperation'; and 'equity' (Human Development Report, 1996: 55–56). Though the report does not relate specifically to work but rather to the entire set of life spheres,[15] these five dimensions adequately sum up what is at stake in reformulating the issue of professional development in the language of capability. They provide a frame of reference for evaluating existing policies, and they indicate what would be required to realise alternative scenarios.

Empowerment

Empowerment involves obtaining some control over one's own destiny. It is the alpha and omega of the capability approach. The power (in the sense of capability) to choose and accomplish the options a person values is an important condition for the *sustainability and security* of that person's professional pathway. *Cooperation and equity*, meanwhile, make this power a collective attribute governed by justice principles. Proceeding out of the interdependence of these five dimensions, human development results from a collectively distributed power to act. It conjoins negative freedom, conceived as the absence of hindrances to action, with the positive freedom of having access to means for doing and being. Because freedom conditions people's power to be and do and yet cannot be determined solely by the individual, it constitutes a matter of social responsibility (Sen, 1999), and this includes the sphere of work.

The extension of the range of choice available to people at work raises the eminently political question of company governance and employee participation. Being an active agent of one's own development presupposes being able to participate in making decisions that affect one's existence; that is, being able to have some degree of control over one's environment, a control that is not only technical but also moral and political. During the twentieth century, union organisations gradually made this possibility available to employees, instituting employee participation through the principle of representation. Such participation promoted collective control over individual futures within the framework of institutionalised socio-occupational categories. Employee participation under management (rather than union) control, as at Bigtrucks, favours individualised empowerment based on individual direct participation against the collective tactic of unions. While making the singular individual its focus and source, participative management is also a means of collectively structuring the company. Flexible work exacerbates tensions between these two modes of collective construction in that it challenges the different work-sphere actors – i.e., entrepreneurs, unions and employees – to reconfigure work identities and memberships. The decline of class-based unionism raises the question of how to renew collective approaches to employee empowerment, and the question of developing alternative counterweights to managerial approaches to participation that individualise employees. This issue far exceeds the world of work; it touches on the more general problem of how people whose only capital is their labour power can gain access to the political. By translating individual causes into a collective one and playing on strength in numbers, collective empowerment approaches foster access to the political for the economically and socially disadvantaged. They make it possible to support mobilisation far beyond the perimeter of the company, thus functioning as a lever for raising the level of political generality, whereas management is either (depending on the circumstances) playing the card of individuals' irremediable singularity or, on the contrary, the omnipotence of capital and its inexorable rules.

Cooperation and Equity

Cooperation and equity bring the political dimension of capabilities to the fore by firmly attaching them to principles of justice. Cooperation and equity refer to the constitution of a 'we' at various scales ranging from the work team to the society at large. They refer to the interactions between this 'we' and an 'I' or 'self', interactions in which 'we' and 'I' mutually constitute each other, alternately identify with each other and distance themselves from each other, and alternately see each other as a resource or a constraint. At Bigtrucks, how this 'we' is defined and how the 'I' relates to it are likely to vary by individual persons and pathways, but they also exhibit constants that have been fashioned by the collective values governing cooperation within the factory. The point here is to *distinguish the notion of cooperation from that of coordination*. This distinction coincides with what distinguishes a factory like Bigtrucks, where what prevails is a sense of the group founded on more than mere market values, from most of the other companies in our sample. Coordinated action requires shared conventions but not necessarily shared values. Cooperation, on the other hand, goes beyond sporadic moves to adjust action; it demands commitment and includes a relational dimension. The point of coordination is for an action involving several actants – beings or objects – to succeed or otherwise unfold correctly. Cooperation extends beyond this: its aim is shared achievement. Cooperating for the purposes of achieving or realising something – a product or a major work, for example – implies having reached agreement on the characteristics and qualities of the thing to be achieved, how to accomplish it, how to assess each person's contribution to it and what he or she can expect in the way of returns. These different aspects mobilise a sense of fairness and raise the question of what justice principles are called upon to govern work. Different principles may coexist within one and the same company, as illustrated by the tension between equality and equity related to merit that characterises Bigtrucks.

Whereas the equality principle governs distributive justice of a sort that applies equally to all (e.g., a 2 per cent pay rise for all), the equity principle modulates distribution by taking into account variations with regard to a given attribute. This attribute may be merit (in which case the raise is a reward proportionate to such merit) or need (in which case it is a corrective measure where priority is given to low wage-earners or persons clearly in need). In the company, merit-based equity is promoted as compensation for the company's efficiency demand; 'Each according to his merit' replaces here Marx's famous formula, 'From each according to his ability, to each according to his need.'[16] But making merit a justice principle means there must be criteria and procedures for assessing merit and that these be known to all – this is the first requirement (that obviously is not reached at Bigtrucks as Rose's case shows). The capability approach adds a second requirement, however. It cannot settle for the idea that merit is the sole foundation of equity but turns as well to a conception of justice that aims to correct unequal access to opportunities. Equity in handling access to opportunities may imply providing stronger support to particularly disadvantaged persons by way of arrangements aimed to correct unequal distribution of means and resources. Formulated in capability approach terms, then, equity is not only a distributive justice dimension but also a corrective one. The fact is that this last dimension is seldom dealt with at the level of the company; companies tend instead to accentuate existing inequalities in access to professional development.

Achieving capability development at work calls for combining different justice principles that involve different regulatory levels, the company being only one of them. Procedures and practices defined at the level of a single company cannot be made to converge with more general principles applicable to other companies without the existence of a greater regulation space, where equivalencies between situated practices can be determined. Given that in 'the culture of the new capitalism' (Sennett, 2006), employees' pathways are called upon to intersect with different companies, sectors, activities and indeed occupations, this question is crucial for ensuring employees' security.

Sustainability and Security

Ensuring the durability of capabilities is central to securing workers' pathways. Sustainability in a flexible world implies, on the one hand, readily transferable knowledge (i.e., knowledge that is useful above and beyond a single company), on the other hand, the capability to learn and to adjust to changing situations. Adaptability, which management has made the primary virtue of the flexible worker, completely fails to satisfy this condition. It represents a short-term approach in which specific, tailor-made knowledge is adapted solely for corporate needs, neglecting completely its potential value on the broader job marker, value that a worker could activate in the long run. In the absence of such conversion possibilities, adaptability amounts to a permanent race against knowledge obsolescence that proves antinomical to any purpose of acquiring lasting, sustainable knowledge. Knowledge acquisition sustainability requires work experience that is not 'disposable' but rather recognised; work experience that will add to people's stock of knowledge.[17] Thus conceived, sustainability means that the future of the company and the future of its employees must be imagined jointly. The case of Bigtrucks attests not only that fitting the two together is possible, but also that this is beneficial for company and employees alike. A capability-friendly company is a company that workers find attractive, as well as a company that gives its managers the means of selecting and keeping individuals they would like to be able to count on in the future. The collectively constructed quality of the Bigtrucks' employee inscribes his or her pathway in the long term by fostering the continuity of that pathway inside and outside the company, thereby working to ensure its security.

Training as such is not enough to make employees' pathways secure if it does not lead to development potential or strengthen their capability to move around on and situate themselves on both internal and external labour markets. The Bigtrucks' case reveals that granting considerable latitude to expression of worker knowledge and creativity-in-action is an important feature of professional development. It illustrates the degree to which providing workers with even a limited possibility of controlling their work environment helps ensure both their objective security and their feeling of security. This leads to a close convergence between the issue of workers' security and the issue of freedom – conceived not in terms of individual responsibility, as in most adaptability and employability approaches, but in terms of shared social responsibility.

One might reasonably object that in a context of economic and financial crisis, the security of individuals' pathways is first and foremost a matter of companies' sustainability and solidity. This is true, but the crisis context also makes workers' capability for moving about on the job market a more sharply discriminating criteria. While it cannot be denied that employees' freedom of movement is even more limited in a crisis situation than during an ordinary period, the capabilities they have been able to develop in the course of their past experience become even more decisive for the continuity and quality of their occupational lives, and therefore for the continuity and quality of their lives outside work.

(Translation by Amy Jacobs)

NOTES

[1.] I conducted the 2005 studies with Delphine Corteel as part of the European Union research project 'Eurocap: Dialogue Social, Emploi et Territoire: Pour une politique européenne des capacités' (http://www.idhe.ens-cachan.fr/Eurocap/ (accessed 16 August 2011)) and the 2009 studies with Dilip Subramanian as part of the EU research project 'Capright: Resources, Rights and Capabilities: In Search of Social Foundations for Europe' (www.capright.eu (accessed 16 August 2011)).

[2.] See European Commission, 2000, *Labor directives 2001*, COM 548 final.

[3.] This is also shown by Jean-Michel Bonvin; see Chapter 7, this volume.

[4.] Arranging for pathways' linking one temporary work position or activity to the next is a main dimension of the transitional markets idea: 'Transitions include all possible differences from the reference situation of permanent full-time employment' (Gazier, 2003: 131).

[5.] The present analysis does not include youth unemployment, which raises its own problems precisely because young people are by definition not in a position to have developed employability through work experience.

[6.] On how sociology can make the capability approach operational, see Zimmermann, 2006.

[7.] I have broadened the meaning Robert Castel (Castel and Harroche, 2000) attributed to this last notion: by collective supports, I mean entitlements and the material and symbolic resources provided by groups of various types, entitlements and resources ranging from factory workshop regulations to national and EU policy and including company policy and union action.

8. Overall, only 10.5 per cent of the 4800 companies covered by the French component of the European Union's 'Continuing Vocational Training Survey 3' (CVTS3) have implemented capability developing policies for their employees (Lambert et al., 2009: 136).

9. Work at Bigtrucks is organised so that anyone who wishes to can leave the assembly line a few hours a month to work at other tasks – this is Toyota production system-type delegation and it is part of participative management at the company. The tasks in question are organised at the level of each cluster, and they range from keeping assembly workers supplied with consumables (gloves, small tools, etc.) to spotting and dealing with production anomalies to quality monitoring. Work time allotted varies by task: some tasks involve one to two hours a week, others as much as 45 minutes a day.

10. These points are analysed in depth in Zimmermann, 2010.

11. Not every type of participation is capability friendly.

12. The company's *potential list* is drawn up by the human resources department with the help of managers who have been asked to identify the most 'promising' employees regardless of whether there are any job openings. The persons identified then become the focus for company training efforts, with the aim to get them ready in case of higher internal vacancies.

13. These sets were drawn up with Delphine Corteel and two Swedish colleagues, Christina Garsten and Jessica Lindvert, as part of the EU's *Eurocap* research project.

14. Law of 16 November 2001.

15. The conclusions of the United Nations' annual global *Human Development Report* are based on health, education and living standards data.

16. Slogan formulated by Karl Marx to get beyond 'the narrow horizon of bourgeois right' (Marx 1970 (1891 [1875]), 27).

17. The idea of experience as a 'stock of knowledge' is borrowed from Alfred Schütz (Schütz and Luckmann, 1973).

REFERENCES

Bérêt, P. (2009), 'Formation continue, salaires et transformation des marchés internes', *Travail et Emploi*, 117, January–March, 67–80.

Castel, R. and C. Haroche (2000), *Propriété Privée, Propriété Sociale, Propriété de Soi*, Paris: Fayard.

Corteel, D. and B. Zimmermann (2006), 'Employability, Voice and Security: An inquiry into the capabilities of workers in French firms', Paris: Document de Travail de l'IDHE, no 06–01.

Corteel, D. and B. Zimmermann (2007), 'Capacités et développement profession-nel', *Formation et Emploi*, **98**(2), Special issue: Pour une approche par les capacités, 25–39.

De Munck, J. (2008), 'Qu'est-ce qu'une capacité?', in J. de Munck and B. Zimmermann (eds) *La liberté au prisme des capacités. Amartya Sen au-delà du Libéralisme*, Paris: Editions de l'Ecole des hautes études en sciences sociales, Coll. Raisons pratiques, 21–49.

De Munck, J. and B. Zimmermann (eds) (2008), *La liberté au Prisme des Capacités: Amartya Sen au-delà du Libéralisme*, Paris: Editions de l'Ecole des hautes études en sciences sociales, Coll. Raisons pratiques.

Dewey, J. (1991 [1939]), 'Theory of valuation', in *John Dewey: The Later Works, 1925–1953 (Vol. 13, 1938–9)*, Carbondale and Edwardsville: Southern Illinois University Press, pp.189–251.

Dodier, N. (2003), *Leçons Politiques de l'Epidémie du Sida*, Paris: Editions de l'Ecole des hautes études en sciences sociales.

Dubar, C. (2008), 'Les changements possibles du système français de formation continue', *Formation Emploi*, **10**(1), Special issue: Regards croisés sur les relations formation-emploi, pp.167–182.

European Commission (2007), *Towards Common Principles of Flexicurity: More and Better Jobs through Flexibility and Security*, Communication, Brussels: European Commission, COM (2007) 359 final.

Gasper, D. (2002), 'Is Sen's capability approach an adequate basis for considering human development?', *Review of Political Economy*, **14**(4), 435–461.

Gazier, B. (2003), *Tous 'Sublimes': Vers un Nouveau Plein Emploi*, Paris: Flammarion.

Human Development Report (1996), *Economic growth and human development*, New York: United Nations Development Program.

Lambert, M., J. Vero, D. Corteel and B. Zimmermann (2009), 'Capability for life long learning in French companies', in P. Bartelheimer and N. Moncel (eds) *Sensitising Life Course Research? Exploring Amartya Sen's Capability Concept in Comparative Research on Individual Working Lives*, Cereq, Net.doc, **50**, 115–157.

Marx K. (1970 (1891 [1875])), 'Critique of the Gotha Programme' (Written: April or early May, 1875. First Published in the journal Die Neue Zeit, Bd. 1, No. 18, 1890–91), in K. Marx and F. Engels, *Selected Works, Volume Three*, Moscow: Progress Publishers, pp.13–30.

Paugam, S. (2000), *Le Salarié de la Précarité*, Paris: Presses Universitaires de France (PUF).

Schneuwly, B. (2002), 'Le développement du concept de développement chez Vygotski', in C. Yves (ed.) *Avec Vygotski*, Paris: La Dispute, pp.291–304.

Sen, A. (1993), 'Capability and well-being', in M. Nussbaum and A. Sen (eds), *The Quality of Life*, Oxford: Oxford University Press, pp.30–53.

Sen, A. (1999), *Development as Freedom*, Oxford: Oxford University Press.

Sennett, R. (2006), *The Culture of the New Capitalism*, New Haven: Yale University Press.

Schütz, A. and T. Luckmann (1973), *The Structures of the Life-World*, Evanston: Northwestern University Press.

Zimmermann, B. (2004), 'Competence-oriented logics and the politics of employability', in R. Salais and R. Villeneuve (eds) *Europe and the Politics of Capabilities*, Cambridge: Cambridge University Press, pp.38–53.

Zimmermann, B. (2006), 'Pragmatism and the capability approach. Challenges in social theory and empirical research', *European Journal of Social Theory*, **9**(4), 467–484.

Zimmermann, B. (2010) *Ce que travailler veut dire: Une sociologie des capacités et des parcours professionnels*, Paris: Economica.

7. Reframing the issue of responsibility in labour market activation policies[1]

Jean-Michel Bonvin

INTRODUCTION

Most activation policies are based on a simplistic conception of responsibility: behaving responsibly boils down to quick reintegration into the labour market. Local welfare agents are called to push beneficiaries to actively endorse this goal. But the issue of responsibility is much more complex and multi-faceted. Drawing on Sen's capability approach, this chapter suggests that responsibilisation of recipients requires both empowerment programmes improving their employability and the recognition of their real freedom to choose the life and job they have reason to value. Against the present trend toward hypertrophying individual responsibility, it calls for a more equilibrated balance between individual and social responsibility. The objective is not to define an impracticable ideal of responsibility, but to provide an analytical and normative yardstick for assessing activation programmes and reforming them in the direction of what could be labelled 'capacitation' strategies. The trend towards activation in contemporary social policies is by now well documented. Departing from the so-called decommodification mission of conventional welfare states, a great variety of reforms were passed in most OECD countries in the last decades with a view to transforming welfare into an instrument of activation (e.g. RMI in France, TANF in the United States, the New Deal programmes in the UK, the Hartz reforms in Germany, etc.). This evolution entails a threefold transformation: a) in contrast with cash benefits widely interpreted as a purely passive device, social expenditure is to be activated and become productive in line with the social investment state. In this new perspective, increasing the recipients' purchasing power is not identified as an economic investment (as was the case in the Keynesian welfare state), since investment exclusively relates to professional reintegration or recommodification; b) accordingly, benefit recipients have to be

138

induced (e.g. via the financial incentives of 'making work pay' pro-grammes) or constrained (via workfare schemes) to quickly reintegrate into the labour market; c) local agents of the welfare state as well as private contracted-out providers are pushed to act as intermediaries towards such quick and, possibly long-lasting, professional reinsertion, which implies in certain cases a profound change in professional practice.

At the core of all these changes, there is an implicit and undisputed view of what objectives individual recipients and local welfare agents are expected to pursue within the field of social policies. In a nutshell, these targets are strongly connected with increasing the employment rates at a macro level, and accelerating reintegration into the labour market at a micro level. As a result, acting responsibly coincides with getting people back to work as quickly as possible, and the issue of employment quality is given much less attention. This being settled, the main challenge faced in social policies becomes finding the most efficient modes of governance in order to promote such responsible behaviour among both the local agents of the welfare state and the beneficiaries. In other terms, how can these actors be induced or constrained (via sticks and/or carrots) to endorse such a view of responsibility? In this way, the issue of governance is reduced to a technical question of efficiency, and all political and normative issues dealing with equity, social justice or the adequate combination of indi-vidual and collective responsibility are left aside. This chapter contends that the issue of responsibility is much more complex and needs to be carefully re-examined. Drawing on Sen's capability approach (Sen, 1999), the first section identifies the main prerequisites of genuinely responsible behaviour, i.e. adequate resources and opportunities on the one side, real freedom of choice on the other one. The following two sections apply this framework to the case of local agents and beneficiaries in activation policies. They propose an analytical and normative grid to assess present activation programmes and reform them in the direction of 'capacitation' strategies. The first of these focuses on the notion of empowerment, while the next tackles the difficult issue of freedom of choice in activation policies. The final section synthesises the main findings of the chapter and concludes.

THE PREREQUISITES OF RESPONSIBLE BEHAVIOUR IN THE CAPABILITY APPROACH

The capability approach insists on two necessary preconditions for respon-sible behaviour: adequate means and power to act, and real freedom to choose one's way of life. Hence, if someone is not adequately equipped in terms of capacity to act, s/he cannot be expected to act responsibly. In Sen's words, the responsible person should then be provided with sufficient resources or commodities (e.g. goods, services, incomes, social transfers, etc.) and with appropriate factors of conversion (i.e. competencies, available social and economic opportunities, etc.) allowing him/her to convert these resources into a real capacity to act. Extensive collective responsibility is required in all these respects. However, such empowerment is not sufficient to foster individual responsibility. Indeed, if a person adequately empowered is not free to use his/her capacity in the way s/he chooses to (or to use Sen's recurrent formula, 'in the way s/he has reason to value'), it still does not make sense to speak of responsible or irresponsible behaviour. Benevolent dictatorships or paternalistic practices are not conducive to responsible behaviour, insofar as their efforts in the field of empowerment are not matched by a corresponding recognition of the beneficiaries' freedom to choose their way of living. In Sen's language:

> *Without the substantive freedom and capability to do something, a person cannot be responsible for doing it.* But actually having the freedom and capability to do something does impose on the person the duty to consider whether to do it or not, and this does involve individual responsibility. In this sense, freedom is both necessary and sufficient for responsibility. (Sen, 1999: 284, emphasis added)

Here lies the very dilemma of collective responsibility in the capability perspective: while the state (or any other collective body) is called to act extensively on the side of empowerment, it needs to remain modest in terms of normative expectations vis-à-vis its beneficiaries. The objective of public action is the enhancement of capabilities or real freedoms to choose one's way of life, it is not a top-down specified aim such as the increase of the employment rate or the quick reintegration into the labour market. This calls for a situated view of public action, where objectives are negotiated in context and not exhaustively defined and imposed on beneficiaries and public agents from above. These extensive requirements placed on collective responsibility do not imply that individual responsibility is discarded altogether. As Sen insists in the quote above, if these conditions are fulfilled, then the individual can legitimately be called upon to act responsibly.

In the field of social policy, the enhancement of the capacity to act, or empowerment, entails taking into account at least two dimensions: the cash resources made available (i.e. are they sufficient in amount and duration? What conditions are recipients subject to? Is there a risk of moral hazard if welfare programmes are too generous or unconditional?); and the opportunities – for training, professional reintegration, etc. – open to the recipients (i.e. what is their quantity and quality? Are they available for all beneficiaries? etc). In active labour market programmes (ALMPs), these two issues of resources and opportunities are tackled in a great variety of ways. Indeed, if activation always implies a higher focus on individual responsibility, this may coincide either with more extended collective interventions (close to the perspective suggested by the capability approach) or with the retreat of the state. And this variety within the field of ALMPs indicates a significant diversity in the ways the balance between individual and collective responsibility is conceived, which in turn impacts heavily on local agents' practices and on their expectations towards beneficiaries. If the state is called to retreat, the whole burden of responsibility will be placed on the individual with very limited support from the collective agencies. Local welfare agents are then required to endorse such a view of individual responsibility that is clearly at odds with the capability approach. By contrast, if extensive means are deployed to empower the beneficiaries (in line with Sen's perspective), this supportive view will help develop other kinds of expectations and relationships with the recipients.

With regard to freedom of choice, Sen's capability approach sets a very high standard of responsibility. Indeed, real freedom of choice, which is interpreted as a prerequisite for responsible behaviour, depends on the availability of the three options identified by Hirschman (1970): loyalty, exit and voice. In such a perspective, then, local actors, i.e. welfare agents and beneficiaries, should not be constrained to *loyalty*, but they should be allowed not to comply with the official view of activation without incurring unbearable penalties as a consequence (i.e. *exit*), and they should also be able to negotiate and somewhat influence the content of ALMPs (i.e. *voice*). Hence, the extent to which local actors are allowed to reinterpret the centrally designed conception of activation and adjust it to local circumstances is a necessary condition of their behaving responsibly.

To sum up, for Sen (1999) responsibility necessitates a combination of capacity to act (opportunity freedom) and freedom to choose (process freedom). As Sen repeatedly emphasises, these two dimensions are deeply interrelated: indeed 'It is hard to escape the general conclusion that economic performance, social opportunity, political voice and public reasoning are all deeply interrelated' (Sen, 2009: 350). The next two sections examine how these two dimensions of freedom that are the prerequisites of responsibility, are tackled in the case of activation policies.

RESPONSIBILITY AND OPPORTUNITY FREEDOM IN ACTIVATION POLICIES

The local actors' capacity to act depends on at least three complementary dimensions. First, the way financial redistribution is organised within the welfare state clearly impacts on the conception of responsibility in social integration policies. Indeed, according to the amount and duration of social security benefits, as well as the eligibility conditions and other requirements imposed on recipients, the expectations in terms of responsibility will vary significantly. In countries such as the US or the UK, where benefits are envisaged as potential sources of poverty traps, redistribution of cash resources is limited both in amount and duration, and strict conditionalities are imposed (Handler, 2004; King, 1999). This implies that benefit systems are carefully reviewed in order to eliminate such traps and set up appropriate financial incentives. In these countries, a specific normative reference is imposed with regard to the link between cash redistribution and activation (i.e. too many redistributed resources = less capacity or willingness to act on behalf of the recipients, along the lines of the moral hazard argument), and competing views of the 'welfare-activation' nexus are discarded by decision-makers (Bonvin, 2006). Such ambition to make welfare policies more dissuasive also shapes the work of local welfare agents who have to work in shorter time spans and are pushed to privilege quick-fix remedies and avoid long-term and expensive schemes aiming at long-lasting professional reintegration (Peck and Theodore, 2000). This especially holds for the most disadvantaged groups. Indeed, retrenchment measures inducing benefit reductions often coincide with a corresponding reduction of the time available for activating recipients, and a consequent risk of creaming and selective practices at local level (Benarrosh, 2006). Such budget pressures negatively impact on both beneficiaries and local agents, who are equally pushed to privilege quick reintegration into the labour market, whatever the quality of this professional reintegration. Such an approach is clearly at odds with the capability perspective. If Sen recognises some relevance to the moral hazard argument, he also clearly sets the limits of this relevance: when assessing the individual responsibility of benefit recipients, the degree of motivation and effort applies only insofar as other variables such as gender, age, or asymmetry of information, do not interfere (Sen, 1992; Bonvin and Farvaque, 2008). In other words, if the failure to find a job can be related to such factors and not to a lack of commitment, then the individual cannot be taken as responsible for his/her situation.

By contrast, programmes providing generous and long-lasting benefits, e.g. in Scandinavian countries, endorse the opposite view (i.e. more redistributed resources = more capacity to act), which allows for more ambitious and longer-term interventions at local level. Local agents also enjoy larger budget envelopes and longer time spans for organising the modalities of their action. In this case, access to adequate resources appears as a prerequisite for fostering responsible behaviour. This does not imply that the moral hazard argument is discarded altogether, but that its relevance is strictly delimited in much the same way as in the capability approach. This alternative conception of the (re-)distribution of resources and its impact on beneficiaries and local agents, also entails another division of responsibilities between individual actors and collective bodies: whereas, in countries such as the UK or the US, responsibility is interpreted first and foremost as a matter of individual will, with the state mostly playing a moralising part in this direction, it is here envisaged as a joint mission of the individual and the state.

Second, the design and content of activation measures is also far from uniform. In strictly quantitative terms, the amount of resources devoted to ALMPs greatly differs along countries (e.g. European Commission, 2006). Besides, ALMPs may endorse very different views of activation promoting respectively quick return to work, the enhancement of employability, the necessity to keep people busy (activation as occupation), or looser objectives such as autonomy or social integration (for an illustration of such diversity in OECD countries, see Tergeist and Grubb, 2006). And this diversity in turn plays a key role in shaping local agents' practices. Indeed, if the normative reference underlying ALMPs focuses on the development of qualifications, and considerable financial resources are mobilised to this purpose, long-term programmes may be designed to foster durable professional integration in a qualified job. By contrast, if work is considered to be a short-term objective with a view to reducing the caseload and public expenditure, reintegration into the labour market will take much less account of the issue of job quality (Bonvin and Moachon, 2007). Depending on the normative reference of activation selected, local agents' responsibility will then coincide either with pursuing quick professional reintegration (possibly in a precarious job), or with promoting a long-term reintegration in an attractive job. A key issue in this respect is linked to the degree of precision of the administrative view of activation: the more specified it is (e.g. all recipients should go back to work as quickly as possible), the less margin of manoeuvre is left to local agents, and consequently the less scope for exercising their responsibility; by contrast, the less specified it is (e.g. promote all recipients' social integration or autonomy), the more margin of manoeuvre and the higher the scope for responsibility, provided adequate funding and means are made available. According to the capability approach to responsibility, the problem is not activation in itself but the ambition to impose one and the same conception of activation on all beneficiaries (Bonvin and Farvaque, 2007). In this perspective, incompleteness (i.e. lack of specification of ALMPs and their objectives) is considered as the very condition of situated public action and as such it is a prerequisite for the genuine exercise of responsible behaviour by both local agents and beneficiaries.

Finally, the capacity to act also depends on the opportunities for social and professional integration open to benefit recipients. In most OECD countries, market actors are increasingly deemed responsible for job creation, as well as for the quality of the jobs created. As a consequence, the availability of working opportunities strongly depends on these market actors' readiness and ability to create enough jobs. In this context, the state is called to re-deploy its interventions from a market-steering to a market-supporting orientation (Levy, 2006), and this may be achieved in a plurality of ways. The state might be confined to creating the appropriate conditions to foster entrepreneurship and promote competitiveness and job creation (e.g. via financial incentives such as job subsidies). This option has been severely questioned since the beginning of the financial crisis. Or it can act as a kind of last resort employer via the development of an extended public sector (which has somehow been the case of Scandinavian countries, whose share of public employment amounts to double of the OECD average – see Esping-Andersen, 1999). Or it may choose to subsidise the creation of a so-called secondary labour market or of an extensive third sector. These various options impact differently on the quality and quantity of working opportunities, and especially on their availability to diverse categories of benefit recipients. If the market is the ultimate provider of working opportunities, access to such jobs may prove difficult for the most disadvantaged groups. By contrast, if job creation is a task commonly assumed by the market, the state and the third sector, then these groups will have more opportunities for professional integration under adequate conditions in terms of employment quality. The capability approach clearly advocates this last option, insofar as it is more inclusive and socially equitable. The responsibility for creating opportunities for everyone's social and economic integration should not be left to market actors alone. The recent financial crisis has certainly contributed to arousing the policy-makers' awareness with regard to the necessity of a more extensive public intervention in this respect.

To sum up, with regard to the 'capacity to act' side of responsibility, a high level of resources, a great variety of activation programmes aiming at providing appropriate solutions for all target groups, as well as plenty of valuable opportunities created by diverse actors (the market, the state and the third sector) qualify as more capability-friendly than their opposite, i.e. few resources, very specified activation schemes and opportunities of variable quality provided mainly by the market. Hence, the way these three issues (resources, content of ALMPs, employment opportunities) are framed, determines to a large extent the possibility to efficiently support all target groups, and it also defines the balance between collective and individual responsibility and the version of the enabling state – closer to activation in the harsher sense (workfare, learnfare, etc.) or to 'capacitation' (enhancement of capabilities) – that will prevail in the end (Gilbert, 2004). If equipped with appropriate resources and opportunities, local welfare agents and beneficiaries may rightly be considered as accountable for their actions; in contrast, public policies marked by retrenchment offer poor resources and opportunities, and requirements imposed on local agents and beneficiaries to behave responsibly appear as much more questionable when viewed from the capability perspective.

The Paths to Empowerment and Opportunity Freedom in the Academic Debate

In current academic research and debate, two alternative conceptions seem to be valid candidates when it comes to implementing the capability perspective of opportunity freedom. The following paragraphs contrast these two views with the capability approach.

First, the so-called 'asset-based welfare' (ABW) approach insists on the necessity to *equip people for the market* (Gautié and Gazier, 2003), and it emphasises the importance of individual initiatives and responsibility in this respect. In this perspective, the state has to supply 'assets' (mainly human and social capital) or to help individuals acquire these assets. Ideally, each member of society should be able to constitute him/herself as an *entrepreneur self* (Périlleux, 2005), i.e. an active and competitive individual able to responsibly manage all spheres of his/her life and to increase all forms of resources or capitals (monetary, affective, cognitive, behavioural, social, etc.) s/he possesses. The responsibility of empowerment mostly relies on individuals, and less attention is paid to the dimensions that are out of his/her control such as the creation of valuable employment opportunities. The ABW approach certainly takes some steps towards developing people's employability. However, when confronted with the capability approach, it appears that: a) it is clearly biased towards supply-side interventions (people are equipped for the markets, but nothing or very little is suggested to equip the markets for the people); b) the development of employability is envisaged as a duty for all welfare recipients and workers, rather than an opportunity; c) entitlement to cash benefits is conditional upon compliance with specific conditions defined by public administration. In short, empowerment tools are reinforced, but biased in favour of supply-side instruments, and they imply significant limitations of the beneficiaries' freedom to choose.

By contrast, the 'transitional labour markets' (TLM) approach insists that the possession of capitals or 'assets' is not sufficient to empower people and increase their employability. It is necessary to envisage the labour market not exclusively on the supply side, but in terms of adjustments between supply and demand. So-called 'interactive employability' is presented as an apt substitute for the ABW approach insofar as it adds to the issue of individual capitals (both human and social) that of the organisation and regulation of the demand side on the labour market (Gazier, 2001, 2006). The TLM approach still emphasises individual initiative, but it insists at the same time on the necessity to introduce collective arrangements in order to secure transitions within the individual's life course and professional career. If they are organised via collective arrangements, such transitions may result in a more equitable distribution between work, family life, leisure and other dimensions of the human life. The TLM approach contrasts with the ABW in three main respects: first, the supply and the demand sides are envisaged as complementary dimensions of an employability strategy; second, the individual, the state and numerous other actors are considered as jointly responsible for developing employability, i.e. for securing smooth professional transitions for every member of society; finally, work is not considered as the *sine qua non* condition of human flourishing, but as one component of human life, among others. Therefore, the ABW motto, i.e. 'equipping people for the market', has to be completed with interventions aiming at 'equipping the markets for the people' (Gazier, 2006). Günther Schmid's concept of 'embedded employability' takes further steps in this direction, by advocating that the notion of employability should also encompass the firms' capacities to employ people. In other words, the *'sustained capability to work* on the supply-side' needs to be complemented by the *'sustained capability to employ* on the demand-side', e.g. via 'the ability to make flexible capacity adjustments rather than relying solely on a *hire and fire* policy' (Schmid, 2006: 26, passim). In Schmid's view, such a demand-side perspective allows us, at least to some extent, to avoid the negative by-side effect of approaches focusing exclusively on the supply side and on individual responsibility, namely that they often result in blaming the victim. Hence, Schmid's insistence on the necessary embeddedness of employability 'addresses the need to establish functioning opportunity structures to guarantee meaningful and decent employment over the life course' (Schmid, 2006: 23). Hence, the enhancement of opportunities features as a central dimension of both interactive and embedded employability, as is illustrated by the key notion of 'functioning employability', which 'can be defined as the capability to realize in the labour market one's own life-plans, having the opportunity to change these plans and to make transitions between various kinds of employment' (Schmid, 2006: 23).

However, the lack of concern for the issue of cash resources in the two TLM perspectives may be detrimental in terms of opportunity freedom and responsibility. Indeed, the payment of unconditional cash benefits appears as a necessary condition for enhancing the bargaining and negotiating power of benefit recipients when it comes to the definition and implementation of activation strategies. Without such unconditional rights to what Sen calls passive empowerment, the exit and voice options might be very difficult to implement for deprived individuals (or for those that are threatened to be deprived of their benefits in case of non-compliance with the official view of activation). Hence, if interactive employability or embedded employability are implemented in a context of high benefit conditionality, they may end up in promoting people's adaptability rather than the development of their opportunity freedom and responsibility.

RESPONSIBILITY AND PROCESS FREEDOM IN PUBLIC EMPLOYMENT SERVICES

However, responsibility comprises a second dimension in the capability perspective, namely real freedom to choose. A key topic in this respect is what we labelled elsewhere 'capability for voice', i.e. the real freedom to express one's concerns and make them count in the course of collective decision-making (e.g. Bonvin and Farvaque, 2006). Sen repeatedly emphasises the huge significance of the practice of democracy when it comes to promoting social justice, i.e. development as freedom (e.g. Sen, 1999, 2009). Indeed, there is 'extensive evidence that democracy and political and civil rights tend to enhance freedoms of other kinds (such as human security) through giving a voice, at least in many circumstances, to the deprived and the vulnerable' (Sen, 2009: 348). In this perspective, democracy does not boil down to public balloting, it encompasses all exercises of public reasoning. The following paragraphs assess to what extent practices in public employment services, especially with regard to activation programmes, can be defined as democratic.

The main issue at stake here is whether the modes of governance used to monitor the relationship between the central and the local level in activation policies leave enough margin of manoeuvre to allow local actors to express their wishes, concerns, expectations, etc. and make them count. Two levels of public action, both increasingly marked by contractualism, will be considered in the next two subsections: the relationship between central level and local agents on one side (that is ruled by provision agreements and the like), that between local agents and beneficiaries on the other side where individual action plans or similar devices are designed.

Contractualism between Central Administration and Local Actors

Bureaucratic provision of services, along standardised lines of intervention, is not adapted to ALMPs insofar as it is unable to take into account local and individual circumstances (Varone and Bonvin, 2004). Therefore, bureaucracy needs to be substituted by other modes of governance in which local agents are called to take on more responsibilities. However, in order to avoid the potential arbitrariness of purely local decisions, the state needs to monitor these interventions, i.e. to secure that the beneficiaries' fundamental rights are respected and that local action keeps in line with centrally designed objectives. With regard to this role of the central state in ALMPs, three configurations can be identified (see Bonvin and Moachon, 2007; Borghi and Van Berkel, 2007; Newman, 2007), which I suggest to name 'hierarchical', 'marketised' and 'capability-friendly'.

In the first one, the state keeps a strong hold over local practices, mainly via the tools of new public management: quantitative objectives are fixed with financial penalties for local agents not fulfilling them, budgets are allotted on a short-term and revisable basis, precise indicators of performance are elaborated, etc. In some cases, this pattern of public action somewhat paradoxically contributes to reinforce the features of bureaucratic administration. Indeed, via benchmarking the various local employment services, best practices are identified and then imposed on the least performing local agents. Then, contrary to the NPM focus on outputs and outcomes, not only the results of public employment services are carefully compared and monitored via output indicators, but also the means and processes of public action are determined and controlled via input indicators (such as the sanctioning rate, the number of monthly interviews with jobseekers, etc.). As a consequence, local agents are not only held accountable for unsatisfactory results in terms of outputs or outcomes, but they are also responsible for respecting the processes identified by the central administration as the best practices. And they have to abide by the sanctions that can be imposed on them for both reasons. In such cases, behaving responsibly implies full compliance with administrative directives: it leaves very limited space for situated public action. The knowledge, sense of justice and competence of local actors are not recognised as such. Management by objectives within the public administration, when it is implemented along these strict lines, is certainly the purest illustration of such a pattern (the implementation of ALMPs in the Swiss unemployment insurance go a long way on this managerial path – see Bonvin and Moachon, 2007 – but this is a common way of governing public employment services in many OECD countries, as emphasised by Sol and Westerveld, 2005a). However, private suppliers of social services, whether for profit or not, may also be subjected to this hierarchical configuration, especially when their financial dependency vis-à-vis the state is high. Under these circumstances, they are equally unable either to contest the official view of activation when they think it irrelevant (i.e. Hirschman's voice option), or to refuse the conditions defined in the provision agreement (i.e. the exit option). In such cases, loyalty is the only available option also for local private actors. Viewed from the capability perspective, local actors placed in such a configuration do not enjoy substantive freedom of choice, and therefore cannot be held fully responsible for what they do. Indeed, responsibility in the capability approach does not boil down to compliance.

In the second instance, the state retreats and leaves a higher margin for manoeuvre to local actors. In such a model, the state as a provider of ALMPs and employment services is considered to have failed. Thus the responsibility of running efficient professional reintegration services is left to market actors equipped with appropriate financial incentives (often higher than the means granted to public employment agencies). In this configuration, the state is responsible for providing sufficient funding and for evaluating the efficiency of local action against rough indicators of performance (e.g. reinsertion rates). Competition between service providers, it is claimed, will improve the quality of the services as well as their quality-price ratio. As evidenced by Sol and Westerveld (2005b), the potential advantages of this formula are greater flexibility in the use of contractors (whose inefficiency can be sanctioned via the non-renewal of the provision contract), focus on outcomes rather than processes, and lower costs. All these are supposedly connected with higher efficiency in the pursuit of centrally fixed targets. In this model, normative issues related to activation are considered as the exclusive prerogative of policymakers, and the whole problem is reduced to a matter of technical efficiency in implementing ALMPs. Market modes of governance are envisaged as the most appropriate tool to improve efficiency via competition and tendering. However, due to their tendency to lower costs (i.e. give precedence to cheaper providers for the same tasks) and standardise programmes (scale economies are an efficient way to decrease costs and propose cheaper services), they cannot guarantee that a situated view of activation, i.e. one taking into account local circumstances and individual features, will be implemented at local level. Indeed, such a configuration based on market modes of governance risks favouring creaming and selective practices, i.e. local providers will focus on the beneficiaries that allow them to reach the targets (fixed in the provision agreement), at the expense of more disadvantaged groups (Sol and Westerveld, 2005a, provide illustrations of this risk).

In the third instance, central administration and local agents act as partners in the implementation of ALMPs. The central state keeps an essential twofold function as a guarantor of the beneficiaries' fundamental rights and as a monitoring body of local action, but these tasks are interpreted in such a way as to promote local actors' active participation in the implementation of ALMPs. This entails a twofold move from bureaucratic public action and from the hierarchical model identified above: first towards a more participative definition of the aims and performance indicators of public action (which also entails an exercise of public reasoning when it comes to defining the notions of quality and performance of public employment services); second towards the formulation, by the central level, of more incomplete objectives and directives in order to leave a higher margin for manoeuvre and interpretation to local actors. For instance, if the objectives of ALMPs are not defined in terms of employment rates, but in terms of improving the beneficiaries' autonomy or of enhancing their capabilities, then the scope for situated public action and for genuinely responsible behaviour on behalf of local actors is extended. Hence, an incomplete definition of activation at central level makes space for a 'politics of needs interpretation' at local level (Fraser, 1989). This third configuration is barely mentioned in Sol and Westerveld's survey (2005a) of contractual practices in employment services. Yet, this innovative path, which implies less controlling power for the central administration and more genuine autonomy for local actors, is not incompatible with the pursuit of efficiency in ALMPs. Quite the contrary: by giving local agents the means and freedom to act responsibly (in line with the capability approach), it makes them truly responsible and accountable for the results obtained. In this last pattern, responsibility and accountability do not boil down to efficient implementation of exogenously defined objectives, but encompass participation to the definition of the most adequate modes of activating, or rather 'capacitating', people. This entails another distribution of power between the state, local agents and beneficiaries, more in line with the so-called participative model of new public management (Monks, 1998). According to the capability approach, contractualism in employment services should leave the restrictive view of principal-to-agent relationships (which dominates in most present implementations of NPM principles) and embrace a more participative and truly reflexive conception of public action, in line with the conception of democracy as public reasoning.

Contractualism between Local Agents and Beneficiaries

The place of the benefit recipient in individualised activation policies needs also to be questioned. In the hierarchical pattern, the beneficiary's responsibility is fostered via obedience to the injunctions of the central administration relayed by local agents acting as 'driving belts'. Individual wishes and expectations are taken into account only insofar as they correspond to the official conception of activation, otherwise it is the local agents' task to reform them and make them coincide with the institutional expectations. The chain of governance is conceived as a top-down transfer of specific normative contents that need to be endorsed and actively pursued by local agents and beneficiaries alike (Bonvin and Moachon, 2007). Such practices are clearly at odds with the capability perspective and its idea of democracy as public reasoning.

In certain instances of the marketised configuration, the individuals are equipped with more freedom of choice via the provision of vouchers or personal budgets (e.g. Bruttel, 2005). Beneficiaries can then express their wishes more freely since they are allowed to choose their ALMPs. At the core of such practices, there are two problematic postulates: first, the respect of the beneficiary's freedom of choice passes via the attribution of a freely disposable income, i.e. the issue of freedom of choice is framed in terms of consumer choice; second, it is assumed that a free choice by consumers, in this case benefit recipients, will result in a higher quality of the services provided by employment agencies. As Sol and Westerveld (2005b) emphasise, there are many practical obstacles to overcome before this twofold promise can be fulfilled: the great similarity of the solutions provided in marketised employment services (which considerably restricts the beneficiary's actual freedom of choice), the asymmetry of information about the quality of these services (which facilitates cheating on customers) and most importantly the frailty of the recipient's consumer position. The key issue lies here in the capacity of the beneficiary to influence the definition and content of ALMPs, and it is doubtful whether s/he will really be allowed to have his/her say in this respect. In comparison with the hierarchical pattern, this configuration takes some steps toward giving more responsibility to benefit recipients (additional means are provided and some freedom of choice is granted), but it still remains in the middle of the road.

In the capability-friendly model, the beneficiary is considered as an active citizen and invited to take part in the definition of ALMPs and the modalities of their implementation. Provided adequate means are granted to empower him/her and improve his/her capacity to act, this pattern engages him/her in a self-reflexive process (Borghi and Van Berkel, 2007) on how to best develop his/her capabilities. The main difference with the marketised pattern lies in the possibility granted to the beneficiary to co-define and co-implement activation programmes. The capability-friendly model recognises that rationality is not detained by single actors presumably more competent than all others, and that the informational role of multi-levelled actors is essential in any actual policy-making situation. If rationality is distributed or shared in such a way, then local employment agencies have to be seen as 'informational agencies' (White, 1990), and beneficiaries are informational sources to be mobilised in the collective definition of ALMPs. What matters then is not how the central state may impose more efficiently its own normative references on local actors, it is rather how it can promote the co-definition and co-implementation of activation programmes at local level.

With regard to the 'freedom to choose' side of responsibility, our analysis shows the importance to take into account local expertise and knowledge, as well as local circumstances and individual preferences when it comes to designing and implementing ALMPs. The role of the state, no more as a provider but as a guarantor and a monitoring body, is key in this respect. Indeed, local action by itself will not necessarily result in enhancing the capabilities of all local actors, i.e. providers and all groups of beneficiaries alike. A finely tuned balance needs to be found in the way the central level connects to local actors. In the capability perspective, the normative references defined by central bodies ought to be both incomplete in order to allow for local initiatives, and quite strict and precise in defining fundamental rights, in order to prevent local arbitrariness and all forms of unduly intrusion in the beneficiaries' private sphere that may lead to 'shameful revelations' (Wolff, 1998).

These two subsections on contractual practices in public employment services aptly demonstrate the necessity of democracy and public reasoning in the field of ALMPs. Instead of taking for granted some postulates and present them as undisputable evidence (activation as the panacea for all jobseekers, the necessity to increase the employment rate, etc. – see Bonvin and Rosenstein, 2009), these should be systematically submitted to public reasoning in the context of situated public action. The notion of 'positional objectivity', developed by Sen (e.g. 2002), emphasises the epistemological foundations and the normative relevance of process freedom and of democracy and public reasoning. Following this conception, all observations or descriptions of social reality depend on the observer's position vis-à-vis the objects (persons, situations, etc.) observed or described. In decision theory, such positional objectivity implies that a person makes her decisions on the basis of her specific position, i.e. her past experience, her education, her social status, etc. Sen insists that positional objectivity also applies to ethics as some positional characteristics are inevitably relevant for evaluation and choice. Democracy and public reasoning are then envisaged as the most appropriate ways to confront multiple positional objectivities and build socially acceptable compromises between these. In this perspective, attention needs to be paid to who defines policies, who is allowed to participate in the decision-making and implementing processes, thereby distinguishing policies and procedures that are developed and implemented with a view to imposing top-down managerialism from policies that result from negotiation and compromise-building.

CONCLUSION

The capability approach provides the tools for a renewed analysis of the issue of responsibility in activation policies. First, on the 'capacity to act' side of responsibility, an application of Sen's perspective allows for an identification of the importance of providing sufficient resources and adequate opportunities to local ALMP agents and beneficiaries. If they are not appropriately equipped in these two key respects, the call for responsibility remains formal in the Marxist sense, i.e. local actors are invited to behave responsibly, but they do not have the necessary means to that purpose. In the capability approach, collective interventions are envisaged as necessary prerequisites for fostering individual responsibility, and not as factors producing dependence and irresponsibility. This implies, for instance, that workfare programmes and all measures exacerbating individual responsibility without providing adequate collective support are not able to promote responsibility as understood by the capability approach.

Furthermore, a precise administrative definition of activation plays a key role for the issue of responsibility. If the centrally designed definition of activation is restricted to solutions of quick reintegration into the labour market, it does not allow taking into account local circumstances and individual characteristics and preferences. If targets are defined too precisely, they may prove inappropriate or even unrealistic, especially for the most disadvantaged groups. In contrast, unspecified objectives, such as the enhancement of capabilities, allow for more diversified interventions at local level. Although return to work or the promotion of employability are useful measures, they only constitute solutions amid a more extensive set of active labour market policies. In any case, in order to promote policies that enhance the 'capacity to act', three prerequisites are necessary for a successful promotion of responsibility among local actors: sufficient resources, adequate opportunities and broad definitions of activation.

Second, the 'freedom to choose' dimension of responsibility greatly depends on the organisation of coordination between the different actors involved in activation policies. This encompasses the relationships between central administration and local level on the one hand, local providers and individual beneficiaries on the other. If one level prevails over the others and imposes its own specific definition of activation (or its own positional objectivity), the freedom of choice of other partners is reduced and, consequently, the conditions for genuine responsibility are not adequately fulfilled. In the capability perspective, all such interventions are counterproductive when it comes to fostering responsibility, and the role of the state is to prevent them. What is suggested is not an unconditional respect of the local agent's and the beneficiary's freedom to choose (whatever their preferences), but that the opportunity is offered to them to take an active part in the design and implementation of ALMPs and to make their voice heard.

In the capability approach, the assessment of responsibility in activation policies necessitates taking into account two main questions: a) the balance between individual and collective responsibility, b) how the two core issues – capacity to act and freedom to choose – are framed within this context. The objective is not to define an impracticable ideal of responsibility, but to provide a yardstick for assessing activation programmes (e.g. given specific resources and opportunities, and a determined degree of freedom to choose, what level of individual responsibility can reasonably be expected from the local actors?) and to suggest possible improvements in the direction of fostering more genuine responsibility among the local agents and the beneficiaries. In our view, such a conception calling for more realistic claims to individual responsibility could well represent the way out of the pitfalls (paradoxical injunctions, double binds, etc.) of most present managerialist practices and prepare the ground for the setting up of truly innovative 'capacitation' programmes in the place of the present activation strategies.

NOTE

[1.] This chapter draws on and elaborates the article 'Activation policies, new modes of governance and the issue of responsibility', *Social Policy and Society*, 7(3), 367–377, May 2008 © Cambridge University Press, reproduced with permission.

REFERENCES

Benarrosh, Y. (2006), *Recevoir les chômeurs de l'ANPE: L'institution entre don et contrat*, Paris: L'Harmattan.

Bonvin, J.-M. (2006), 'Assessing the European social model against the capability approach', in M. Jepsen and A. Serrano (eds), *Unwrapping the European Social Model*, Bristol: The Policy Press, pp.213–232.

Bonvin, J.-M. (2008), 'Activation policies, new modes of governance and the issue of responsibility', *Social Policy and Society*, **7**(3), 367–377.

Bonvin, J.-M. and N. Farvaque (2006), 'Promoting Capability for Work: the Role of Local Actors', in S. Deneulin, M. Nebel and N. Sagovsky (eds), *Transforming Unjust Structures: The Capability Approach*, Dordrecht: Springer, pp.121–143.

Bonvin, J.-M. and N. Farvaque (2007), 'A capability approach to individualised and tailor-made activation', in R. Van Berkel and B. Valkenburg (eds), *Making it personal. Individualising activation services in the EU*, Bristol: The Policy Press, pp.45–66.

Bonvin, J.-M. and N. Farvaque (2008), *Amartya Sen, Une Politique de la Liberté*, Paris: Michalon.

Bonvin, J.-M. and E. Moachon (2007), 'The impact of contractualism in social policies: the case of active labour market policies in Switzerland', *International Journal of Sociology and Social Policy*, **27**(9/10), 401–412.

Bonvin, J.-M. and E. Rosenstein (2009), 'Al di là delle politiche basate sull'evidenza: Strutture cognitive e implicazioni normative nelle politiche di integrazione sociale', *La Rivista delle Politiche Sociali*, **3**, July–September, 85–106.

Borghi, V. and R. Van Berkel (2007), 'Individualised service provision in an era of activation and new governance', *International Journal of Sociology and Social Policy*, **27**(9/10), 413–424.

Bruttel, O. (2005), 'Delivering active labour market policy through vouchers: experiences with training vouchers in Germany', *International Review of Administrative Sciences*, **71**(3), 391–404.

Esping-Andersen, G. (1999), *Social Foundations of Postindustrial Economies*, Oxford: Oxford University Press.

European Commission (2006), 'Employment in Europe 2006', Luxembourg: Office for Official Publications of the European Communities.

Fraser, N. (1989), *Unruly Practices*, Cambridge: Polity Press.

Gautié, J. and B. Gazier (2003), 'Equipping Markets for People: Transitional labour markets as a central part of a new social model', paper presented at the 15th Annual Meeting of the Society for the Advancement of Socio-Economics (SASE), Aix en Provence, 26–28 June.

Gazier, B. (2001), 'L'employabilité: la complexité d'une notion', in P. Weinert, M. Baukens, P. Bollérot, M. Pineschi-Gapenne and U. Walwei (eds), *L'Employabilité: De la Théorie à la Pratique*, Brussels: Peter Lang, pp.3–28.

Gazier, B. (2006), 'Promoting employability in the context of globalisation in the EU and Japan', Background Paper, 11th EU-Japan Symposium, 20–21 March.

Gilbert, N. (2004), *Transformation of the Welfare State: The Silent Surrender of Public Responsibility*, Oxford: Oxford University Press.

Handler, J.F. (2004), *Social Citizenship and Workfare in the United States and Western Europe: The Paradox of Inclusion*, Cambridge: Cambridge University Press.

Hirschman, A.O. (1970), *Exit, Voice and Loyalty: Responses to Decline in Firms, Organizations and States*, Cambridge, MA: Harvard University Press.

Jessop, B. (1994), 'The transition to post-fordism and the Schumpeterian workfare state', in R. Burrows and B. Loader (eds) *Towards a Post-fordist Welfare State?* London: Routledge, pp.13–37.

King, D. (1999), *In The Name of Liberalism: Illiberal Social Policy in the United States and Britain*, Oxford: Oxford University Press.

Levy, J. (ed.) (2006), *The State after Statism: New State Activities in the Age of Liberalization*, Cambridge, MA and London: Harvard University Press.

Monks, J. (1998), 'La nouvelle gestion publique: boîte à outils ou changement paradigmatique?', in M. Hufty (ed.), *La pensée comptable*, Genève/Paris: Les nouveaux cahiers de l'IUED/PUF, pp.77–89.

Newman, J. (2007), 'The "double dynamics" of activation: institutions, citizens and the remaking of welfare governance', *International Journal of Sociology and Social Policy*, 27(9/10), 364–375.

Peck, J. and N. Theodore (2000), 'Beyond "employability"', *Cambridge Journal of Economics*, 24(6), 729–749.

Périlleux, Th. (2005). 'Se rendre désirable. L'employabilité dans l'Etat social actif et l'idéologie managériale', in P. Vielle, P. Pochet and I. Cassiers (eds) *L'Etat social actif: vers un changement de paradigme?*, PIE-Pieter Lang: Brussels, pp.301–322,

Schmid, G. (2006), 'Social risk management through transitional labour markets', *Socio-Economic Review*, 4(1), 1–33.

Sen, A.K. (1992), *Inequality Reexamined*, Cambridge, MA: Harvard University Press.

Sen, A.K. (1999), *Development as Freedom*, Oxford: Oxford University Press.

Sen, A.K. (2002), 'Positional objectivity', in *Rationality and Freedom*, Cambridge, MA: The Belknap Press of Harvard University Press, pp.463–483.

Sen, A.K. (2009), *The Idea of Justice*, Cambridge, MA: The Belknap Press of Harvard University Press.

Sol, E. and M. Westerveld (eds) (2005a), *Contractualism in Employment Services: A New Form of Welfare State Governance*, The Hague: Kluwer Law International.

Sol, E. and M. Westerveld (2005b), 'Contractualism: concluding remarks', in E. Sol and M. Westerveld (eds), *Contractualism in Employment Services: A New Form of Welfare State Governance*, The Hague: Kluwer Law International, pp.383–402.

Tergeist, P. and D. Grubb (2006), 'Activation strategies and the performance of employment services in Germany, the Netherlands and the United Kingdom', Paris: OECD Social, Employment and Migration Papers.

Varone, F. and J.-M. Bonvin (eds) (2004), 'La nouvelle gestion publique', Special Issue of *Les Politiques Sociales*, 1–2/2004.

White, M. (1990), 'Information et chômage des jeunes', *Sociologie du Travail*, 90(4), 529–541.

Wolff, J. (1998), 'Fairness, respect, and the egalitarian ethos', *Philosophy and Public Affairs*, 27(2), 97–122.

8. Creating collective capability: historical perspectives on co-ordinating public action[1]

Noel Whiteside

Individual human beings, with their plural identities, multiple affiliations and diverse associations are quintessentially social creatures with different types of societal interactions. (Sen, 2009: 246–247)

INTRODUCTION

The financial crash of 2008 demonstrated that markets are neither self-stabilising nor the most efficient means of distributing goods and services. Yet the crash has not generated new analysis to change the direction of public policy. Much goes on the same as before. Bankers' bonuses are restored even as unemployment escalates: future cuts in public services and higher taxation are the price to be paid for bailing out financial institutions 'too big to fail'. Yet this crisis necessarily must cause us to rethink the principles of social justice that co-ordinate the administration of social policies – to allow new solutions to permeate political discussion, to change the orientation of both political leaders and the publics they serve. In this, Europe's rich historical experience in co-ordinating public action can inform discussion by demonstrating the different principles on which social rights were (and are) founded. In light of recent events, public administration should question the automatic adherence to market paradigms that have underpinned policy delivery in recent years. For, as this chapter will demonstrate, there are alternatives.

Evidence drawn from earlier forms of public intervention in urban economies shows how major industrial and commercial centres achieved the modernisation and co-ordination of economic and social action under varied political agendas. Such experiments reflected particular conceptions of social order and social justice that legitimated behaviour understood to be conducive to the promotion of the common good. Such conceptions reflect what Sen calls the Informational Bases of Judgement in Justice (IBJJ) that pertain to specific situations. What criteria, set against which principles, determine rights to public help – and under what conditions? How are such criteria drawn up, by whom and in accordance with what conception of authority? In combination, using this analytical double helix and by linking Sen's arguments on the IBJJ to concrete examples of past arenas of public action, we witness how a reflexive discourse between individual preferences and freedoms and the social situations within which they were found enabled (or not) communities to flourish. In so doing, the chapter demonstrates how situated public action created the contexts within which personal capability might flourish and the considerable overlap that existed (and exists) between economic and social spheres of political discourse. What emerges from our study is how personal opportunity and collective well-being were promoted by the provision of public services, ranging from transport, to communications, to guarantees of democratic accountability, stretching the sphere of the social well beyond the provision of social protection *tout court*.

This causes us to question the assumption that public welfare services damage economic growth. Social policy's critics still define them as a burden on market activity. This conception needs to be challenged. The state is implicated in all market exchange: it defines fraud, regulates technical standards of products, guarantees essential services and determines the legitimacy of financial transactions. In terms of labour markets, European governments mediate qualifications, safety standards, hours of work, paid holidays as well as parental leave and equality of treatment in terms of gender and ethnicity. It is in the public interest for governments to guarantee the efficient operation of labour markets, albeit that the terms under which 'efficiency' is constructed are widely varied. This variance is explored below and offers insights into the ways in which varieties of capitalism (Hall and Soskice, 2001) took root and flourished.

The following section addresses key concepts, drawn from the work of Amartya Sen, that link spheres of public judgement ('informational basis of judgement in justice', IBJJ) to address social rights. In the next section, historical evidence is used to illustrate how principles of public action in specific situations shaped varied frameworks within which human capability was understood and developed. Reflecting current policy preoccupations with labour market activation, this focuses on the development of placement agencies (labour bureaux, exchanges or registries) as public services: on the principles of social justice they embodied as interpreted by the objectives they claimed to serve. A capability approach reveals multiple typologies of social participation and creates comparative social histories that, shifting from national accounts, move beyond a simple listing of legislative achievements and the measurement of outcomes. In so doing, this chapter addresses issues pertinent to the varieties of capitalism debate. By focusing at the sub-national level, the analysis demonstrates the variability of spheres of public action – and the range of compromises they embodied – that qualifies the national prototypes with which this debate has largely been concerned. Hence we return to Sen, and his emphasis on the multiplicity of factors to be taken into account by public deliberation, as offering a pertinent framework to explore this agenda.

SEN AND FRAMEWORKS OF SOCIAL WELL-BEING

In *The Idea of Justice* (2009), Amartya Sen stresses the importance of public reasoning (the plurality of reasons and the compromises to be reached between them) in shaping an evaluation of social rights: reasoning and deliberation among actors create collectively respected values. Here, Sen offers a very different concept of rationality to that offered by rational choice theorists, with their emphasis on individual action devoted to maximising personal ends. We move beyond utility maximising explanations of human agency to focus on the reasoned development of a moral environment within which agents can develop personal projects they have reason to value. As in his earlier work, Sen resists any listing of the reasons to be taken into account, pointing instead to the significance of collective discourse in determining agreed judgement. The development of personal capability is situated in an environment shaped by collective democratic reasoning. The informational basis of judgement in justice (IBJJ) – the environments within which individuals make choices and have their actions assessed – are necessarily multiple and varied, reflecting complex compromises reached through different forms of public deliberation accepted by particular communities at specific points in time. In the accumulation of publicly reasoned argument we reach the founding principles that co-ordinate social and economic action, shaping the environment within which personal projects can be realised by condemning anti-social behaviour (sometimes through legal sanctions) and fostering welcome social contributions (through public acclaim: honours or prizes, as well as higher remuneration).

In this way the development of individual capability is linked to the creation of collective values: social structures and institutions shape personal capabilities. For Sen, the main focus remains on the individual and her rights; proper spheres for public action are to create environments that enable individuals to develop their capabilities. He uses the provision of public health care, medical care, education and the containment of criminal activity as examples of public duties to achieve that goal (Sen, 2009: 226–227). Here, importance is given to factors that might exacerbate poverty and constrain individual freedom (poor health, innumeracy or illiteracy being obvious examples). The just society, by inference, must offer access to facilities and services that act as resources to enable all to realise latent abilities. Sen denies explicitly that the capability approach implies signing up to social policies aimed entirely at equating everyone's capabilities (Sen, 2009: 232) as the plurality of personal identities and situations makes this impossible. Rather, social obligation rests on the promotion of social rights in terms of guaranteed personal freedom: the resources to be offered being determined by processes of public deliberation. Hence two conceptions of personal freedom emerge from Sen's work: the freedom to act and the freedom to be involved in democratic debate over resources to enable action – also referred to as 'capability for voice' (Bonvin and Farvarque, 2005).

Sen stresses the importance of *reasoning*, exercised by means of a free press, democratic political institutions and public debate as central to the pursuit of justice and the definition of rights (the plurality of reasons that must be accommodated and the compromises required between them) (Sen, 2009, ch. 16). This plurality of reasoning leads him to deny the purpose of measuring outcomes as an evaluation process *tout court* and to stress the multiplicity of principles that may become involved in creating evaluative categories. Recalling the IBJJ, there are multiple bases of judgement against which the justice of given policies may be evaluated; only democratic deliberation should determine what these are. While the means to identify social rights are prescribed, how the ends (the resources) are to be provided is not identified. There is thus no preordained role for the state (central or local), or for commercial competition, or for mutual aid, except in so far as such institutions can promote the realisation of personal capabilities. However, freedom to act cannot be understood independently of the interpretive framework within which action is situated, which structures action and gives it sense in terms of power relations and the consequent capability for self-expression (Zimmermann, 2006).

While it remains in the margins of his writing, Sen acknowledges that social environments shape individual identities, personal preferences and values (the bases from which people decide what action they value and the projects they wish to fulfil) and the possibility of social participation. Those things a person has reason to value are likely to reflect activities that her peers also value. Social cohesion implies the creation of an implicit or explicit accord (shaped by democratic deliberation) of capabilities that all agree should be fostered and encouraged. Hence there are self-evident links between personal attainment and activities of value to wider communities –

most obviously those that enable participation in the labour market. The 'value' to the individual does not only derive from some sort of isolated personal satisfaction: self-worth is linked to the acclaim of others. Here we face the problematic link between the personal and the collective: the individual attributes and activities that the collective may wish to encourage (and, by inference, those it may wish to contain). These foster social integration, allowing the person to gain value and self-esteem (not to mention the ability to earn a living). In this context, capabilities as a *genre* emerge as socially constructed; however, as personal situations are all unique, any capability *set* remains essentially individual.

Social coordination is thus central to collective participation, the realisation of capabilities and social rights. Public action to promote social well-being extends well beyond areas of social protection against personal disadvantage. In complex societies, the possible deprivations that might prevent participation have expanded (and are expanding) exponentially. Personal deprivations that preclude successful integration might today include no access to the internet (broadband, naturally) and its multiple networks – or no mobile telephone. Opportunities that give people freedom to make real choices are increasingly complex. This shifts our focus beyond individual welfare services and into wider spheres of public action. As Sen remarks, the provision of universal services offers the means to by-pass financial resources as the only (or best) conversion factor (Sen, 2009: 267 fn). Although he refers here to social services (to avoid the highly inefficient procedure of means-testing the disabled to determine the extra income needed to purchase required medical and social help), this argument can be extended to examine the general case for public services as the means to secure social rights.

Historical examples of expanding cities in the late nineteenth century reveal that, while urban authorities installed water-borne sewage or efficient public transport, the sphere of public reasoning, the varied justifications that underpinned such initiatives and the compromises reached between competing political interests invoked different conceptions of how collective well-being should be realised and of the role public authority should play in realising it (see next section). This did not necessarily involve widening choice and opportunity for all, but rather aimed at guaranteeing co-ordination from a range of different perspectives. Public services might raise revenue for local authorities, or attract wealthier residents (or new businesses) to the city, or foster efficient performance from established commercial enterprise, or protect poorer citizens from excessive exploitation or disease, or appease dangerous political opposition – or compromise between any or all of these. The gospel of 'civic pride' was founded on multiple texts and formed a focal point for complex political debates. To label these initiatives (as they have been labelled at the time and since) as 'municipal socialism' is both crude and misleading; the objectives served were seldom socialist in intent. In this sense at least, past deliberation over public service provision offers insights into prevailing ideas concerning social rights and public participation, the political processes through which these were determined (the avenues for the realisation of capabilities) and their variance by place and time.

Evaluating the past from this perspective widens our understanding of social welfare, away from income replacement for those too old, ill, or ignorant to find work and towards facilities provided that helped some to realise personal potential. In the analysis of historical public deliberation, divisions between economic and social policy objectives, so beloved of neo-liberal discourse, disappear. Social rights involve not only medical care and education, but also the means to establish contacts, integrate in networks of like-minded people; travel to work; access shelter, warmth, food at reasonable prices – as well as guarantees that property will be protected, contracts respected and law-breakers punished. Public action assumed collective well-being was part of an efficient economy (good telecommunication systems, efficient power supply and transport links and so on). More recent conceptions of public amenities as separate from social policy: seeing the first as a necessary foundation for a market economy and the second as a burden on it, distort our understanding. In recent years, transfers of amenities into commercial hands have fractured co-ordinated social provision that underpinned earlier urban growth. In the late nineteenth century, municipal debates about how facilities should be provided demonstrate how urban projects were realised and the multiple IBJJ involved in the process.

FOUNDING PUBLIC SERVICES

Late Nineteenth-Century Cities and their Governance

The growth of major urban conglomerations in the late nineteenth century threatened social chaos as much as it presaged commercial success. Then as now, technological change (the introduction of electric power, the advent of the telephone) transformed the nature of working lives. The expansion of industrial and commercial towns and cities brought large numbers of people, often strangers, into close proximity and required them to live in harmony. Urbanisation increased reliance on wages for food, warmth and shelter, extending public regulation from earlier preoccupations with public highways and public order towards questions of public hygiene, which in turn spawned interest in the generation of gas and electricity to light streets or drive the pumps for sewage and fresh water. Industrialisation required a more literate workforce (education standards rose as a public concern) as well as a larger one, which raised issues of how urban workers should be housed and transported to and from their place of work. Increased urban circulation (of suppliers, customers and general population) generated bye-laws governing pavements and traffic: concern for public safety extended from factories and commercial premises, to the streets, to prevent accidents as well as control the spread of disease. Demands for public action increased and the powers of municipal authorities expanded accordingly. In multiple ways, modernisation invoked the creation of a networked city (Dennis, 2007, ch.9): the deployment of new technologies to foster collective participation and social integration as central to prosperity, to social harmony and thereby to economic growth.

Personal behaviour (hitherto considered private) commanded increasing professional, and thereby public, interest. Industrial employment introduced new expectations about self-discipline, the virtue of work and the need for household planning. Such perspectives justified an ever-closer inspection of the poor for personal signs, denoted in terms of 'character' or psychological impairment that explained their situation: creating categories of social claimant whose deficiencies merited specific treatments (Mansfield et al., 1994; Mah, 2009). A propensity to drink, gamble, wander or beg all pointed to personal failings requiring correction. The analysis of such anti-social behaviours acquired an increasingly scientific profile with the emergence of new disciplines (medical sciences such as psychiatry and eugenics as well as sociology and criminology) whose administrators (doctors, social workers, social investigators, above all social statisticians) emerged as new coteries of expertise dedicated to securing social improvement by applying specific remedies to social and personal ills. Whether public authorities were prepared to implement their proposals (or leave the task to voluntary action) was a more open question.

Through pan-European networks and congresses, growing professional organisations exchanged knowledge and information. Delegations that had long crossed borders to inspect new farming methods or steam-driven factories now travelled to examine not only sewers, pumping stations, electrical generation plant, but also medical facilities, factories and model industrial communities, publishing results in learned journals. Social issues in particular created more collective evaluative identities, measured in more extensive social statistics (Desrosieres, 1998). Technical and social scientific knowledge challenged established political authority: not only traditional powers derived from land ownership and property or the newly enriched industrialists but also nascent democracy. Compromises made between these different sources of authority shaped how public services were understood and the remit of their activities. As public deliberation might be informed by arguments from all sides of the political spectrum, so understanding its provenance becomes significant to analysing prevailing conceptions of social rights, the way urban improvements were to be promoted and the role public authorities were to play in promoting them.

A word needs to be said about the definition of the public sphere. In the pre-1914 era, public deliberation was limited, thanks to a constrained franchise. In Strasbourg (under German rule at this time) the right to vote was more widespread than elsewhere in Germany and, by the early twentieth century, local Social Democrats and free trade unions collaborated openly in the extension of municipal services and the sphere of public action. In Frankfurt equally, although collaboration between council and unions was less successful, a wider franchise fostered more municipal subsidies for more urban amenities. Conversely, where the franchise was limited, disruption and dissent could result – visible in Liverpool in 1911 (the government sending a gunboat up the Mersey to quell riots). In Leipzig similarly, a skewed franchise allowed property owners and major industrialists to retain control of a city council that ignored the demands of an increasingly powerful labour movement. The political composition of municipal authorities reinforced different conceptions of the public interest and shaped how public services were conceived, the objectives they sought to serve and how the social rights of urban populations were defined. Differing governing principles are illustrated in the following three case studies, each offering a specific vision of how an ideal city was to be created and sustained.

Birmingham

> Birmingham is above all else a business city, run by business men on business principles. (Ralph, 1890, cited in Briggs, 1952: 70)

In the course of the nineteenth century Birmingham expanded from 102,000 (1821) to over 300,000 (1861), to reach half a million by 1900, acquiring a further 320,000 in 1911, on the formal extension of the city boundary (Briggs, 1952: ch.5). By 1914, this was Britain's second largest city, its economy originating in the manufacture of small metal wares (from bathroom accessories and heating radiators to jewellery, small arms, saucepans, nuts, bolts, screws, nails) that poured from multiple small quasi-artisanal workshops. The mark 'Made in Birmingham' was known world wide, making the city a global trading centre, with active interests in Imperial affairs. By the late nineteenth century, the foundation of Austin automobiles signalled the first large factories and a supply chain focused on the mass production of standardised components. New production systems (based on imported American machinery) employed not tens but thousands, divided masters from men and marginalised the outworkers and casual employees that had hitherto absorbed fluctuating demand. By 1914, small workshops, although still numerous, no longer dominated Birmingham's industrial structure: names like Austin, Dunlop and Cadbury were increasingly prominent.

The small workshop legacy founded traditions of production flexibility and social mobility; skilled journeymen became small masters, retaining membership of unions that recruited masters and men alike and offered trade benefits (for sick or unemployed members) rather than organising industrial action. The arrival of compulsory social insurance in 1911 caused not a ripple of dissent in Birmingham (unlike the furore it provoked on the Clyde) as the reform represented a consolidation of established voluntary practice. Equally, trade societies (over 80 by 1914 – Briggs, 1952: 50–52) alleviated trade depressions by sharing work and fixing prices. Reputation and profit were founded not on cut-throat competition, but in the consolidation of – and co-operation between – similar manufacturing ventures. In Birmingham's politics, industrial business united successfully to overthrow Conservative landed interests. A Liberal Caucus, in power from the 1870s until 1914, embodied a politics of religious Dissent (a Quaker heritage standing in opposition to Anglican hierarchies) that promoted the mutual obligation of employer and employed as the foundation of collective prosperity and social harmony.

The city council (aptly called the Corporation) was controlled by men who used it to secure collective social improvement by adapting business methods to public service. The Corporation aimed to promote the health, wealth and happiness of the population it governed, to allow them to pursue the fruition of their labour and the realisation of their objectives. The object of both voluntary institution and local authority was the same: an alliance between Dissenting churches and local council representatives to promote philanthropy and achieve the domestic mission of prevention (of disease, ignorance, crime, social disaffection) and reclamation of the downfallen. Here, urban authority was central. 'All private effort, all individual philanthropy,' the Liberal Mayor of Birmingham said in 1875, 'sinks into insignificance compared with the organised power of a great representative assembly such as this' (cited in Hennock, 1973: 143). The benefits of prosperity would reach all orders of society; the civic mission offered opportunity to enable the community to develop the talents of all its members. This was a clarion call to business to take up its social responsibilities as part of a moral duty to the community on which its wealth depended.

Birmingham earned itself the sobriquet of 'the best governed city in the world' (Ralph, 1890): its MPs pioneered the cause of national education and its Corporation redeveloped the city centre (to attract customers for Birmingham's wares), created one of the first civic universities and spread the advantages of gas (later electric) lighting and public transport throughout the city and into surrounding urban areas. Achievement was grounded on municipal trading. The Corporation was majority shareholder in the urban gas company and used profits from this venture to fund the city art gallery, a large public library as well as the urban improvement project, a majority shareholding in the local electricity company and a major investment in water supply. Selling gas and, later, electricity to neighbouring local authorities without the means to manufacture their own allowed cross-subsidy to protect the rates (local taxes) while improving Birmingham's amenities and cultural facilities to promote the city as a desirable place to do business.

Creative as these initiatives proved, the labour market remained off-limits for the Corporation. Birmingham could boast a world-class patent library, but it also had some of the worst slum housing whose inhabitants, casual and unskilled workers, were among the poorest in the UK. The politics of Dissent favoured opportunities for all, but confined personal interventions to voluntary action for deserving cases. Employers claimed that labour management was private business; trade unions repudiated any intervention that interfered with control over access to key skills and jobs. The Liberal Caucus relied on electoral support from both. More fundamentally, for Dissenters personal responsibility remained a moral duty: public authority could offer opportunities to secure advancement, but the individual had to be capable of taking them, of achieving salvation through personal effort. Punitive poor laws had long enforced this message of self-sufficiency: Birmingham's poor law authorities remained among the strictest in the country.

This moral environment underpinned Birmingham's response to national reforms to organise urban labour markets. In 1905, legislation required British cities to create a labour bureau or exchange, to distinguish those destitute from want of work from the rest of the pauper host. The 'unemployed' were to be recruited onto public works (almost an early labour market activation programme). Birmingham's Distress Committee, representing charity, poor law administrators as well as the Corporation, determined the criteria against which applicants would be evaluated. To gain access to a job, sound moral character (evidenced by a clean and tidy house, cared-for children, previous thrift) combined with need (married applicants with dependants) and proper market behaviour (a history of regular employment) identified those meriting help. In addition, to demonstrate a positive desire to work, applicants laboured for two weeks breaking stones prior to referral to the municipal exchange. This punitive approach deterred all but the most desperate and, when a national labour exchange was introduced in 1910, it took over this clientele and the methods by which they were assessed. It was also shunned by regular workers and their employers. In 1918, a survey of 3,000 firms in the Birmingham Chamber of Commerce found only 170 able to report favourably on the exchanges.[2] In Birmingham, legacies derived from a market-based economy proved hard to shift.

Leipzig

Leipzig was a trading centre between the German states and the Russian provinces well before its industrial development. From a population of 106,000 in 1871, Leipzig swiftly expanded to 589,000 in 1910, making it Germany's fourth largest city (Brandmann, 1998: 32). This increase reflected mass immigration from rural areas, and the incorporation (in the early 1890s and in 1910) of surrounding parishes, in many cases themselves already urban centres (Dobson, 2001). Leipzig's bankers sparked the city's industrial expansion. Local capital financed entrepreneurs in textiles, machine-construction and mining. Serving ever larger markets created by the establishment of the North German Confederation (1866) and then the Empire (1871), Leipzig attracted large joint stock companies from Berlin and the Ruhr. Reserves of brown coal (lignite) were cheaply extracted from open cast mines, following the advent of mechanical excavators in the 1880s. Here as elsewhere in the *Reich,* large companies formed cartels, fixing price and output to prevent competition damaging firms. An agreement between the region's different brown coal producers, formalised in 1905, worked closely with the national German Brown Coal Syndicate. Cartels secured high tariffs on foreign imports, giving industry a huge captive home market (Dobson, 2001: 8–12). As with Birmingham we cannot attribute success to unfettered free-market competition. Like Birmingham again, Leipzig was a world player, a local economy embedded in a global market, sustaining trading links with the Far East and the Balkans as well as Russian and East European provinces.

Leipzig possessed no dominant, driving city council like Birmingham's Corporation, with its confident interventions to promote the city's well-being. Rather the 'poverty of civic discourse' in informal and formal bourgeois politics was noted (Dobson, 2001: 74). Unlike Birmingham, the influence of landowning and propertied interests increased during these years. By 1894, Leipzig was among the most politically regressive cities in the Reich, as the existing local electoral franchise was abolished and replaced by a three class voting system: the top 5 per cent of taxpayers and those in the next 15 per cent each elected 33 per cent of council deputies. The remaining 80 per cent elected the final third (Schäfer, 1998: 275–276), thereby undermining any possible domination of the city council by a rising Social Democrat movement. The influence of high tax payers generally worked against big spending interventionist local government of the Birmingham type.

Broadly speaking the council attempted to meet escalating housing demand within the parameters of its existing strategy of land purchase. A major source of council income derived from the purchase of agricultural land on the city outskirts. When the expanding economy increased the land value, this was sold to entrepreneurs for development. Largely unregulated private housing companies who developed the land cut corners to increase profits; workers' safety was compromised during construction, and the finished buildings were structurally unsound. In order to maximise occupancy and their returns on rents, the companies only built four or five storey tenement blocks, cramming working families into cellar and loft space (Kreuzkam, 1897: 587–591). Housing remained expensive and homelessness among the low paid haunted the public authorities (begging and vagrancy being criminal offences), forcing them to build barracks to house poorer workers adjacent to the poor law workhouses. Lodging workers on the city outskirts necessarily required the construction of tramlines to get the inhabitants to work. Sporadic disputes between privately owned tram companies, forced by their contracts to sustain low fare structures while paying high city rents, illustrates another mechanism by which the council minimised local taxation by creating new streams of revenue.

Education policy in Leipzig structured the labour market in a disciplinary manner, confining access to secondary education and skill training to the offspring of families already in the trade (Dale, 1897). Thanks to a sustained hierarchical structure, educational self-improvement was minimal and social mobility consequently low. Outside the field of education and training, the municipality showed little interest in employment issues, aside from supporting employer-run labour bureaux closely associated with strike breaking. In extremis, Polish workers were imported across the border under police escort and repatriated when the need for their services disappeared. Unsurprisingly, industrial relations, in contrast to Birmingham, were characterised by mutual suspicion that occasionally erupted into open hostility. Employers, including master artisans, formed employer organisations. Workers, especially skilled workers, increasingly turned to the Social Democrats – affiliated free trade unions, rather than the traditional guilds (in protestant Saxony, no competing Catholic labour organisation existed). Strikes were relatively common. In construction, for example, workers downed tools to force a collective agreement on hours and wages from employers in 1895, in 1898 and again, following a lock-out, in 1910. Liebknecht and Luxemburg, among Germany's most radical socialist thinkers, were regular contributors to the socialist *Leipziger Volkszeitung.* In general, however, it appears that the unions grew less willing to use union funds to finance strikes, preferring instead to invest in welfare for their members to strengthen organisation.

This shift in SPD policy was partly a response to the social insurance laws of the 1880s that, although introduced to undermine support for the labour movement, were adapted in Leipzig to strengthen labour organisation. There were few official alternatives: Leipzig's poor law remained excessively punitive. Claimants who could not be deflected to private charity (again reducing local government costs) were stripped of their civil rights and given subsistence level handouts. The indolent, along with beggars, vagrants and unlicensed prostitutes, were incarcerated. The advent of social insurance witnessed the creation of new institutions that offered trade unions two-thirds of the seats on local administrative boards of the health and invalidity insurance funds. In Leipzig, SPD and union functionaries integrated this support within a network of institutions organised by the labour movement to fill the vacuum left by local government. The city offered no municipal support for the unemployed (bar emergency soup kitchens in exceptionally hard winters), the *Volkshaus* union headquarters took over the role. Over and above the administration of health and invalidity benefits, it acted as placement agency for those seeking work and a legal advice centre – open to all, not just union members. In addition, the SPD ran workers' libraries and the Leipzig-Plagwitz co-operative society, one of the largest in Germany with a membership of over 40,000 by 1905, ran its own bakery and butchers' outlets. In this manner, the SPD created labour market organisation founded on collectivist principles that were designed to strengthen the appeal of the party and its affiliated trade unions.

By 1914, two municipal authorities operated in Leipzig, each grounded on very different principles. The official city council remained a strong defender of traditional hierarchies founded on property ownership and its associated privileges. The advent of industrialisation and the accelerated growth of the city created tensions between these and the rising demands of social democracy, to which the city authorities responded with disciplinary and increasingly repressive measures. Rival public authorities remained inherently unstable: at the end of the First World War, Leipzig erupted as a major centre of communist revolt, generating a comparatively smooth transition of power to an established socialist authority grounded in the principles of technical and scientific socialism.

Strasbourg[3]

In 1872, Strasbourg was, as capital of Alsace Lorraine, handed over to German rule following the Franco-Prussian war. Under German auspices, the process of integrating the region into the *Kaiserreich* transformed both previous authority structures and the logics underpinning them. The provincial economy of Alsace Lorraine, centred on village-based small factories (well over 2,000 by the 1880s), had previously been run by French employers virtually as a personal fiefdom. Paternalism had dominated industrial relations: manufacture was largely organised under family labour. The transfer of sovereignty was accompanied by a transformation in social relationships as German authorities imposed technical standards of employment, promoting workplace organisation and a more cohesive labour movement, giving women workers a voice in the workplace for the first time (Kott, 1995).

As for Strasbourg itself, the city was transformed from a backward garrison town into a prototype of the modern city (Claude, 1985: Zimmermann, 2001: ch. 6). Unlike both Leipzig and Birmingham, Strasbourg was not a major manufacturing centre. Its commercial origins as a port on the Rhine had been abandoned when industrialisation fostered the growth of larger ports down river. The city became a garrisoned administrative centre, with interests in the processing and distribution of local produce. Under Napoleon III, Strasbourg's rulers (local landowners and their acolytes), successfully resisted efforts from Paris to promote general urban improvement: the city remained a warren of medieval backstreets with its sanitation dependent water from the rivulets emanating from the Rhine. Effluent not sold to local farmers as fertiliser was deposited back into ditches loosely connected to the waterways that criss-crossed the urban area. The place was an unhygienic stagnant backwater in need of the planners' attention.

Transfer to German rule required the city to be rebuilt: the railway line that had connected Strasbourg to Paris was torn up, replaced by a link to Berlin and existing railways were networked into the German system. Fortifications facing one way were rebuilt to face the other. Financed by Berlin, a new coterie of young technical experts – water, gas and electricity engineers – modernised the city: building new suburbs, paving and lighting the streets, creating a water-borne sewage and fresh water system that replaced the antiquated sanitation of the old town. The population of Strasbourg expanded: from 80,000 inhabitants (both within and without the city walls) in 1875 to 179,000 in 1910, including some 4,600 foreigners (non-German Belgian and Italian labourers, attracted by the employment on these projects of urban reconstruction) and 61,000 Germans from outside Alsace Lorraine. Under direct rule of Berlin for nearly 20 years, urban development encountered little resistance and, once democratic rule was restored (on a more extensive franchise than that found elsewhere in Imperial Germany) an enlarged population, more appreciative of the higher standard of life now available, continued to support projects of reform and renewal.

The technical expertise that had raised urban living standards and integrated Alsace Lorraine into the *Kaiserreich* also underpinned the transformation of labour market organisation that made Strasbourg a prototype for social reformers from all over Europe. By the early twentieth century, a central labour bureau co-ordinated the work of established trade union registries under joint management of employers and employed. All itinerant workers were obliged to register. In collaboration with local poor law authorities, the bureau categorised jobseekers and prescribed suitable treatment: reference of the drunk and mendicant to the police, penal work under the poor law for those deemed deliberately idle, publicly funded work (ditch digging, street repairs etc.) for general labourers in slack seasons, placement with an employer for regular skilled men. Strasbourg's bureau eventually became a call centre for a network of telephone-linked labour exchanges across Alsace Lorraine. The city created projects of road construction, forestry and similar public works to absorb idle labour and obliged subcontractors to hire through the exchanges. From 1907, the exchanges placed business and clerical employees. The central bureau also arranged apprenticeship placements for school-leavers: master artisans recruited through the exchanges and the municipality subsidised apprenticeship dues for poor families. Municipal allotments were allocated to able-bodied poor law claimants to offer the industrious poor the possibility of reintegration into the labour market.

All this was feasible thanks to very close links with a growing trade union movement – particularly after 1899, when the local SPD endorsed the system. Reformist free trade unionists associated with the SPD, like their Christian counterparts, sought to restrict job opportunities to their members. Their registries were absorbed into the municipal labour bureau's network: their representatives were present on all administrative processes. Unions offering benefits for unemployed members were subsidised by the municipality from 1907. This necessitated a reappraisal of the meaning of unemployment as Strasbourg's bureau disallowed the municipal supplement to claimants on strike, ill or dismissed for misconduct.

In the years immediately preceding the First World War, Strasbourg emerged as a 'model city'. The city was hardly unique; in the Netherlands and in Belgium cities such as Liege, Antwerp and Ghent also created alliances between trade union registries and city authorities that determined the organisational principles on which labour markets should function. Older trading centres along the Rhine had long fostered co-operative methods of urban management in order to keep business from their rivals: this is simply another manifestation of an established tradition. Additionally, these cities did not experience any sudden industrial expansion; quasi-artisanal trade organisations were more easily accommodated when creating systems of labour market co-ordination. The mutual hostility between employers and employed that characterised industrial relations in heavy industry on the Ruhr and the Clyde was notably absent.

In Strasbourg, a successful compromise was forged between city governance based on technical competences and democratic representation in decision-making. The transfer of public authority and the introduction of different policy logics required the local government to legitimate new systems, incorporating all interests. In other cities, similar initiatives to embrace the total organisation of the labour market did not manage to bridge such divisions. In Frankfurt, for example, the free trade unions refused to amalgamate with the municipal exchanges; in consequence, the latter focused largely on the unorganised (female) workforce (Schmidt, 2010). Here collaboration was tacit, not open. However, the reception available at exchanges in Strasbourg and Frankfurt stands in stark contrast to Birmingham. Reading rooms, legal advice, help with accommodation, and restaurants were provided; separate waiting rooms were available for skilled and unskilled, for male and female workers to entice customers to register with the official exchanges in preference to their commercial competitors. Applicants were classified in accordance with not only their professional aptitude and previous work experience but also in terms of bodily health and psychometric assessment. These more successful German experiments created a public service of labour market placement whose legitimacy rested on normative scientific values based on criteria ostensibly independent of vested interest.

CONCLUSIONS

Each city outlined above had its own imaginary in the minds of its citizens: its own coherent vision of the perfected form of itself that determined the nature and purpose of public services and thus the location of specific social rights. No single vision was universally shared, but it is possible to identify prevalent policy logics for each city on which principles of public action rested and respect for public authority was sustained. This approach allows us to get behind a simple institutional observation (the adoption of labour exchanges) to witness how new initiatives were adapted to prevailing political circumstances. Here lie the roots of varieties of capitalism: less a duality of political systems than multiple compromises between prevailing policy perspectives to form foundations for urban co-ordination. This perspective also offers the means to appraise current systems of labour market management that have been promoted in recent years in the context of the European Employment Strategy (EES).

None of the cases outlined above represents an ideal towards which past or present authorities could or should strive. In each city we witness traditional paternalist authority derived from property being replaced by something else: market authority (Birmingham), or technical expertise reinforced by representative democracy (Strasbourg) or (eventually) scientific socialism (Leipzig). In each case, co-ordinating principles of urban governance in general and of labour market management in particular were rooted in these different policy logics, which offered different locations for socio-economic participation and different roles for public authority. Hence, for example, we witness how multiple systems of labour market classification emerged that consolidated moral and professional judgements about the worth of each individual, embodying different compromises between competing values that were heavily moderated by the role public authority played in the creation of such judgement – and by the ability of interested parties (not only trade unions but psychometric experts, doctors and religious authorities) to participate in deliberation and evaluation. In this regard, the situation in Birmingham contrasts with that in Strasbourg: in the former, the interested parties are market actors (trade unions and businessmen): in the latter, professional experts and social statisticians who adopt scientific methods to reach impartial (and thus unassailable) conclusions.

What lessons can we learn from the labour market policies of the past? There are basically three. First, the cities discussed here all enjoyed a higher degree of coherent governance than cities do today. Local determination of local outcomes facilitated processes of public deliberation over the nature and purpose of reforms, allowing all parties to internalise their rationale and conform to their stipulations. This fostered a high degree of interpenetration of economic and social spheres, visible in the management of labour markets. City councils employed multiple methods to attract business; the provision of amenities necessarily served social and economic objectives, even if these were designed to serve specific interests (as in Leipzig). The electricity that powered industry also lit the streets, pumped sewage and powered the tramlines taking workers to and from the work-place, thereby facilitating labour market participation for all while also (in Birmingham) allowing the city to create profit by selling surplus to surrounding local authorities. This local concentration of authority improves coordination: hence the labour bureau at Strasbourg could structure labour markets from apprenticeship onwards, facilitating mobility between jobs and between different categories of jobseeker. The diversity of local systems is not a sign of weakness or incomplete development: on the contrary, in the context of democracy, it reflects and reinforces collective local practices understood by all participants. In the creation of local co-ordination, the overlap between economic and social objectives is complete.

This leads to the second point. The recent advent of New Public Management (NPM), used by the Commission to monitor the EES, has reinforced central authority and notions of 'best practice' to be realised through the transfer of market principles into public administration. Benchmarks and targets allow central authorities to monitor the sub-contracted provision of public services in tangled networks of responsibility. Service providers meet predefined targets rather than cater for the needs of a public, who, as clients, are denied any voice in the nature of service provision. This has several negative consequences. First, local co-ordination disappears. Finding a pathway between multiple providers becomes a personal responsibility and if the 'client' abandons hope that is fine as it is one less customer to be served. In this way, those most in need (the least qualified, the disabled, the mentally ill) are liable to slip through the net and disappear. The growing army of (largely young and disaffected) workers deemed Not in Education, Employment or Training (NEETs) in the UK bears testimony to this outcome. Second, associated with this, NPM systems transform the nature of public accountability (Whiteside, 2000). The citizen is no longer a voter able to change policy but a consumer who is offered a choice between service providers. The problem of perverse incentives noted above is not subject to public deliberation, but to professional (meaning audit) regulation. This accumulates over time to result in growing complexity: a thicket of regulatory requirements impenetrable to all bar well-versed experts. These undermine the original object of the exercise. Growing complexity raises compliance costs, making such systems bureaucratic and expensive (Whiteside, 1997, for an historical example). The concentration of expertise over time vests authority in a small oligarchy, unaccountable to anyone but themselves. For finally, regulation and its costs undermine signals of quality and price that are ostensibly the advantages of market-based systems of service delivery.

Third, historical study exposes how similar institutions functioned within different policy logics that created different locations of public participation and possibilities for public reasoning to shape social rights. Of course it does not do to idealise history: in no case cited here is the voice of the poor represented in debate and, in Leipzig particularly, repression of opposition was the more common response than accommodation of popular demand. That said, very different forms of appraisal, using different criteria, shaped access to labour market opportunities. Social rights in terms of labour market access were not only structured in accordance with professional qualification or work record but were heavily mediated by moral and medical judgements that reflected (and reflect) assumed capability for work. How such IBJJ was exercised reflected (and reflects) the state of the labour market: the level of labour demand has long shaped rates of sickness, disability, inaptitude and so forth detected among adults of working age (Whiteside, 1988). The growing use of medical sciences as primary among IBJJ has proved constant; the objective, however, has changed a great deal. While nineteenth-century urban authorities sought to organise and stratify labour markets, thereby determining rightful access to waged employment, current pre-occupations with rising welfare burdens and programmes of labour market activation have reversed the object of the exercise by persuading those previously considered 'economically inactive' or 'incapacitated' to return to the world of work.

When considering the implications of the EES for such people, a host of new public service and welfare issues emerge. We cannot assume 'the market' will provide sufficient support for those with additional responsibilities or disadvantages that stand in the way of such a return to work, as neo-liberal argument suggests. The history of Birmingham, easily the most market-oriented of the cities studied here, stands out as a reminder of the consequences of such assumptions. This city had the worst poverty and the worst slums of all in pre-1914 Britain, in spite of a very active local council run on business principles. Sen argues that policy should aim to remove impediments to real personal freedom that constrain people from fulfilling their latent capabilities. Historical perspectives on economic growth and prosperity in the late nineteenth century demonstrate the significance of locally co-ordinated public services for promoting local welfare and collective well-being. Economic prosperity did not spring from unfettered market competition: rather it derived from active support from public authorities capable of supplying amenities essential for collective co-ordinated action. Nowhere can we witness advantages in minimal state intervention or fractured social provision. Through the lens of capability, we can discern how past systems illustrate multiple different compromises that evaded the spurious alternative of 'state or market'. We would do well to understand what these alternatives are.

NOTES

1. This chapter draws extensively on the ideas and writing of historical researchers working within the CAPRIGHT (FP6) Work Package 4 'Between Nations and Localities' group. I particularly acknowledge the help and research of Dr Alice Mah, Dr Jürgen Schmidt, Dr Roland Atzmuller and Dr Simon Constantine, the last being a research associate who worked on Leipzig under the FP5 EUROCAP programme. The interpretation of their evidence remains my own.
2. Evidence of Homer (West Midlands Division of the Ministry of Labour) to *Committee of Enquiry into the Work of the Employment Exchanges: evidence* (Barnes) Cmd. 1140 / 1921 P.P.XI. 3rd August 1920, pp.338–339, qs. 6009–16.
3. For a detailed account of Strasbourg see Whiteside, 2007.

REFERENCES

Bonvin, J.-M. and N. Farvaque (2005), 'What informational basis for assessing job-seekers?', *Review of Social Economy*, **LXIII**(2), 269–288.

Brandmann, P. (1998), *Leipzig zwischen Klassenkampf und Sozialreform*, Cologne: Böhlau.

Briggs, A. (1952), *History of Birmingham, Volume II: Borough and City*, Oxford: Oxford University Press.

Buchner, T. (2010), 'Organising the market? Reflections on the relations between labour exchanges and labour markets', unpublished paper presented at European Social Science History Conference, Ghent.

Claude, V. (1985), *Strasbourg 1850-1914: Assainissement et Politiques Urbaines*, doctoral thesis, Paris: EHESS.

Dale, F.H. (1897), 'The Continuation Schools of Saxony', in *Education Department, Special Reports on Educational Subjects*, 1896–7, London, 479–509.

Dawson, W.H. (1914), *Municipal Life and Government in Germany*. London: Longmans.

Dennis, R. (2007), *Cities in Modernity*, Cambridge: Cambridge University Press.

Desrosieres, A. (1998), *The Politics of Large Numbers: A History of Statistical Reasoning*, Harvard: Harvard University Press.

Dobson, S. (2001), *Authority and Upheaval in Leipzig 1910–1920: The Story of a Relationship*, New York and Chichester: Columbia University Press.

Edling, N. (2008), 'Regulating unemployment the continental way: the transfer of municipal labour exchanges to Scandinavia, 1890–1914', *European Review of History*, **15**(1), 23–40.

Friedrich, E. (1914), 'Der Ausbau der Arbeitsämter in Elsass-Lothringen', 3 January 1914, Armenrecht (Elsass), *Straßburger Blatter für Sozialpolitik u. Armenwesen*, 1913/14–1918 ZC 2735 Leipzig Universitätsbibliothek.

Hall, P. and D. Soskice (eds) (2001), *Varieties of Capitalism*, Cambridge: Cambridge University Press.

Hennock, E.P. (1973), *Fit and Proper Persons: Ideal and Reality in Nineteenth Century Urban Government*, London: Edward Arnold.

Hennock , E.P. (2006), *The Origins of the Welfare State in Germany and Britain, 1850–1914*, Cambridge: Cambridge University Press.

Kott, S. (1988), 'Les industriels et la sante des ouvriers. L'example du Haut-Rhin dans la seconde moitie du xix siècle', in *Colloque sur l'histoire de la Sécurité sociale de Lyon en 1987*, Paris: Association pour l'étude de l'histoire de la Sécurité sociale, pp.263–282.

Kott, S. (1995), *L'Etat social allemand: representations et pratiques*, Paris: Editions Belin.

Kreuzkam, T. (1897), 'Das Baugewerbe mit besonderer Rücksicht auf Leipzig', *Schriften des Vereins für Socialpolitik*, LXX , 543–628.

Mah, A. (2009), 'Moral judgements and employment policies in Birmingham (1870–1914)', *International Journal of Sociology and Social Policy*, **29**(11/12), 575–585.

Mansfield, M., R. Salais and N. Whiteside (eds) (1994), *Aux Sources du Chômage*, Paris: Editions Belin.

McGibben, D. (1992), 'Who were the German Independent Socialists? The Leipzig City Council election of December 1917', *Central European History*, **25**(4), 425–443.

Ralph, J. (1890), 'The best-governed city in the world', *Harper's Monthly*, **81**, 99–110.

Schäfer, M. (1998), 'Die Burg und die Bürger. Stadtbürgerliche Herrschaft und kommunale Selbstverwaltung in Leipzig 1889–1929', in W. Bramke und U. Heβ (eds) *Wirtschaft und Gesellschaft in Sachsen im 20. Jahrhundert*, Leipzig: Leipziger Universitätsverlag, pp.269–292.

Schmidt, Jürgen (2010), 'Public Services in Erfurt and Frankfurt am Main Compared (c.1890–1914)', unpublished paper researched for the Capright network.

Sen, A. (2009), *The Idea of Justice*, London: Allen Lane.

Steinmetz, G. (1993), *Regulating the Social: The Welfare State and Local Politics in Imperial Germany*, Princeton: Princeton University Press.

Whiteside, N. (1988), 'Unemployment and health', *Journal of Social Policy*, **17**(2), 177–194.

Whiteside, N. (1997), 'Regulating markets', *Public Administration*, **75**(3), 467–485.

Whiteside, N. (2000), 'Accounting and Accountability: an historical case study of a public-private partnership', in R. Rhodes (ed.) *Transforming British Government*, Vol. 2. London: Macmillan, 167–182.

Whiteside, N. (2007), 'Unemployment in comparative perspective', *International Review of Social History*, **52**(1), 35–56.

Zimmermann, B. (2001), *La constitution du chômage en Allemagne. Entre professions et territoires*, Paris: EHESS.

Zimmermann, B. (2006), 'Pragmatism and the capability approach. Challenges in social theory and empirical research', *European Journal of Social Theory*, **9**(4), 467–484.

PART II

What future for European employment
policies?

9. Occupational structures and social models in European societies[1]

Colin Crouch

Occupational structure has always been a major constituent of the wider social structure, differences and changes in it being linked to other, wider social differences and changes. During the early 1970s Daniel Bell (1973) drew attention to the changes in occupations attendant on the transition that he observed from industrial to post-industrial society. Throughout Europe it may now be said that we are living in post-industrial societies, in the specific sense that the proportions of the workforce engaged in the production of material goods is declining. Even countries which continue to maintain large populations working in the primary sector (agriculture and extractive activities) experience shifts towards services rather than manufacturing and related employment as their primary-sector workforces decline. What, then, are emerging as the main shapes of occupational structures in post-industrial societies? And are they all the same, or do they exhibit major differences? What patterns are emerging among European societies?

To seek differences among societies leads very rapidly to a search for different 'types', into which individual nation states (for we continue to regard nation states as constituting societies) can be placed. This will not be my approach here, unless the evidence leads us to identify types. I am seeking variables that might be more or less present in different countries, and this will certainly enable us to talk about differences. But when various items of a cluster of variables come together in different patterns across different societies, we do not necessarily have differences of types. These may possibly appear, at a later stage of analysis, if variables seem to hang together in distinctive ways, setting whole groups of countries apart from each other, rather than simply ranking differently along various continua. Here, existing classifications of European societies will be treated as hypotheses for exploration, not as established facts.

For the purpose of this inquiry I shall use the division of post-industrial occupational structures into the five or six sectors that were developed during the 1980s. The more familiar division into three sectors leaves 'services' as an over-large and undifferentiated tertiary sector, when within post-industrial societies it is change and diversity within this sector that reveals to us important differences and changes. When economists first developed the concept of a tertiary sector, seen as post-industrial, in the inter-war years (Clark, 1940), they had in mind a straightforward movement from primary as the extraction of materials (whether food or raw production materials) from nature, through secondary as the fashioning of natural resources into products, to tertiary as the subsequent handling and distribution of those goods. At each stage there was a movement away from 'raw nature', but there was always a contact with its products. The 'services' sector was therefore primarily seen as distribution, transport and communications. Observers were not at that stage very interested in services further removed from distribution – what we today call 'services to business' – and services provided to persons through social policy and therefore not concerning material products much at all. Both these sectors were too small to be considered separately. These originators of the idea of a tertiary sector were also not much interested in personal services to households: the vast armies of men and, mainly, women engaged in domestic service in the 19th century and earlier were seen as a declining group of no particular economic significance.

In the 1970s observers began to concentrate on services provided to business, primarily but not solely financial services, as a sector of activities one further stage removed from the manufacture and distribution of goods, and identified what was then a very small quaternary sector (Katzovien, 1970; Singelmann, 1978).

Also during the 1970s observers separately identified a range of activities further removed still from dealing with goods and services: the provision of social and community services such as health, care, education, law, public administration (see again Katzovien, 1970; Singelmann, 1978).

I therefore define the main sectors as follows, broadly following (for a more detailed discussion, see Crouch, 1999: Part I):

I   Agriculture (and related activities like fishing and forestry) and extractive industries;

II   All manufacturing; construction; provision of gas, electricity and water;

III The transport and distribution of goods, persons and messages, including electronic means;

IV   The provision of services to enterprises;

V   The provision of services to social collectivities or to individuals who are primarily concerned with their welfare.

Several authors make a distinction between V and a sixth sector concerned with personal services, distinguishing between those services that have a collective or public aspect and those that are purely personal. Elsewhere (Crouch, 1999: ch. 2) I have tried to operationalise this distinction by constructing a sector VI from a combination of services provided directly to households, leisure and cosmetic services (normally included within sector V) and restaurants and hotels (normally included in sector III). Such a distinction reveals workforces with very different demographic character- istics in sectors V and VI, so the distinction is worth making. On the other hand, it is in practice very difficult to distinguish services provided for individual purposes that nevertheless include some collective gain from pure individual services. Partly for this reason, partly because it has not been possible to get up-to-date and internationally comparable data at the levels of disaggregation needed, I have not tried here to account for a full sector VI. This has involved keeping restaurants and hotels in sector III, and leisure and similar services in sector V. I have removed 'the provision of private services directly to households' from sector V and excluded it from the main analysis. It is a very small sector, though there will be some discussion of its size and how it varies across countries at a later point.

Of course, share in employment does not necessarily indicate economic importance. Different kinds of activity vary considerably in the role of labour in their value added. In general, services (all activities except those in sectors I and II) involve an interaction among persons. While there may be efficiency gains from replacing labour by technology, the presence of human labour is necessary at some point in the delivery of these activities. For the primary and secondary sectors this is not always the case; complete robotisation would not necessarily involve any deterioration in the quality of the product. Similarly, while most secondary-sector activities can be easily imported from other societies, their consumption not depending on the existence of any employment in the first country, this is not the case for most services – though it is for some. There is often a need for some geographical proximity between provider and consumer of a service. In looking at the relative sizes of sectors as employment we are therefore not looking at relative economic importance in any way; we are however looking at relative social importance, as the conditions under which goods are produced and services delivered through occupations tell us something about the way in which lives are being lived within societies.

We shall here examine employment in the various sectors, asking two sets of questions: how do cross-country differences match up to different types of society that have been observed in recent sociology? And how do they match up to various indicators of socio-economic sustainability?

In doing the former of these I am attempting something against which I have just warned: we should not necessarily expect to find types. Furthermore, the authors of the main typologies in use for the analysis of advanced societies have not claimed that these have any relevance to occupational structures; so one is in no way 'testing' these typologies. Nevertheless, a certain approach to classifying advanced capitalist societies has been found useful in much recent comparative sociology. When observers talk of different 'social models' among advanced societies they usually have in mind one or other of two schemes. The first is a simple division between the Anglophone world and one based in continental western Europe but often extended to include Japan. This division was first made by Albert (1991), who distinguished culturally between 'Anglo-Saxon' and 'Rhenish' economies; Hall and Soskice (2001) later formalised it as liberal market economies (LMEs) versus coordinated market economies (CMEs).

The second scheme is what one might call the revised Esping-Andersen model. Gøsta Esping-Andersen's (1990) original model identified three forms of welfare states, which had a combined political and cultural (geographical or linguistic) significance: liberal or Anglophone, based on residual social welfare safety nets; social democratic or Nordic, based on universal, egalitarian and high levels of welfare guarantees; and corporatist or continental, based on non-egalitarian, occupation-based welfare.

It is important to note that the original reach of Esping-Andersen's typology, based on an earlier one by Richard Titmuss (1958), was concerned solely with one aspect of social policy: the provision of income guarantees in cases of unemployment, ill health or old age. It was not about health services, or education systems, or care services, let alone whole social formations. It acquired a wider meaning, partly because behind it lay an explanatory theory of the differences which went beyond Titmuss's account of forms of welfare provision and drew on earlier Scandinavian research on different forms of class cleavage that had helped form industrial society (Korpi, 1983; Rokkan, 1999). This has given the model considerable purchase on other aspects of social life. For example, authors in the transitional labour markets school of analysis have found it useful when considering different patterns of labour-market transition typical of different groups of countries (Muffels et al., 2002; Muffels, 2008). However, this extended use has also brought a vulnerability to the Esping-Andersen model. While forms of social welfare might be classified into three relatively neat forms, it was quite another step to press into an equal simplicity the whole pattern of class relations during industrialisation. To take the most obvious instance, France and Germany might have similar systems of social insurance, but can the social confrontations of post-revolutionary France and those of 19th-century Prussia really be put into the same box?

However, another reason for the continuing power of the Esping-Andersen model came when he applied it to account for differences in female labour-force participation, the most significant social change of all in the occupational sociology of advanced countries in the late 20th and early 21st centuries (Esping-Andersen, 1999). Both the 'liberal' and 'social democratic' forms of post-industrial society found it far easier to facilitate a two-gender workforce than the 'corporatist' form. This has proved to be one of the most important advances to have taken place in the study of work in post-industrial societies, in particular its distinctive gender structures. But this only strengthened what was already becoming a problem with the original analysis: the difficulty of assimilating southern European economies into the corporatist or continental box designed primarily around Germany and Austria, but also including Belgium, France, the Netherlands and Switzerland. In Greece, Italy, Portugal and Spain welfare provision continued to depend upon families' resources and recognised mutual obligations, with very strong implications for women's employment and indeed employment as a whole. This difference has become generally accepted, such that the literature now mainly uses the four types of an amended Esping-Andersen model to classify the countries of western Europe (European Commission, 2008; Ferrera, 1996; Naldini, 2003):

1.   Liberal (represented within Europe by Ireland and the UK);
2.   Social democratic (the Nordic countries);
3.   Corporatist (Austria, Belgium, France, Germany, Netherlands, Switzerland);
4.   Familistic (Greece, Italy, Portugal and Spain, Turkey).

Since this model subsumes the Albert and Hall and Soskice dichotomy (LMEs or 'Anglo-Saxons' form category 1; CMEs or 'Rhenish' all the others), we shall use it here. If it proves to be the case that only the two (LME/CME) categories are needed, we can apply Occam's razor and collapse the other categories.

So much for the European 'first world'. To include the second world of former Soviet bloc countries, we could simply treat them as one group, all sharing a similar past of a state socialist planned economy, moving into capitalism from the start of the 1990s. Potentially we might however identify three separate groups:

1.   Ex-Soviet Union countries, which had experienced state socialism from 1917 onwards (within Europe: Russia itself, the Baltic states, Belarus, Moldova, Ukraine);

2.   Countries absorbed into the Soviet economic system only from the 1940s onwards (Bulgaria, Czech Republic, Hungary, Poland, Slovakia);
3.   Countries which experienced a form of state socialism, but outside the Soviet system (the countries of former Yugoslavia; Albania).

In addition to discovering whether these classifications have any relevance to differences in occupational structure, we can explore whether any particular occupational structures are likely to be more capable than others of sustaining themselves. We can operationalise this by asking whether some kinds of occupational structure are more associated than others with:

1.   *A high capacity to provide employment.* With some reservations about differences between full- and part-time work, and about different sizes of shadow economies, we can get some estimate of this through statistics for the proportions of populations of working age in gainful employment.
2.   *A positive relationship to innovation.* Three measures can be taken here: of proportions of GDP spent on research and development; of proportions of enterprises involved in innovative activity; and of patent applications.

Ideally, one would add some measures of environmental sustainability, but it is difficult to find appropriate measures, especially as environmental damage is rarely limited to the territory of the nation state that produces it.

For data on employment by sector, we use the most recent ILO statistics, which relate to 2007. Unfortunately, no reliable statistics are available for Belarus or the Ukraine, and Belgium has not provided data to the ILO for this period. With these exceptions, we shall examine statistics for all countries in the ILO classification of Europe, apart from the very small ones (Luxembourg and smaller).

Data on overall employment rates and on innovation are contained in the Eurostat Yearbook (Eurostat, 2009), though not for all countries of interest to us. The data provided include:

• overall employment rates for 2006 (Eurostat, 2009: 250);
• public and private expenditure on research and development activities (mainly for 2005 or 2004) (Eurostat, 2009: 473);
• the proportion of firms in a country considered to be engaged in 'innovative' activities (2004) (Eurostat, 2009: 477). Eurostat defines this datum as follows:

An innovation is defined as a new or significantly improved product (good or service) introduced to the market, or the introduction within an enterprise of a new or significantly improved process. Innovations are based on the results of new technological developments, new combinations of existing technology, or the utilisation of other knowledge acquired by the enterprise. Innovations may be developed by the innovating enterprise or by another enterprise. However, purely selling innovations wholly produced and developed by other enterprises is not included as an innovation activity, nor is introducing products with purely aesthetic changes. Innovations should be new to the enterprise concerned: for product innovations they do not necessarily have to be new to the market and for process innovations the enterprise does not necessarily have to be the first one to have introduced the process. (Eurostat, 2009: 476)

• numbers of patent applications to the European Patents Office per million inhabitants (2003) (Eurostat, 2009: 481);
• numbers of high technology patent applications to the European Patents Office per million inhabitants (2003) (Eurostat, 2009: 481);
• numbers of patents granted by the US Patents Office (2000) (Eurostat, 2009: 481).

EUROPEAN EMPLOYMENT BY SECTOR

With the exception of three southeastern countries (Moldova, Romania and Turkey), the proportion of European workforces engaged in the primary sector has become very small (see Table 9.1). It is notable that state socialist countries that had not been part of the Soviet bloc retain far higher agricultural workforces than nearly all other countries, but this sector is not central to our interests in studying patterns in post-industrial society.

The proportion engaged in the secondary sector ranges widely from 18% to 39%, the lower levels being occupied both by countries which have never industrialised much (Moldova) and by those which have lost their earlier high levels of industry (the Netherlands) (Table 9.2). There is complete overlap across western European countries in the expanded Esping-Andersen categories. When we examine the newly added former state-socialist ones – which overall include both the lowest and highest levels – we do find one distinctive group: the non-USSR Comecon countries have the highest levels of manufacturing employment, joined at levels of over 30% only by some parts of the former USSR.

Table 9.1 Employment in Sector I, 2007

'Regime' type	Percent of total employment																														
	2	3	4	5	6	7	8	9	10	11	12	13	14	15	16	17	18	19	20	21	22	23	24	25	26	27	28	29	30	31	32	33
Liberal	UK				IE																											
Social democratic		SE DK	NO	FI																												
Corporatist		DE NL	FR CH		AT																											
Familistic			IT	ES							GR, PT															TR						
Ex-USSR					EE				LV	LT RU																						MD
Ex-Comecon				CZ SK, HU				BG							PL																	
Other ex-state socialist									SI			HR						MK			RS									RO		

Note: Abbreviations: AT: Austria; BG: Bulgaria; CH: Switzerland; CZ: Czech Republic; DK: Denmark; EE: Estonia; ES: Spain; FI: Finland; FR: France; DE: Germany; GR: Greece; HR: Croatia; HU: Hungary; IE: Ireland; IT: Italy; LV: Latvia; LT: Lithuania; MK: Macedonia; MD: Moldova; NL: Netherlands; NO: Norway; PL: Poland; PR: Portugal; RO: Romania; RU: Russia; RS: Serbia; SE: Sweden; SI: Slovenia; SK: Slovakia; TR: Turkey; UK: United Kingdom.

Source: ILO Yearbook.

Table 9.2 Employment in Sector II, 2007

'Regime' type	Percent of total employment																					
	18	19	20	21	22	23	24	25	26	27	28	29	30	31	32	33	34	35	36	37	38	39
Liberal					UK					IE												
Social democratic		NO		SE		DK			FI													
Corporatist			NL			FR	CH			AT		DE										
Familistic					GR			TR				ES	IT, PT									
Ex-USSR	MD									RU	LV		LT				EE					
Ex-Comecon												PL				HU	BG					CZ, SK
Other ex-state socialist										RS			HR, MK, RO				SI					

Note: See Table 9.1 for abbreviations.

Source: ILO Yearbook.

189

Transforming European employment policy

Today the tertiary sector as originally conceived remains one of relatively unchanging size, but with some variation among countries (between 19% and 31%, though most are bunched between 21% and 29% (Table 9.3)). This stability persists despite large changes that have taken place in the constitution of the sector, ranging from changes in retail distribution to those in telecommunications. There is little diversity according to the typology. Within western Europe, it is relatively but not outstandingly small in the social-democratic countries, and the lowest levels are found among some former state socialist lands, but overall there is again heavy overlap among all the expanded Esping-Andersen classes, including the extension to CEE. Any earlier tendency for state socialist economies to employ fewer people in distribution and communications has almost disappeared.

Table 9.3 Employment in Sector III, 2007

'Regime' type	Percent of total employment												
	19	20	21	22	23	24	25	26	27	28	29	30	31
Liberal								UK, IE					
Social democratic			SE			DK, NO	FI						
Corporatist					DE	FR		NL	CH	AT			
Familistic						PT		IT, ES, TR					GR
Ex-USSR			MD					EE	LT, RU		LV		
Ex-Comecon						CZ, SK			HU	BG	PL		
Other ex-state socialist	RO			SI	MK			HR, RS					

Note: See Table 9.1 for abbreviations.

Source: ILO Yearbook.

The expanded Esping-Andersen categories are more relevant when it comes to the relatively small sector of business services (Table 9.4). The sector remains relatively small, but in several countries it has grown to more than 15% of employment, while in others it remains at the low (about 5%) levels that used to be general.

The 'familistic' welfare states of southern Europe, and even more so, all sub-types of the former state-socialist countries, clearly score lower than the other groups. That this is the case for the ex-state-socialist countries is not very surprising, given that many of these services did not exist in their former economic model. Meanwhile, the complete overlap between the

Table 9.4 Employment in Sector IV, 2007

'Regime' type	Percent of total employment													
	4	5	6	7	8	9	10	11	12	13	14	15	16	17
Liberal											IE		UK	
Social democratic										DK, NO	FI			SE
Corporatist									AT				DE, FR, NL	CH
Familistic		TR			PT	GR			ES		IT			
Ex-USSR	MD		LT		RU	EE, LV								
Ex-Comecon			BG		SK	CZ, HU, PL								
Other ex-state socialist	MK	RS		HR		SI								

Note: See Table 9.1 for abbreviations.

Source: ILO Yearbook.

three original Esping-Andersen categories, including Italy and Spain, might be considered surprising, if we follow a common view that sees high levels of financial and similar activities as particularly associated with 'liberal', Anglophone economies. It might also seem surprising that they are also particularly high in the 'social democratic' cases.

Finally, Sector V has become a large sector in many economies, in several cases being the largest of all as an employer of labour (Table 9.5). It is also the sector presenting the widest range among our countries (from 16% to 39%). We also now find some fit with the Esping-Andersen categories, though with some surprises. With very little overlap, the social-democratic countries have the highest levels here, which is of course completely as we should expect from the designation of them as welfare-state-based social democracies; this is the original heartland of the Esping-Andersen categories. We also find distinctly low levels in familistic southern Europe, the members of which group do not overlap at all with any other western European group. However, the corporatist and liberal groups present no differences from each other at all. All sub-groups of the former state-socialist countries also have distinctly lower levels than the first three western groups, but they overlap heavily with the southern Europeans.

Overall, we can conclude that the original Esping-Andersen categories continue to help us to account for some distinctiveness in the occupational structure of the social-democratic countries, i.e. the strong role of sector V, as Esping-Andersen himself predicted in 1999. Beyond that however it is

Table 9.5 Employment in Sector V, 2007

'Regime' type	Percent of total employment																							
	16	17	18	19	20	21	22	23	24	25	26	27	28	29	30	31	32	33	34	35	36	37	38	39
Liberal												IE							UK					
Social democratic																		FI				DK	SE	NO
Corporatist											AT	CH				DE			FR	NL				
Familistic		TR					ES, PT			GR, IT														
Ex-USSR								MD	LV		EE	LT	RU											
Ex-Comecon								BG, CZ, PL	SK			HU												
Other ex-state socialist	MK, RO				RS	HR				SI														

Note: See Table 9.1 for abbreviations.

Source: ILO Yearbook.

192

not informative, in particular revealing no differences between the liberal and corporatist cases. It is only when we expand the original categories to add the southwest European countries that we identify a distinct cluster, in terms of both sectors IV and V. Expanding the model even further to embrace eastern Europe, we have more distinctiveness, again concerning sectors IV and V, though overlapping with southwestern Europe. In general it is unnecessary to use the sub-types of the CEE group.

These patterns suggest some familiar popular stereotypes, in terms of an 'advanced' northwestern Europe (and especially the social-democracies) and a 'backward' south and east. On the other hand, they do not support stereotypes based on a contrast between liberal Anglophone and corporatist continental Europe, or LMEs and CMEs, as nothing has emerged to distinguish Ireland and the UK from either the corporatist or the social-democratic group. In fact, the UK fits very comfortably within the social-democratic category, having levels of employment in both sectors IV and V within the social-democratic range. It is the extended form of the Esping-Andersen categories, rather than its original one, that has some explanatory relevance.

INDICATORS OF SUSTAINABILITY

We can now try to fit these groups of countries to the various indicators of sustainability, before relating models of occupational structure to these latter. Unfortunately we now have to restrict the range of countries that we consider, as the best data for our issues of concern are those of Eurostat. These are restricted to EU member states, plus for several purposes Croatia, Norway, Switzerland and Turkey. We can now however start to include Belgium.

In terms of capacity to provide employment, Esping-Andersen's predictions of a superior capacity of both liberal and social democratic countries is partly borne out by recent statistics (Table 9.6), in that no country in these groups has employment levels as low as some countries in the others. There is however considerable overlap with the corporatist group, rendering questionable the tendency of many observers to regard this group as distinctly inferior on this issue. Familistic southwest Europe is distinctly lower still, though with some overlap with the corporatist – but not with the liberal and social-democratic groups. Again, as with occupational structure, southwest Europe appears as rather similar to the various CEE groups. Among these, indeed, the small Baltic states of the former USSR appear as more successful in providing employment than the countries of southwest Europe.

Table 9.6 Percentage of population aged 15–65 in employment, 2006

'Regime' type	Percentage of population aged 15–65 in employment																							
	46	55	56	57	58	59	60	61	62	63	64	65	66	67	68	69	70	71	72	73	74	75	76	77
Liberal																IE			UK					
Social democratic																FI				SE		NO		DK
Corporatist									BE	FR					DE		AT							
Familistic	TR				IT			GR				ES			PT						NL			
Ex-USSR											LT		LV	EE										
Ex-Comecon		PL		HU		BG SK						CZ												
Other ex-state socialist			HR			RO								SI										

Note: See Table 9.1 for abbreviations.

Source: Eurostat (2009).

Some similar patterns appear in the indicators of innovation, though also with important differences (Tables 9.7 to 9.11). The corporatist and social-democratic groups appear clearly as the strongest for research and development, for the proportion of innovative companies, and for all indicators of patents. There is total overlap between them. It is also notable that most of their members rank above the two liberal countries in all cases, except for proportion of innovative companies, where there is complete overlap. This is a surprising finding, as most observers claim an hypothesised Anglophone liberal model as superior in innovation to continental Europe, though some more perceptive experts have noted the particularly strong capacity of the Nordic countries (Amable, 2000; 2003; Boyer 2004a; 2004b). Certainly for virtually all earlier observers there had been an important distinction between the innovative capacity of countries in the corporatist group and the liberals and/or social democrats (see, for example, several contributions in Hall and Soskice, 2001). This does not seem to be the case in the early 21st century.

Familistic Europe again lags clearly behind even the liberal group – except in the high proportion of innovative companies in some cases. Again all groups of CEE countries lag further behind, though there is strong overlap between them and the southwest group.

If we now explore any relationships between our indicators of sustainability and those of occupational structure, we can finally free ourselves from the a priori allocation of cases to categories. The results are summarised in Table 9.12.

Employment in sector II (manufacturing, etc.) correlates negatively with all our sustainability measures, except for one of the indicators (proportion of innovative companies), though the correlations are weak. To a considerable extent this result is explained by the predominance of both manufacturing and low innovation in CEE countries. If we take account of the western countries alone, the correlations become even weaker, though all signs (except for the proportion of innovative companies index) remain negative. In general, high levels of employment in manufacturing are no longer associated with a strong capacity either to provide employment overall or to innovate. They may even be negatively associated with these indicators of sustainability. This does not necessarily mean that there are not individual manufacturing industries that form exceptions to this, but they will be minority cases. This constitutes major grounds for arguing that we do now live in post-industrial societies.

Table 9.7 Percentage of GDP spent on R&D, 2005

'Regime' type	Percentage of GDP spent on R&D																																			
	0.4	0.5	0.6	0.7	0.8	0.9	1.0	1.1	1.2	1.3	1.4	1.5	1.6	1.7	1.8	1.9	2.0	2.1	2.2	2.3	2.4	2.5	2.6	2.7	2.8	2.9	3.0	3.1	3.2	3.3	3.4	3.5	3.6	3.7	3.8	3.9
Lib.										IE				UK																						
Social-democratic											NO									DK											FI					SE
Corporatist															BE, NL			FR			AT	DE				CH										
Familistic			GR	TR	PT			IT, ES																												
Ex–USSR			LV	LT	EE																															
Ex–Comecon		BG, PL SK				HU					CZ																									
Other ex-state socialist	RO								HR, SI																											

Note: See Table 9.1 for abbreviations.

Source: Eurostat (2009).

Table 9.8 Percentage of enterprises engaged in innovative activity, 2004

'Regime type'	Percentage of enterprises engaged in innovative activity					
	<20	20–30	31–40	41–50	51–60	61–70
Liberal				UK	IE	
Social-democratic			NO	FI, SE	DK	
Corporatist			FR, NL	AT, BE		DE
Familistic			ES, IT, GR	PT		
Ex-USSR	LV, LT			EE		
Ex-Comecon	BG	HU, SK, PL		CZ		
Other ex-state socialist		RO, SI				

Note: See Table 9.1 for abbreviations.

Source: ILO Yearbook.

Table 9.9 European patents per million inhabitants, 2003

'Regime' type	European patents per million inhabitants								
	<50	51–100	101–150	151–200	201–250	251–300	301–350	351–400	401–450
Liberal		IE	UK						
Social democratic			NO		DK	SE	FI		
Corporatist			BE, FR	AT	NL		DE		CH
Familistic	GR, PT, ES, TR	IT							
Ex-USSR	EE, LV, LT								
Ex-Comecon	BG, CZ, HU, PO, SK								
Other ex-state socialist	HR, RO	SI							

Note: See Table 9.1 for abbreviations.

Source: ILO Yearbook.

Table 9.10 High-tech European patents per million inhabitants, 2003

'Regime' type	High-tech European patents per million inhabitants						
	<20	21–40	41–60	61–80	81–100	101–120	121–140
Liberal	IE	UK					
Social-democratic	NO		DK	SE			FI
Corporatist		AT, BE, FR	DE, NL, CH				
Familistic	GR, IT, PT, ES, TU						
Ex-USSR	EE, LV, LT						
Ex-Comecon	BG, CZ, HU, PL, SK						
Other ex-state socialist	RO, HR, SI						

Note: See Table 9.1 for abbreviations.

Source: ILO Yearbook.

Table 9.11 US-registered patents per million inhabitants, 2000

'Regime' type	US-registered patents per million inhabitants						
	0–25	26–50	51–75	76–100	101–125	126–150	151–175
Liberal		IE	UK				
Social-democratic		NO	DK		FI	SE	
Corporatist			AT, BE, FR	NL		DE	CH
Familistic	GR, PR, ES, TR	IT					
Ex-USSR	EE, LV, LT						
Ex-Comecon	BG, CZ, HU, PL, SK						
Other ex-state socialist	RO, HR, SI						

Note: See Table 9.1 for abbreviations.

Source: ILO Yearbook.

Table 9.12 Correlations for employment in various sectors with sustainability indicators (data excluding former state socialist countries in brackets)

Correlation (r)	Sector II	Sector III	Sector IV	Sector V
with proportion employed	–0.4109 (–0.3651)	–0.1472 (–0.3801)	0.6887 (0.6942)	0.7568 (0.7757)
R&D spending	–0.4898 (–0.2569)	–0.2274 (–0.5534)	0.7810 (0.6702)	0.6938 (0.6080)
innovative companies	–0.2458 (0.1313)	–0.1678 (–0.3264)	0.6899 (0.5924)	0.5778 (0.4700)
European patents	–0.5360 (–0.2338)	–0.1651 (–0.4111)	0.8092 (0.7177)	0.6435 (0.5179)
European hi-tech patents	–0.5093 (–0.2772)	–0.2482 (–0.5278)	0.6796 (0.5403)	0.6635 (0.5702)
US patents	–0.5321 (–0.2232)	–0.1792 (–0.4393)	0.8097 (0.7299)	0.6252 (0.4948)

Employment in the original tertiary sector (transport, distribution and communications) has a similarly negative, but weak, relation to sustainability indicators. The weakness of the relationship is partly the result of the small size of this sector in the CEE countries. Among western European countries there is a clearer negative relationship between employment in this sector and overall innovative capacity, especially in relation to R&D expenditure and high-tech patents.

A very different picture emerges when we examine sector IV, business services. Here the relationships are universally positive and strong, in relation to both employment and the indicators of innovation. The correlations for innovation are reduced somewhat when only western countries are considered, but that for employment remains high.

We find a similar profile when we consider sector V (community and social services). Again the correlations are reduced slightly when only western countries are considered, and those for innovation are not as strong as those for employment, or for the scores for sector IV, but they are always positive.

This evidence confirms suspicions engendered by examination of the groupings of countries in the earlier discussion. Sectors IV and V are associated with 'advance', or perhaps as we can better describe it now, 'sustainability'. (Not surprisingly, there is also a strong positive correlation between employment in the two sectors IV and V (r = 0.7684), though lower for western countries alone (r = 0.6710).)

In some respects these are findings that we should expect; these are the two sectors that employ the highest proportions of highly educated people; they also employ high proportions of women, an important indicator of a sustainable economy. There is however one element that jars with prevailing orthodoxy. Sector V is the part of the economy that is most removed from the capitalist market. Large numbers of the people working in it are employed by public authorities (public administration, the administration of justice, education, health, social care), or by foundations and charitable organisations working at least in part outside the market. Even where, as in an increasing number of cases, workers in this sector are employed by private firms, the funding that rewards their activities is funded by the state or the charitable and voluntary sector. This is outstandingly the case in Europe, but even in the USA (outside our present scope), where the market plays a bigger role in some of these services (particularly health care), there are large elements of public or charitable funding. Sector V in the USA may be more market-oriented than in Europe, but within the USA sector V is the least market-determined sector. It contains all public administration, the education system, health and all other care services.

Something even more surprising emerges if we look more closely at the sub-sectors of sector V. The two largest and relatively most homogenously defined are health and social care, and education. Tables 9.3 and 9.4 present the array of countries for these cases. Health and care employment follows the pattern set in Table 9.5 for the sector as a whole: the Nordic countries and the Netherlands rank higher than the rest; there is complete overlap between the liberals and the corporatists; and among southwestern Europe and CEE. Employment in this sub-sector correlates even more highly with the indicators assessed in Table 9.12 than does sector V employment overall (total employment: 0.7708; R&D 0.7519; innovative companies: 0.5779; EU patents: 0.8079; high-tech EU patents: 0.7326; US patents: 0.7841). Employment in education shows a far less distinctive pattern. The Scandinavian countries, the UK and the countries of the former Soviet Union show the highest levels; some southwest Europeans and non-COMECON state socialist ones (southeast Europe) show the lowest levels, but most countries are grouped around 6–7%. There seems to be less discretion in the size of this sector than for health and social care. The correlations with the Table 9.12 indicators are weak (overall employment: 0.4345; R&D: 0.2784; innovative companies: 0.2822; EU patents: 0.2038; high-tech EU patents: 0.1886; US patents: 0.2048).

Table 9.13 Employment in health and social care services, 2005

'Regime' type	Percent of total employment																
	3	4	5	6	7	8	9	10	11	12	13	14	15	16	17	18	19
Liberal								IE		UK							
Social democratic													FI	SE		DK	NO
Corporatist							AT		CH	FR, DE					NL		
Familistic	TR		GR	ES	IT, PT												
Ex-USSR		LV	MD	EE	LT, RU												
Ex-Comecon			BG	PL	CZ, HU, SK												
Other state socialist		RO		HR, MK, RS, SI													

If the dynamism of modern economies is primarily determined by the strength of market forces, why is there a positive association between employment in their least market-oriented sector, and within that a sub-sector remote from the main activities of the market economy), and indicators of both employment and commercial innovation? Should this relationship not be negative? Even Esping-Andersen (1999: 179–180), who drew attention to the employment-creating capacity of the social-democratic welfare state, considered that this might be doomed by its dependence on taxation-based, government-generated demand. He saw more potential dynamism in the private services model of the liberal countries, where wealthy people could afford to pay poor people to provide services for them generated in the market.

It is not clear, at least in Europe, that Esping-Andersen was right about this difference between types of employment. According to the ILO (2009) data, private services to households account for more than 1% of employment only in the following countries: Estonia: 5.5%; France: 2.2%; Greece: 1.52%; Italy 1.50%; Portugal: 3.24%; Spain: 3.78%; Switzerland: 1.13%. They are not significant in either of the European liberal countries, the figure for Ireland being 0.46 and for the UK 0.41. Further, the larger of these, the UK, has a share of overall employment in sector V only very slightly lower than that of the social-democratic countries.

Table 9.14 Employment in education services, 2005

'Regime' type	Percent of total employment							
	4	5	6	7	8	9	10	11
Liberal				IE		UK		
Social democratic				FI	DK	NO		SE
Corporatist		AT	DE, CH	FR, NL				
Familistic	TR	ES	PT	GR , IT				
Ex-USSR				LV	EE	RU, MD	LT	
Ex-Comecon			CZ	BG, PL, SK	HU			
Other state socialist	RO, RS		HR, MK		SI			

ANALYSIS AND CONCLUSIONS

The foregoing account has given us good reason to doubt the importance assigned in much of the literature to the different so-called types of industrial society. Several studies achieve an impression of differences between these types by comparing the average values for the cases in a type. Consequently, if, say, the average proportion of the adult population in employment in a particular type is higher than that in another type, the validity of the classification is deemed to have been confirmed. This is a methodologically illegitimate conclusion if there has been considerable overlap across the values of members of different types. Attention has to be paid to these ranges at least as much as to averages. This has been our procedure in the above analysis, which is why we have found less support for the reality of types than much other literature.

Types are abstract concepts, Weberian ideal types; such types are constructed by assuming that certain independent variables cluster together in clearly differentiated, strongly articulated ways. Actual empirical cases will correspond to types only to the extent that they possess these clusters as predicted by the type. A case may only be considered to be an example of a particular type if it has the expected cluster. It may well possess some characteristics of one type and others of another; or the expected characteristics may be found but only weakly. The process of deeming cases to constitute members of a type by averaging the possession of the expected characteristics among them conceals the extent to which some cases may in fact not possess the characteristic in question. This is bad practice. Further, by treating cases as though they possessed a characteristic in the average quantity of their group of cases, we may well miss any independent impact of that characteristic outside the frame of the typology.

We can illustrate this by turning back to the pair of variables that we have explored: proportion of the workforce engaged in sector V and proportion of the relevant population employed across all sectors. In eight countries the proportion of sector V employees exceeds 30%; seven of these countries are also among the eight with the highest overall employment rates (France drops out of the top eight and Austria enters the list). Three of the four Nordic countries (the three Scandinavians, in fact) occupy the first three positions in the sector V list and three of the four top positions for overall employment rates. This is consistent with hypotheses based on the social-democratic group. However, the fourth to sixth places in the sector V list are occupied by the Netherlands (a 'corporatist' case), and by France and the UK (respectively corporatist and liberal). The eighth place is occupied by Germany (another corporatist). Scandinavian countries (Denmark and Norway) hold the first two places in the employment rankings, after which comes a 'corporatist' (Netherlands), then Sweden, the UK, and a further mix of corporatist cases and the other 'social-democratic' country (Finland).

The sector V variable is more closely associated with the employment rate than is the social-democratic category. Whereas membership of the social-democratic category is geographically fixed, countries' employment of persons within sector V can change. It is also a precisely specified variable in the way that membership of the types is not. In fact, we can see that the social-democratic type exists to the extent that it includes, inter alia, the sector V variable. Some countries in the group might possess that characteristic (and a high position on the employment rate) more weakly than others – as is the case with Finland; while countries outside the group (mainly the Netherlands, but also the UK and, far less strongly, France and Germany) might also show strong combinations of sector V employment and overall employment. Concentrating on the types rather than on the variables exhibited in cases draws our attention away from the connection, and probably leads us to misunderstand the dynamics of the British and Dutch cases. Are these correctly specified as 'liberal' and 'corporatist' at all? The original allocation by Esping-Andersen (1990) was based on countries' ways of providing for periods of lost income through unemployment, disability or old age, and he convincingly showed (Esping-Andersen, 1999) that doing this through universal policies, as in the Nordic countries, made for generally strong welfare states based on the provision of services, which in turn provided employment (especially for women). But this is not necessarily the only way in which countries can acquire strong welfare states. The Dutch system of public subsidies for the activities of church-based welfare, and the strong symbolism in the UK of the National Health Service, may provide functional equivalents. These are not captured if we make a priori allocations of countries to types on the basis of one or two indicators of policy model.

Of course, this kind of analysis cannot establish any causative links between employment in sector V (or IV) and overall employment. We certainly cannot predict that increasing the proportion of the workforce engaged in administrative, educational and care activities – or health and care in particular – will produce an increase in overall employment. Indeed, as Burroni and Keune (2009) have shown, policies to increase numbers of public employees in southern Italy without their employment being linked to public demand for services had if anything a negative effect. On the other hand, we can probably reject the contention that any causative relationship flows the other way, i.e. that overall economic strength (reflected in a high employment rate) makes it possible to spend on sector V. The strong welfare states of the Nordic countries, the Netherlands and the UK date back to an earlier period.

To return to a point already made, we can cast considerable doubt on the current orthodoxy that sees employment in activities funded other than on market principles as likely to be inefficient, leading to lower levels of overall employment and reduced innovation. Amable (2003) has made a similar but far more detailed and rigorous challenge to the orthodoxy, though staying within the framework of an analysis of types rather than of variables within cases.

When Daniel Bell (1973) originally drew our attention to the occupational structures of post-industrial society, the characteristic forms of employment that he stressed were primarily those in non-market, or at least less marketised, industries and services: education, health and scientific research. At first sight it seems strange that such a leading role can be played in market economies by these least market-oriented activities. Some years ago, discussing the problem of identifying a paradigmatic sector in post-industrial society to correspond to the role of manufacturing in industrial society, I made an argument of this kind. Noting that sector V was becoming the largest in several countries, I said that it obviously could not be paradigmatic given that the economy was a market one (Crouch, 1999: ch. 4).

Increasingly I think that I was wrong. Sociologists are of course familiar with the proposition that, just because an economy is a market one, we cannot characterise the whole of *society* as 'market society'. Such a description is valid only if the market can be shown to penetrate all aspects of life in that society. Perhaps, however, we can take the argument further and into the economy itself. Just because an economy is primarily a market one, we should not conclude that everything within that *economy* conforms to market principles, or even that its efficiency depends on the dominance of market forces. Adam Smith considered that the market economy depended on certain underlying beliefs, or 'moral sentiments', that were not reproduced by the market itself, which might indeed have tendencies to destroy them. In other words, the sustainability of the market might depend on forces outside itself.

The point being made here is similar, though it does not immediately concern moral sentiments: it is possible that the efficiency of the market depends on the existence of other activities, which the market cannot easily create for itself. If that is true, then it will not be the case that the market economy will be more efficient, the purer that its market characteristics are. Certain kinds of non-market activities may be supportive of it. This is a large theme and can extend to many aspects of the economy. There is space here to draw attention to just one of them. The market economy requires labour to accept considerable flexibility, which can create uncertainty and insecurity concerning income flows and the continuance of employment itself. At the same time, the market economy also needs the public to be confident consumers, purchasing the flow of goods and services that it produces. Labour market uncertainty does not encourage confident consumption. It is of course possible for this puzzle to be resolved by exporting the product of a flexible workforce to countries with less flexible labour markets and therefore more confident consumers. But the achievement of the advanced economies has been to combine work and consumption in the same population.

The market can provide solutions to the puzzle, if the resources that people use for consumption can be separated from the incomes that they derive from their (flexible) labour. This was the great achievement of the system of unsecured debt, in particular mortgage debt, developed by the UK and US banking sectors from the 1980s onwards. Doubts now exist over its sustainability. Other approaches to the puzzle require some compromise between the market and other forms of governance. Among these a certain role is played by employment in the non-market sector. But this is a theme that has to be pursued elsewhere (Crouch, 2009).

NOTE

[1.] This chapter is based on my plenary address for the opening session of the conference of the European Sociological Association in Lisbon, 2–5 September 2009. It has been prepared as part of my work for European Union Framework Programme 7 project 'The

Governance of Uncertainty and Sustainability: Tensions and Opportunities' (GUSTO) (grant no. 225301).

REFERENCES

Albert, M. (1991), *Capitalisme Contre Capitalisme*, Paris: Seuil.

Amable, B. (2000), 'Institutional complementarity and diversity of social systems of innovation and production', *Review of International Political Economy*, **7**(4), 645–687.

Amable, B. (2003) *The Diversity of Modern Capitalism*, Oxford: Oxford University Press.

Bell, D. (1973) *The Coming of Post-Industrial Society*, New York: Basic Books.

Boyer, R. (2004a), 'New Growth Regimes, But still Institutional Diversity', *Socio-Economic Review*, **2**(1), 1–32.

Boyer, R. (2004b), *The Future of Economic Growth: As New becomes Old*, Cheltenham: Edward Elgar.

Burroni, L. and M. Keune (2009), 'Understanding the multiple sources of and relationships between flexibility and security: towards a governance approach', Working Paper, European Trade Union Institute, Brussels: ETUI,

Clark, C. (1940), *The Conditions of Economic Progress*, London: Macmillan.

Crouch, C. (1999), *Social Change in Western Europe*, Oxford: Oxford University Press.

Crouch, C. (2009), 'The flexibility/security trade-off: incorporating the lessons of the financial crisis', paper presented at ESA conference, September 2009, Lisbon.

Esping-Andersen, G. (1990), *The Three Worlds of Welfare Capitalism*, Cambridge: Polity Press.

Esping-Andersen, G. (1999), *Social Foundations of Postindustrial Economies*, Oxford: Oxford University Press.

European Commission (2008), *Industrial Relations in Europe 2008*, Luxembourg.

Eurostat (2009), *Eurostat Yearbook 2008*, Luxembourg.

Ferrera, M. (1996), 'Il modello Sud-Europeo di welfare state', *Rivista Italiana di Scienza Politica*, **1**, 67–101.

Hall, P.A. and D. Soskice (eds) (2001), *Varieties of Capitalism: The Institutional Foundations of Comparative Advantage*, Oxford: Oxford University Press.

International Labour Organization (2009), *ILO Yearbook*, Geneva: ILO.

Katzovien, M.A. (1970), 'The Development of the Services Sector: a New Approach', *Oxford Economic Papers*, **22**(3), 362–382.

Korpi, W. (1983), *The Democratic Class Struggle*, London: Routledge.

Muffels, R., T. Wilthagen and N. van den Heuvel (2002), *Labour Market Transitions and Employment Regimes: Evidence on the Flexicurity-Security Nexus in Transitional Labour Markets*, WZB Discussion Paper FS I 02–204, Berlin: Wissenschaftszentrum Berlin für Sozialforschung.

Muffels, R. (ed.) (2008), *Flexibility and Employment Security in Europe: Labour Markets in Transition*, Cheltenham: Edward Elgar.

Naldini, M. (2003), *The Family in the Mediterranean Welfare States*, London: Frank Cass.

Rokkan, S. (1999), *State Formation, Nation Building. And Mass Politics in Europe: The Theory of Stein Rokkan*, edited by S. Kuhnle, P. Flora and D. Urwin, Oxford: Clarendon Press.

Singelmann, J. (1978), *From Agriculture to Services: The Transformation of Industrial Employment*, Beverly Hills, CA: Sage.

Titmuss, R. (1958), *Essays on the Welfare State*, London: Allen and Unwin.

10. Corporate social responsibility and employment: a plurality of configurations*

Claude Didry

The principal of corporate social responsibility is frequently presented as the basis for a new way of regulating working conditions and the environment (Sobczak, 2002). This type of regulation, initiated by multinationals, is considered to be an alternative, or at very least a supplement (European Commission, 2001), to legal norms in place within nation states and even continental areas (in the case of the EU). As a form of 'soft law', this model would avoid the use of a legislative intervention that would prohibit behaviour deemed harmful for the community, and would contribute to what some negatively term 'legislative inflation'.[1] Indeed, this new form of regulation would reflect *the firm's role* in the monitoring of working conditions and environmental awareness. Accordingly, through the theme of social responsibility we see how the perception of multinational firms has changed radically. Once denounced by political leaders in the 1970s as a threat to national sovereignty, they are now celebrated as economic agents whose declarations of principle could moralise globalisation. In its current form, corporate social responsibility has been rendered visible through 'codes of conduct' and 'international framework agreements', many of which are catalogued on the ILO website concerning the 'Tripartite declaration of principles concerning multinational enterprises'.

This evolution corresponds with the advent of a new kind of company model, that of the 'networked firm', a firm which outsources its production activities in order to focus on management and design. Codes of conduct allow these firms to establish minimum standards regarding working conditions and the environment for their subcontractors, sometimes operating in territories all but lacking the rule of law. These codes reflect a strong trend of relocation to areas where economic activities are more profitable.

A lexical analysis of these codes of conduct shows, however, that the emergence of a 'merchant firm', which abandons jobs in developed countries in favour of outsourced production in developing countries, is not the only possible model to which corporate social responsibility applies: other models are emerging. This plurality of models, identifiable through their different codes of conduct, requires a deeper analysis which would take into account the social movements addressed through these codes, declarations of principles, and agreements. In truth, codes of conduct have very little to do with a sudden appearance of 'angelic' firms struck by a sudden need for philanthropy. They form part of a communication strategy aimed at restoring a firm's 'image' when it has been challenged by the exposure of abusive practices by unions and non-governmental organisations (particularly human rights and consumer associations).

After reviewing the role of international norms in codes of conduct and social responsibility, we will consider the plurality of firm models that can be observed. We will then discuss the different configurations as they relate to the issue of employment.

CODES OF CONDUCT FROM THE 1970S TO THE 2000S: AN INCREASE IN NUMBER BUT A DECREASE IN IMPACT

The increase during the 1970s of initiatives aimed at regulating the activities of multinationals viewed as a threat to democracy, resulted in the 1990s in a policy based on 'principles' rather than a real legal framework. Declarations of principles became the starting point for observing firms' initiatives, which sought to promote the emulation of 'best practices'. This movement clearly contrasts with the movement towards 'social harmonisation'[2] which accompanied and reinforced the creation of a European society by laying the foundations of European social legislation (Didry, 2009). This contrast leads us to centre our discussion on the dialectic between the initiatives undertaken by international organisations and the codes of conduct created by multinationals, whose impact was used by the European authorities as a reason justifying the halt of the legislative movement propelled by Jacque Delors.[3]

From a Proposed Code in the 1970s to an Inventory of Codes in the 2000s

The 1970s was a period when the power of multinationals throughout the world was being questioned, notably with respect to nation states. President

Allende underlines this sentiment in his passionate and premonitory speech before the United Nations' General Assembly on 4 December 1972:

> We are faced by a direct confrontation between the large transnational corporations and the states. The corporations are interfering in the fundamental political, economic and military decisions of the states. The corporations are global organisations that do not depend on any state and whose activities are not controlled by, nor are they accountable to any parliament or any other institution representative of the collective interest. In short, the world's whole political structure is being undermined.

From that point onward, international organisations began reflecting on the means necessary to control the excesses of multinational firms, culminating with a proposed Code of Conduct for Multinational Enterprises presented to the UN in 1974. This Code, however, eventually gave way to declarations and principles, sparking the proliferation of 'codes of conduct', both monitored and encouraged by international organisations.

UN, ILO, and OECD Initiatives in Reaction to Multinationals

In 1947, a social clause (art. 7) was included in the Havana Charter on the Organisation of International Trade adopted by the UN, but the charter was abandoned in favour of the GATT at the request of the United States.[4] It wasn't until the 1970s that the international community, both on a political level and through union action,[5] mobilised against the activities of multinationals, giving rise to initiatives from the UN as well as from the ILO and the OECD.

The ILO's Tripartite Declaration

In 1973, the ILO published a report entitled *Multinational Enterprises and Social Policy*. This raised the issue of multinational firms causing competition between countries, creating a risk of a negative impact on working conditions. Discussions within the ILO led to an initial Tripartite Declaration on Principles concerning Multinational Enterprises and Social Policy adopted in 1977.

The UN's code of conduct concerning multinationals

In general terms, discussion in the UN focuses on ways in which the activities of multinationals might be controlled within the different countries in which they are established. This was the aim discussed during the planning of a Code of Conduct for Multinational Enterprises put forward by the United Nations[6] with the intent to sanction multinationals in their country of origin for their abusive practices throughout the world. The goal was to create the conditions necessary for multinationals to be held legally accountable, in other words liable,[7] for their actions. This project led to a lasting process of reflection. The creation of the UN's Global Compact at the end of the 1990s is one of the later results of this reflection. Sometime between the 1970s and the 1990s, the term 'code of conduct' ceased to refer to a plan to regulate and sanction multinationals, and began to apply instead to initiatives of firms employing 'best practices' as defined by the principles set out by international organisations.

OECD Guidelines

In the OECD, the issue of the power held by multinationals led to the creation of Guidelines aimed at these firms. These guiding principles are laid out in 10 chapters, including a chapter dedicated to 'Employment and industrial relations' (chapter 4). The 'promotion' of the Guidelines is the responsibility of National Contact Points, institutions where individuals may report multinationals within their national territory that fail to comply with these principles. These Guidelines, voted in 1976, were revised in 2000, giving rise to the collection of data of various types. Designed as a starting point in the larger picture of promoting best practice in firms, these Guidelines were paired with the institution of National Contact Points (NCP) available for legal recourse in cases of infringement. Paradoxically, the normally liberal OECD seems to have gone a step further than the ILO or the UN in regulating firms' abusive practices. However, NCPs are independent of each other and are free to adopt divergent positions, as was the case with the brutal closure of Marks and Spencer in France and Belgium in 2001. Indeed, the French NCP decided that the firm had violated the Guidelines whereas its Belgian counterpart deemed that it did not have sufficient evidence to ascertain whether a violation had in fact occurred.

The ILO's Tripartite Declaration as the Basis for an Inventory of Codes of Conduct

Condensing international regulations

International organisations have slowly abandoned their aim of creating a single code of conduct to regulate the behaviour of multinationals. Progressively, international norms have taken the form of 'declarations' proclaiming a limited number of principles taking into account established legislative change.

The ILO declaration concerning Fundamental Rights and Principles at Work adopted in 1998 is a combination of other ILO conventions and covers five main principles: freedom of association, recognition of the right to collective bargaining, the abolition of forced or obligatory work, the abolition of child labour and the elimination of discrimination at work. It is focused primarily on nation states, whether they have ratified ILO conventions or not, by monitoring changes in legislation and practices within their borders.

Launched in 2000, the Global Compact outlines 11 principles ranging from the respect of human rights, to the fight against corruption, to the protection of the environment. These principles are written in the form of wishes rather than laws.[8] They are part of an incentive strategy based on the formal recognition of firms that commit to the application of the principles.[9]

Revising the Tripartite Declaration concerning Multinationals

The ILO Declaration on the Fundamental Rights and Principles at Work gave rise in 2000 to a revision of the Tripartite Declaration of Principles concerning Multinational Enterprises, adopted initially by the ILO in 1977. Article 8 was revised to read that parties:

> should contribute to the realization of the ILO Declaration on Fundamental Principles and Rights and Work and its Follow-up, adopted in 1998. They should also honour commitments which they have freely entered into, in conformity with the national law and accepted international obligations.

In this way, the ILO's principles have taken on the role of guidelines for initiatives originating from firms. With their mention in the Tripartite Declaration, the efficacy of the principles has diminished in intensity but increased in scope: they no longer apply solely to the behaviour of nation states but also to the relationship of multinationals to individuals.[10] The initiatives undertaken by multinational firms and catalogued on the ILO's website[11] make up the corpus for this study.[12]

Characteristics of the ILO Corpus

Among the initiatives catalogued by the ILO, only the codes of conduct and collective agreements[13] of single firms were examined, which excludes documents establishing norms for whole industries such as the toy industry. These codes were compiled to form a corpus, and were characterised by variables such as the firm name and associated industry, variables which were analysed as information additional to the body text of the codes themselves.

The corpus is composed of 175 framework agreements and codes of conduct representing 151 firms (see Table 10.1); the difference is due to the fact that certain firms have several reference texts in the ILO's database.

Of these 175 texts, 151 are codes created unilaterally by the firm and 34 are framework agreements negotiated with union associations.

One-third of the firms are based in Europe (33.8%), 62% in North America (the United States and Canada), 2.6% in the Asia-Pacific region and 2% in the rest of the world.

Table 10.1 Industries and origins of firms under study

	Europe	N. America	Asia/ Pacific	Other	Total firms	% firm	Codes
Manufacturing	5	35		2	42	27.8	48
Chemical	5	8			13	8.6	15
Oil	7	4			11	7.3	15
Food-processing	4	4	1		9	6	14
Retail	4	3	1		8	5.3	11
Forestry	3	5			8	5.3	10
Telecommunications	5	3			8	5.3	10
Public works	2	3	1		6	4	6
Aeronautics		5			5	3.3	5
Building	4	1			5	3.3	5
Finance	3	2			5	3.3	5
Construction materials	2	2	1		5	3.3	5
Electronics	3	1			4	2.6	4
Automobile	1	2			3	2	3
Education		3			3	2	3
Information technology		3			3	2	3
Metal working		3			3	2	3
Mining		2		1	3	2	3
Media, culture	1	1			2	1.3	2
Hotel – Catering	1				1	0.7	1
Toy	1				1	0.7	1
Health		1			1	0.7	1
Unknown		2			2	1.3	2
Total	51	108	4	3	166	100%	175

The range of industries present in the corpus shows a clear predominance for manufacturing industry (more than a quarter of the firms), followed by the chemical, oil and food-processing industries. 'Traditional' industries (forestry, building, mining...) represent a similar proportion to hi-tech industries (telecommunications, aeronautics, electronics and information technology). Finally, the presence of public works, represented by distribution networks (water, gas, electricity), should be noted, as should that of the health and education industries.

WORLDS OF CORPORATE SOCIAL RESPONSIBILITY

Codes of conduct convey the existence of a need for multinationals to display the unilateral commitments made as part of their communication policy. This need originates as much from the firms themselves, which react to the initiatives of 'stakeholders' such as non-governmental organisations and unions, as from the partners, subcontractors and employees responding to these firms' requirements. The codes allow a series of commitments to be identified, but also and above all, they underline the plurality of themes that constitute 'corporate social responsibility'. An initial distinction can be observed between commitments related to the environment and those related to fundamental rights at work, but a deeper analysis of the codes reveals an even greater diversity, in which a true plurality of 'worlds of social responsibility' can be seen. These 'worlds' reflect a level of coherence between typical firms and their products, activities and code content, suggesting that beyond the issues of environment (integrative firm), and of work (merchant firm), we should also take into account issues linked to employee responsibilisation (supervisor firms) and the role of ownership in the preservation of a firm's assets (knowledge firm).

Lexical Analysis of the Corpus

The corpus, composed of codes of conduct as mentioned previously, was lexically analysed using software called Alceste. The first phase of this analysis was to classify sentences according to their vocabulary. Eight separate categories were identified as being characterised by certain word groups, i.e., specific lexical fields. A previous presentation of these categories[14] revealed the restricted role[15] played by themes related to the most common conception of corporate social responsibility, namely the regulation of working conditions and the protection of the environment. It also showed the importance of alternative themes concerning work and workers,[16] particularly in regard to ensuring that established principles are effective[17] and to clearly defining the firm's assets to reduce the risk of ownership claims by employees.[18]

A discussion of results of the second phase of the software's analysis, a factorial analysis identifying the principal components, will be used to build on these previous contributions. This phase uses the vocabulary found in the sentences that form the eight categories identified in the first phase. The proximity of sentences to their categories is evaluated according to words shared: the more words that are shared, the closer they are. Consequently, the groupings presented in the 2007 article may now be replaced by the sections of a framework. This framework forms the basis of the design of Table 10.2 (below).

Overview of the Results

The 'classic' themes of social responsibility can be found on the left side of Figure 10.1: the upper left-hand corner contains the theme of the environment and the lower left-hand that of regulating work. Themes related to the application of principles announced in the codes are in the upper right-hand corner. Those themes related to the ownership of a firm's assets can be found in the lower right-hand corner.

The Main Types of Firm

Alceste's classification permits the distinct groupings of sentences and codes of conduct that make up the corpus to be visualised simultaneously, allowing the companies most strongly associated with each of these groups to be observed. It underlines the firms that are the most representative of each group of firms and codes of conduct, as identified during the analysis, by isolating the most significant sentences in their codes.

The integrative firm
A considerable portion of the codes of conduct analysed deal with the idea of creating a dynamic of production through a dual process of integration: internal (the integration of individuals, consumers, and employees into the firm) and external (the integration of the firm into its environment). This process of integration is based firstly on the firm's *product* as a contribution to the common good,[19] notably through attempts to minimise negative effects on health and the environment, as demonstrated by the practices of Philip Morris for example.

Companies operating in the chemical industry are the firm type most associated with this group, the representative code being that of Procter and Gamble.

Table 10.2 The worlds of corporate social responsibility

Internal	
Integrative firm *Typical firms:* Procter and Gamble, Caterpillar, Total Fina Elf, Nestlé, Shell *Industries:* Chemical, oil *Key words (sampling):* Reputation, Ethic, Integrity, Partners, Shareholder, Stakeholder, Consumer, Environment, Product, Community	**Supervisor firm** *Typical firms:* Boeing, Cable and Wireless *Key words (sampling):* Control, Contractor, Subcontractor, Manager, Supervisor, Accident, Misconduct, Report Discipline
Products	***Assets***
Merchant firm *Typical firms:* Kellwood *Industry:* Manufacturing *Key words (sampling):* Vendors, Sourcing, Forced labour, Children, Age, Discrimination, Race, Unions	**Knowledge firm** *Typical firms:* Verizon, IBM, Halliburton *Industries:* Telecom, information technology, public works *Key words (sampling):* Asset, Confidential, Intellectual, Discovery, Invention, Corruption, Bribe, Conflict of Interests
External	

Integration in the code of Procter and Gamble corresponds to a fundamental commitment to provide quality products to consumers in return for a recognition which would allow the enduring success of the firm. It states:

> We will provide products and services of superior quality and value that improve the lives of the world's consumers. As a result, consumers will reward us with leadership sales, profit and value creation, allowing our people, our shareholders, and the communities in which we live and work to prosper.

This openness to external partners leads to a kind of mutualisation of company property allowing the company to succeed, prosper and attain a lasting position of leadership: 'We all act like owners, treating the Company's assets as our own and behaving with the Company's long-term success in mind.'

The use of 'we' and the invitation to assume ownership of company assets convey an approach demonstrating an aspect of 'community', in contrast, as we will see, with the tendency of 'knowledge firms' to defend their assets. In some respects, the workers themselves are reduced to company assets meant to operate facilities 'like' they were owners, the 'like' conveying the distance maintained between the true ownership of assets and the employees.

This process of integration *into the firm* is complemented by an integration process of the *firm itself* into its surrounding 'environment'. This phenomenon can be observed mainly in the oil and food-processing industries, particularly in the codes of Total Fina Elf, Royal Dutch Shell, and Nestlé.

The protection of the environment, particularly by limiting greenhouse gases, is targeted through the improvement of these firms' products:

> TotalFinaElf endeavours to contribute to the efficient and properly managed utilisation of all sources of energy and products that it provides through its activities.

> The Group takes into account the needs of today's consumers and the interests of future generations through an assertive policy of continuous improvement and environmental protection that forms part of its strategy of sustainable development.

The merchant firm

Vendor selection and ways of sourcing production activities carried out by subcontractors are both issues forming a good transition point with the integrative firm in the sense that these issues concern the 'values' of prime contractors operating between the vendors of their products and their subcontractors. This corresponds to the difficulty associated with production activities involving firms that have not participated in establishing the code of conduct. Those most affected by this issue are firms operating in manufacturing industry. The codes of conduct of these firms allow the delimitation of what could be termed as a 'merchant firm agreement', an agreement transposing the mechanics of the relationship between the merchant and craftsman of the 19th-century industrial era[20] to the relationship between Western manufacturing multinationals and their factories in South East Asia, Latin America and even Eastern Europe.

Merchant firms are concerned with ensuring that working conditions in manufacturing facilities are in accordance with ILO fundamental principles. This group of firms can therefore be identified by their references to ILO principles, and is dominated almost exclusively by the codes of manufacturing firms, with the exception of Barclays Bank for issues related to discrimination.

This group contains the codes of firms such as Kellwood, Levi Strauss and C&A. A sentence from Levi Strauss's code is particularly representative of the relationship between sourcing and the respect for fundamental rights at work: 'Our global sourcing operating guidelines help us to select business partners who follow workplace standards and business practices that are consistent with our company's policies.'

The issue of relocation of the manufacturing activities targeted by the codes is reflected through the need to refer to local norms to evaluate whether principles, such as the ban on forced or child labour, have been properly applied, as demonstrated in Kellwood's code:

> Child Labor: The use of child labor is not permissible. For a definition of 'child', we will first look to the national laws of the country in which business is being conducted. If, however, the laws of that country do not provide such a definition or if the definition includes individuals below the age of 14, we will define 'child', for purposes of determining use of illegal child labor, as any one who is:
>
> a.   less than 14 years of age; or
> b.   younger than the compulsory age to be in school in the country in which business is being conducted, if that age is higher than 14.

The supervisor firm

Another group of codes of conduct emphasises the employees' responsibility in the application of principles set forth in the codes. Three codes stand out in particular, that of Cable and Wireless in the telephone line installation industry, that of Boise Cascade Company in the forestry industry and that of Boeing in the aeronautics industry:

> Every employee has the responsibility to ask questions, seek guidance, report suspected violations, and express concerns regarding compliance with this policy and the related procedures. The Boeing Company will maintain a program to communicate to employees its commitment to integrity and uncompromising values, as set forth in the Boeing Values. The program will inform employees of company policies and procedures regarding ethical business conduct and assist them in resolving questions and in reporting suspected violations. Retaliation against employees who use company reporting mechanisms to raise genuine concerns will not be tolerated.

Thus, a dual movement of information is created: the first movement originating from the employees who transmit information concerning the firm's principles, and the other originating from the management who pass on information concerning the employees' application of principles. In this model, the 'anonymous hotline' is the key tool.

The special feature of firms of this kind is that employees of different firms often work together. Boeing, consequently, specifies its code's scope in the following way: 'Applies to: All Boeing company and subsidiary employees, contract labor, consultants and others acting for the company ("employees")'.

Here, as was the case with the merchant firm, this world of social responsibility implies the use of sourcing. However, in the case of the supervisor firm, sourcing involves the coexistence on the same site of different firms involved in the creation of the same product.

The knowledge firm

Codes of conduct of firms connected to information and communication technologies, such as IBM and particularly Verizon, the large American telephone operator, tend to define the extent of company assets both internally and externally.

These firms' codes of conduct put an important emphasis on issues of intellectual property by attempting to anticipate complicated disputes related to sharing the ownership of discoveries, particularly with their employees.

> When you joined IBM, you were required to sign an agreement under which you, as an employee of IBM, assumed specific obligations relating to intellectual property as well as the treatment of confidential information. Among other things in the agreement, you assign to IBM all of your right, title, and interest in intellectual property you develop when you are employed in certain capacities, such as a managerial, technical, product planning, programming, scientific or other professional capacity.

Defending company ownership of assets means focusing primarily on non-material assets, but consequently also implies an interest in maintaining the confidentiality of information controlled by the firm, an essential aspect of Verizon's code:

> We will safeguard the confidentiality and integrity of company systems (including password logons, password-protected screensavers, access codes, network access information, log-on IDs) from improper access, alteration, destruction and disclosure. We will only access or use these systems when authorised.

We will also abide by company standards contained in this section and other company policies regarding protecting data and information stored on these systems.

A PLURALITY OF 'RESPONSIBILITY GENERATING SITUATIONS' AFFECTING EMPLOYMENT

A second look at the codes of those firms most typical of each world of social responsibility, allows us to see past the idyllic vision of codes of conduct as spontaneous commitments.

In each of the four worlds mentioned above, the appearance of codes of conduct is concurrent with the mobilisation or emergence of institutions that challenge the firms' activities. We will examine how codes can be analysed as reactions to 'responsibility generating situations' as described by Fauconnet (1928)[21] and the role played by work and employment. The four main types of situation reveal different relationships to employment in instances where firms' behaviour is called into question by different social actors (governmental organisations, unions). The integrative firm attempts to reintegrate the personnel after extensive restructuring, the merchant firm tries to monitor working conditions after outsourcing all its manufacturing, the supervisor firm seeks to group together workers from a variety of subcontractors on the same site and the knowledge firm endeavours to defend its ownership of products created by its employees.

Environmental Impact: A Challenge for the Integrative Firm

As previously discussed, Procter and Gamble, TotalElfFina and Shell's codes of conduct are prime examples of the socially responsible firm type called here the integrative firm. These codes of conduct are adopted according to their specific situational contexts, their content being influenced particularly by the ongoing adoption of new commitments.

Proctor and Gamble's code was published in 2000. During the previous decade the company underwent an extensive restructuring process, with 10,000 American jobs being downsized and a partnership formed with Chinese firms for the production of washing powder.[22] Proctor and Gamble and Nike were among those challenged by Michael Moore in his 1997 film *The Big One*. The restructuring of Procter and Gamble shows a profound change in the firm's strategy, accompanied by a displacement of standard chemical product manufacturing, such as detergent, to make room for products requiring more R&D, particularly in the pharmaceutical industry. The firm has also expanded the development of its cleaning products with the help of the 'Institut Pasteur', in order to reinforce the antibacterial component of its world famous *Mr. Clean*.[23] Proctor and Gamble's significant product improvements are reflected in its code, which insists on their products' role as contributors to the common good. Further this code of conduct attempts to restore a group dynamic by encouraging a sense of ownership among the employees having gone through the period of restructuring and extensive layoffs during the 1990s.

Oil companies' codes of conduct emphasise commitments that constitute responses to accusations against them, particularly concerning oil extraction and transport. Royal Dutch/Shell, for instance, is a firm well accustomed to public scrutiny.[24] After dealing with accusations of collusion with apartheid in South Africa, the firm was attacked by Greenpeace in 1991 for its actions concerning the Brent Spar platform sunk in the North Sea after being retired from service. The firm found itself in the hot seat once again for turning a blind eye to exactions imposed by the Nigerian dictatorship on the Ogonis. These issues have allowed boycotts initiated by environmentalist organisations to enjoy a measure of success, particularly in Germany. Concerns raised by these accusations are reflected in the 1997 code where special attention is paid to offshore installations for example.[25] In the case of TotalElfFina's code, oil transport was the focus of certain changes adopted in 2000 after the *Erika* was shipwrecked in December 1999. Similarly, the code's focus on the development of extraction areas answers to earlier accusations claiming that the company benefitted from army support to recruit labour for the construction of a pipeline in Burma between 1995 and 1999.[26]

The environment would seem, therefore, to constitute a prominent motif in these firms' codes of conduct; however, beyond this theme lies the way in which workers are treated. Indeed, in the case of the *Erika* for Total or the Brent Spar platform for Shell, environmental catastrophes were linked to the never-ending search for profitability, which also inevitably affected working conditions. For Procter and Gamble or Total in Burma, accused respectively of abusive layoffs and forced work, conditions were affected by the way in which work contracts were broken or established.

Sourcing and Fundamental Rights at Work: An Ongoing Struggle for the Merchant Firm

The issue of fundamental rights at work has been at the heart of series of campaigns launched by associations opposed to poor working conditions in South East Asian or Latin American firms working for multinationals in the clothing and sport shoe manufacturing industries. The firm most affected by these press-promoted, association-led campaigns and investigations has been Nike. This firm was first called into question at the end of the 1980s following strikes in firms working for Nike in South East Asia, instigating the first investigations and formal complaints from human rights associations (including Human Rights Watch). Nike responded by adopting an initial code of conduct in 1992. But the consumer associations continued to uncover numerous violations including the use of child labour,[27] as successive codes were adopted. Finally, the multinational moved towards a system aimed at monitoring firms performing custom work for Nike. One of the culminating points in these movements against Nike came with Michael Moore's interview of Phil Knight in *The Big One* in 1997.

In the face of firms aiming to cut all direct ties with manufacturing to retain only those activities related to model design and product commercialisation, the human rights associations focused their campaigns on exposing ties between multinationals and firms violating ILO principles. Kellwood and Wal Mart were swept up in a scandal in 1998 concerning the manufacturing of the Kathie Lee clothing line, involving a subsidiary of Kellwood called Halmode. The Human Rights Action Service[28] accused them of blocking the creator Kathie Lee's request to monitor the wage and the age of workers in Honduras or in factories located in the infamous Dongguan zone near Shenzhen (Hong Kong's industrial zone). The association acted by publishing a leaflet entitled 'Buyers Guide to Human Rights', which encouraged consumers to write to Kellwood's head office, the address of which could be found printed in the middle of the page containing the article.

For merchant firms, social responsibility corresponds to an ongoing battle between consumer associations and multinationals, a battle linked to the poor working conditions which continually surface in firms newly contracted by multinationals. As is the case for integrative firms, associations play an essential role in calling multinationals into question in their home countries, and likewise their home markets, regarding their practices in developing countries.[29] The result has been a conflictual process through which working conditions in firms manufacturing sports shoes and clothing for multinationals have markedly improved, particularly by means of reinforcing the monitoring procedures that ensure the proper application of codes by subcontractors.

Re-establishing a Community at Work: The Objective of the Supervisor Firm

The importance of monitoring revealed in Boeing or Cable and Wireless's codes reflects these firms' tendency towards extensive outsourcing, which has in turn led to the coexistence on a single site of several firms working on the same product. In Boeing's case, the adoption in 2000 of a code of conduct applying to *all* workers making their airplanes was a continuation of an extensive shift in the firm's activities, caused in large part by competition with Airbus throughout the 1990s. Indeed, at the end of 1995, Boeing was faced with a 69-day strike over the issues of health insurance and ever-increasing subcontracting. The firm's chaotic situation was prolonged by its renewed involvement in the aeronautics market, implying an increased rate of work and simultaneously, the purchase (contested by the European authorities) of MacDonnell Douglas in 1998, which led to job cuts.

Boeing's code of conduct is therefore a reaction to the necessity of organising the coexistence of employees from different subcontractors and, in some cases, even consultants. The code reflects the general orientation in the aeronautics industry towards outsourcing, linked in part to the competition between Boeing and Airbus and in part to financial market pressure on labour costs. Outsourcing in this industry has gone beyond the subcontracting of peripheral activities such as cleaning or building maintenance, extending as far as entrusting some aspects of equipment design to consulting companies, notably in order to prevent contracted engineers from benefitting from collective agreements. This was one of the causes of the 1995 conflict: outsourcing affected the highest paid positions and the balance of the firm's health insurance scheme. In the case of Airbus in Toulouse, France, outsourcing allowed the firm to cut out engineers covered by the metalworker's agreement, provoking a union struggle for the recognition of a 'working community' which would include all workers present on a site in the electoral base for a works council comprising Airbus employees as well as workers from other firms.[30] Thus, the adoption of Boeing's code of conduct is a product of both the outsourcing of tasks on their production sites in the aeronautics industry and the union battles aiming to limit the resulting social consequences.

Intellectual Assets: A Concern for the Knowledge Firm

The codes of firms dealing with 'new technologies' share a common concern over the ownership of assets and more particularly the ownership of discoveries within their firm. This concern is linked firstly with the desire to establish the firm's ownership over what is produced, a priority being that employees must not use instruments or software created by other firms in order to avoid legal disputes with other software and instrument creators. Indeed, the issue of intellectual property is very delicate in the context of this type of firm, particularly in regard to financial valuation. The importance of intellectual assets can be observed to some extent in most firms, including clothing firms such as GAP or Kellwood, which centre their American-based activities on creating patterns which are then sent to manufacturing establishments in Latin America or South East Asia (Davis, 2009). But the information and communication technologies industry is the most sensitive to this issue: even the constituent elements of their software must not be seen to be similar to those used elsewhere in software belonging to another firm. This extreme sensitivity calls into question the seemingly peaceful vision of technological clusters such as the Silicon Valley, by underlining the tensions created by the battle for ownership of discoveries. The emergence of the freeware *Linux*, which caused Intel to ally with IBM against the SCO group, owner of the rights to the *Unix* code used in *Linux*,[31] is a telling example of these tensions.

The defence of intellectual property on the internet has also become an issue. At the end of the 1990s, pressure on internet providers increased, notably in the United States with the adoption of the Digital Millennium Act in 1998. This act accords audio and video recording companies, or their representatives, a right to action allowing them to subpoena users downloading copyright material. In Verizon's code adopted in 2000, there is an emphasis on the confidentiality of information provided to the firm by users (including the Federal government) which reflects the 1998 legislation as well as the Recording Industry Association of America (RIAA) suit against peer-to-peer sharing, involving Naspter and Kazaa, and against its users. The legal battles continued into the 2000s, and in 2003 Verizon's confidentiality policy was challenged in court by the RIAA in hopes that the identities of subscribers suspected of offences would be divulged. This challenge was a response to a development concerning the way in which files are shared, namely that sharing was no longer occurring via an intermediary site, but through software requiring the identification of users and computers suspected of sharing. In 2003–2004, the United States Court of Appeal in the District of Columbia Circuit became the ultimate venue of decision, hosting the appeal of the case opposing the RIAA and Verizon, as well as a suit brought by the American Civil Liberties Association supporting subscriber confidentiality.[32] The result was a ruling in favour of Verizon.[33] The tendency towards increased measures of protection for intellectual property online, however, has continued with the recent ruling against users in the United States[34] and the passing of the HADOPI[35] law in France.

CONCLUSION

Conceptualising corporate social responsibility as a social fact allows it to be understood as something other than the simple proliferation of declarations of principles decreed by multinationals to regulate the evolution of activities on a global scale. Indeed, codes of conduct are not regulations that spontaneously stem from firms, but are reactions to 'responsibility generating situations'. These situations represent, from Facuonnet's standpoint, instances of 'social deliberation', or in other words, situations of tension and conflict in which codes of conduct represent reactions to initiatives of other actors, particularly non-governmental organisations.

Through the analysis of codes of conduct, a typology of firms has been established and, by associating these codes with 'collective mobilisations', a typology of other actors has also been put forward, permitting the codes to be understood according to contexts of mobilisation concerning both collective action, via associations for example, and legal action before the courts. Consumer associations, therefore, play a primordial role in questioning the practices of firms operating in developing countries. After investigation, they act through boycott campaigns which affect firms' sales and profitability, and sometimes through lawsuits in the firm's country of origin, founded on the right of action accorded in the case of basic human rights violations in other parts of the world. But consumer associations are not alone: other firms and unions are also important actors in the creation of 'responsibility generating situations'. Corporate social responsibility, therefore, contains an inherent aspect of negotiation, a trend which is now spreading with the creation of international framework agreements (da Costa and Rehfeldt, 2008; Descolonges and Saincy, 2006). Moreover, rather than challenging positive law by artificially opposing hard law and soft law, social corporate responsibility and the codes of conduct that contribute to it are applied according to existing legal frameworks, whether they be ILO principles, or national legislation (determining the age of majority and minimum wage, for example).

Thus, corporate social responsibility is not a simple unilateral initiative; it is first and foremost a response to the institutional interventions and collective mobilisations inherent to the democratic way of life in a state applying the rule of law. The plurality of configurations denoted by the codes of conduct must be taken into account in order to discern the diverse ways in which the issues of work and workers' rights are involved. In the classic configuration of corporate social responsibility concerning the environment, the role of workers in environmental choices is called into question. In terms of ILO fundamental rights, firms often intervene too late to prevent abuses, the issue being the delayed application of monitoring procedures caused by a constantly increasing number of tiers in subcontracted production. In the 'supervisor' configuration, the objective is to re-establish the concept of the production unit, and consequently a functioning community at work, despite the coexistence of many firms on one site. Finally, in the case of intellectual property, the issue is sharing ownership of products created within the firm.

(Translation by Victoria Surtees)

NOTES

*   This chapter takes up the analysis of data collected for an earlier publication: Béthoux Elodie, Didry Claude and Mias Arnaud (2007), 'What codes of conduct tell us: corporate social responsibility and the nature of the multinational corporation', *Corporate Governance, an International Review,* **15**(1), 77–90. An alternative analysis is proposed here. The author wishes to thank Victoria Surtees for her excellent translation of the original text.

1.   The promotion of 'corporate social responsibility' is an important element of employer discourse that seeks to limit public initiatives seen as limiting firms' manoeuvring capabilities.

2.   On this idea, see Mazuyer (2007).

3.   See European Commission (2001). On the decline of the 'single market' convention, see Robert Salais's contribution to this book.

4.   For more history and a deeper look at international commitments concerning labour law, see Drouin (2005).

5.   With for example, the theme of the 'democratisation of the economy', promoted by the European Confederation of Free Trade Unions (which became the European Trade Union Confederation in 1974), see Didry and Mias (2005).

6.   From a report submitted by a high-level group in 1974.

7.   See Drouin (2005).

8.   For example: 'Principle 3: Businesses should uphold the freedom of association and the effective recognition of the right to collective bargaining'

9.   On French firms' initiatives concerning the application of the Compact's principles, see Mazuyer et al. (2010).

10. On the conditions and details on the efficacy of labour law on national and international scales, see Auvergnon (2008).

11. On the site: http://www.ilo.org/dyn/basi/VpiSearch.Main (accessed from 2003 to 2005).

12. For a presentation of the guidelines used for collecting data from the corpus and corpus expectations, see Diller (1999).

13. Codes of conduct and collective agreements can be differentiated by their method of adoption: the first is adopted unilaterally by the management of a firm whereas the second implies negotiation between representatives from the management and unions respectively.

14. Béthoux et al. (2007).

15. Three categories representing 38% of the sentences.

16. Attested in all the other categories.

17. Two categories representing 25% of the sentences.

18. Three categories representing 37% of the sentences.

19. 'Integrity in a business relationship means that all participants are working together for the common good, and are not making decisions based on self-interest.' (Code Raython Company, 2000).

20. What Alfred Marshall terms 'industrial districts', such as Lyon's silk industry for example, were at the heart of the movement towards collective agreements in France, see Didry (2002).
21. For Paul Fauconnet, responsibility is not simply an idea linked to individual wrongdoings; it is a 'social fact', a characteristic attributed to actors in fixed social and institutional configurations.
22. *Le Monde*, 22 February 1994.
23. *Les Echos*, 13 October 1999.
24. On Royal Dutch/Shell's communications strategy, see Patrick Laprise (2005).
25. 'All major installations having significant environmental risks should have been certified. This includes as a minimum:
    All crude oil and natural gas export terminals, gas plans, offshore platforms, major flow stations, floating production and storage vessels, all Shell operated refineries and chemicals manufacturing facilities'.
26. The firm was later sued in France and Belgium by Burmese victims in 2003 but the case was dismissed after a settlement was reached out of court. At Total's behest, Bernard Kouchner wrote a report on the Burmese situation that can be found on Total's website: http://birmanie.total.com/fr/controverse/p_4_4.htm (accessed 16 August 2011)
27. For a timeline of the main campaigns addressing working conditions in factories producing for Nike, see the following page: http://depts.washington.edu/ccce/polcommcampaigns/NikeChronology.htm (accessed 16 August 2011)
28. http://www.humanrightsaction.net/ (accessed 16 August 2011)
29. Duval (2006) discusses NGOs' role as 'interpellators'.
30. For more on this dispute that has lasted more than a decade, see Boussard and Pétracchi (2008).
31. 'Unix : Intel s'associe à IBM dans la bataille qui l'oppose à SCO', *Les Echos*, 13 January 2004.
32. 'A.C.L.U. Challenges Music Industry in Court', *New York Times*, Monday, 29 September 2003, available at: http://www.nytimes.com/2003/09/29/business/media/29aclu.html (accessed 16 August 2011)
33. 'Les Etats-Unis accentuent répression et prévention', *Le figaro*, Friday 16 July 2004.
34. 'Joel Tenenbaum symbole du téléchargement illégal aux Etats-Unis, reconnu coupable', *Le monde*, 31 July 2009.
35. Concerning the creation of a High Authority Promoting the Distribution and Protection of Creative Works on the Internet.

REFERENCES

Auvergnon, P. (ed.) (2008), *L'effectivité du droit du travail, à quelles conditions?*, Bordeaux: Presses Universitaires de Bordeaux.

Béthoux, E., C. Didry and A. Mias (2007), 'What Codes of Conduct Tell Us: Corporate Social Responsibility and the Nature of the Multinational Corporation', *Corporate Governance: An International Review*, **15**(1), 77–90.

Boussard, E. and X. Pétracchi (2008), 'Regards croisés sur la communauté de travail', *Le droit ouvrier*, July, 361–366.

Crouch, C. (1995), 'La société des savoirs ? Un objectif encore lointain. Les implications des changements dans le commerce international (1976–1989) sur les compétences professionnelles', *Sociologie du travail*, **95**(4), 595–621.

da Costa, I. and U. Rehfeldt (2008), 'Transnational collective bargaining at company level: Historical developments', in K. Papadakis (ed.) *Cross-Border Social Dialogue and Agreements, An emerging industrial relations framework?*, Geneva: ILO, pp.43–64.

Davis, G.F. (2009), 'The Rise and Fall of Finance and the End of the Society of Organizations', *Academy of Management Perspectives*, **52**, 27–43.

Descolonges, M. and B. Saincy (eds) (2006), *Les nouveaux enjeux de la négociation sociale internationale*, Paris: La Découverte.

Didry, C. (2002), *Naissance de la convention collective, débats juridiques et luttes sociales en France au début du XXᵉ siècle*, Paris: EHESS.

Didry, C. (2009), 'Retour sur une innovation institutionnelle méconnue: l'émergence du Dialogue social en Europe', *L'année sociologique*, **59**(2), 417–447.

Didry, C. and A. Mias (2005), *Le moment Delors, les syndicats au cœur de l'Europe sociale*, Bruxelles: Peter Lang.

Diller, J. (1999), 'A social conscience in the global marketplace? Labour dimensions of codes of conduct, social labelling and investor initiatives', *International Labour Review*, **138**(2), 107–139.

Drouin, R.-C. (2005), *International Framework Agreements: A Study in Transnational Labour Regulation*, PhD, University of Cambridge.

Drouin, R.-C. (2008), 'The role of the ILO in promoting the development of international framework agreements', in K. Papadakis (ed.), *Cross-Border Social Dialogue and Agreements, An emerging industrial relations framework?*, Geneva: ILO, pp.237–267.

Duval, G. (2006), 'L'irruption des ONG dans le champ de la négociation', in M. Descolonges and B. Saincy (eds), *Les nouveaux enjeux de la négociation sociale internationale*, Paris: La Découverte, pp.139–154.

European Commission (2001), 'Promoting a European Framework for Corporate Social Responsibility', Green Paper, COM (2001) 366 final.

Fauconnet, P. (1928), *La responsabilité, étude de sociologie*, Paris: Alcan.

Laprise, P. (2005), 'La responsabilité sociale et environnementale de l'entreprise et la pétrolière Shell: une stratégie environnementale de légitimation', Conference Presentation, 'Responsabilité sociale de l'entreprise: réalité, mythe ou mystification?', 17–18 March, Nancy.

Mazuyer, E. (2007), *L'harmonisation sociale européenne, processus et modèle*, Bruxelles: Bruylant.

Mazuyer, E., P. Deumier and S. Laulom (2010), 'L'application du Pacte mondial des Nations Unies par les entreprises françaises', in E. Mazuyer, *Regards croisés sur le phénomène de la RSE*, Paris: La documentation française.

Sobzack, A. (2002), *Réseaux de société et codes de conduite: un nouveau modèle de régulation des relations de travail pour les entreprises européennes*, Paris: LGDJ.

11. Reflexive labour law, capabilities and the future of social Europe

Simon Deakin and Ralf Rogowski

INTRODUCTION

This chapter discusses the role that reflexive labour law has played, and can play in the future, in the development of European social policy. The core of the reflexive law approach is an evolutionary conception of law which provides both an analytical framework for studying the operation and effects of European labour law, and a basis for the evaluation of European social policy. Reflexive approaches to law and governance have informed a number of initiatives over the past two decades, most notably the development of the open method of coordination in various contexts including that of employment policy. Their influence has not, however, been confined to 'soft law' measures, but has extended to the re-design of 'hard law' mechanisms including EU Directives and laws adopted at member state level. These reflexive initiatives, we will argue, have had some success in generating a learning process around the formulation and implementation of social policy, which has helped to re-legitimate labour law at EU and member state level, and has contributed to the adoption of new legal measures in areas which include work-life balance laws. In this regard, reflexive approaches have been complementary to efforts to construct a social right agenda around the concept of labour market capabilities. However, reflexive labour law operates in tension with pressures for the homogenisation of member states' labour law systems which stem from a number of sources. These include the development of the European Court of Justice's internal market jurisprudence in the line of cases beginning with *Viking* and *Laval*, the Court's related tendency to treat Directives as pre-empting member state initiative, and, more recently, in the wake of the global financial crisis, the pressures on member states to adjust domestic welfare state regimes in line with the disciplines imposed by the EU's emerging agenda of financial stabilisation.

In developing these themes, the next section sets out the elements of the theory of reflexive labour law and makes the case for understanding the evolution of EU social policy in terms of the emergence and maturing of reflexive techniques. The following section compares and contrasts reflexive law theory with that of the capability approach, noting points of difference as well as elements of continuity between the two approaches. We then look at the challenges to social policy posed by the *Viking* and *Laval* judgments and the impact of financial stabilisation measures.

REFLEXIVE LABOUR LAW AND THE EVOLUTION OF EU SOCIAL POLICY

The Concept of Reflexive Labour Law

More than 15 years after the publication of *Reflexive Labour Law* (Rogowski and Wilthagen, 1994), its claim that a new labour law theory was needed to match the complexity of labour law systems in the modern world with an appropriately articulated theoretical design has been borne out by experience. The theory of reflexive labour law is based on modern socio-logical systems theory and on post-structuralist approaches to law and society. It transforms the insights of these disciplines into questions which are relevant for the sociology and theory of law. The core of its approach is to view the legal system as an autonomous, functional order, discourse or system, located within society on the same plane as the economy or the political system (Luhmann, 1995, 2004; Teubner, 1993). In common with these other social sub-systems, the legal system is ultimately guided by the need to protect its own autopoiesis, that is, its self-referentiality and self-reproduction. The recognition of this fact provides the basis for a realistic assessment of the limits, but also the possibilities, of law as a mechanism for social change.

The theory of reflexive law argues that the legal system becomes con-sciously reflexive when it recognises that the societal domains which it purports to regulate, and to which it also seeks to respond, are themselves independent autopoietic systems, which have arisen from the most perti-nent characteristic of modern society, namely functional differentiation. The separation of law and politics from each other and from the sphere of the market creates the possibility of a decentred social structure, in which power is diffused among a number of autonomous but mutually linked institutions. The autonomy of the legal system is the precondition for the impersonal and abstract administration of justice, and for the institutional channelling of the state's monopoly on the use of force which is associated with the idea of the state based on the 'rule of law' or *Rechtsstaat*. Dissolving the boundary between the legal system and its external context would be counter-productive, as it would involve sacrificing the abstract and impersonal character of legal rules and their application (Zumbansen, 2008). To the extent that law loses this autonomy, it comes to operate increasingly as the pure expression of political power, or as the simple manifestation of economic advantage in the terms of trade set by the market (Supiot, 2010). At the same time, law's separation from other social sub-systems constrains its use as an instrument of social and economic policy-making and insulates it from societal influences which would ensure its more effective alignment with its economic and political context. This is particularly problematic for areas of law such as labour law which are shaped by instrumental policy concerns and evaluated by reference to their social and economic impacts. The solution lies not in denying the possibility that law can influence, and be influenced by, its external context, but in finding institutional means to express the reality of law's autopoietic nature. In practice this means accepting that law is both enabled and constrained by its autopoiesis.

In an autopoietic perspective, social systems such as law or the economy are conceived to be 'operationally closed' but 'cognitively open'. 'Operational closure' means that the system reproduces itself entirely by reference to its own internal structures and modes of operation: from the internal viewpoint of those involved in the operation of legal acts such as legislation or adjudication, only law can produce law. 'Cognitive openness', on the other hand, implies that the system evolves over time by reference to an external context which consists of other, similarly constituted social systems. Systems are inherently dynamic: they are capable, through their own internal processes, of variation or mutation, and they respond, albeit imperfectly, to selective pressures coming from their social environment to which they are linked by mechanisms of 'structural coupling'. In this way, law, politics and the economy can be said to 'co-evolve', that is to say, to evolve by response to privileged irritations which each creates for the other. The fit between them is incomplete, since 'structural coupling' can only produce various degrees of perturbation between systems, to which the operational processes of self-reproduction may or may not respond in direct terms. However, reflexive law theory is not, deep down, a theory of system closure alone. Systems are simultaneously open and closed in the way just described. Systems mutually influence each other, and causal interactions can be assumed to operate at some level between them. What *is* denied are claims to the effect that the legal system is *completely* open to the influences of other systems, of the kind that are made when the 'inherent' economic or political logic of a given legal measure is invoked.

The theory of reflexive law has concrete implications for regulatory design. Its starting point is that in seeking to influence other autopoietic systems which are operationally closed to their environment, the legal system must have resort to indirect means of regulation. Legal intervention is dependent for its effects on self-regulation within the systems which are the target of legal initiatives. Thus the law can only work in so far as it facilitates self-reflexion and self-regulation. This implies a shift from substantive to procedural law. However, it is important, in this regard, not to confuse legal forms with their regulatory functions. From a reflexive point of view, the use of 'default' rules in place of legal 'mandates' may be appropriate in particular settings as a way of triggering evolutionary responses within the social systems that are the focus of regulation. Rules which are mandatory in terms of their legal form still depend for their effects on inducing certain responses from the actors to whom they are addressed, which will be shaped by the systemic context in which those actors are operating. If the systemic conditions are not right, the law will be evaded or ignored by at least part of the population it is aimed at. Conversely, 'default' rules, which formally give parties to transactions a range of options to choose from in tailoring their reaction to a legal rule, may end up inducing a more or less uniform response in the nature of a 'pooling equilibrium', again depending on context. Thus in general, the form of a legal rule, on its own, tells us little or nothing about how the information it imparts will be received and acted on in another systemic context (Deakin and Carvalho, 2010). For this reason, it is essential to go beyond legal formalism in the sociological or economic study of law: reflexive law is an interdisciplinary discipline, which combines analysis of internal legal processes with an understanding of law's context drawn from the social sciences.

Harry Arthurs has recently put reflexive labour law theory to the test in a paper which looks at the phenomenon of corporate self-regulation. In applying reflexive theory to the practice of corporate codes of conduct, the UN Global Compact and the related idea of 'ratcheting' labour standards, he arrives at the conclusion that 'reflexive labour law may be becoming more commonplace, that it may indeed emerge as the characteristic legal form of the future' (Arthurs, 2007: 28–29). At the same time, applying political economy logic in analysing these developments, he argues that the rise of reflexive labour law goes hand in hand with neo-liberal economic policy-making and with deregulation of labour law and welfare state regimes.

This criticism seems misplaced. Reflexive techniques are in principle capable of being applied to a wide range of policy initiatives. Their use in fields such as labour law was initially stimulated by concerns that 'command and control' regulation of the sort associated with some of the regulatory initiatives of the immediate post-1945 decades had failed to achieve the instrumental goals set out for them. Critiques of the means used to implement the egalitarian and solidaristic aims of post-1945 welfare states were undoubtedly combined, in some cases, with critiques of those aims. However, the link is not inevitable. The concept of reflexive law has been used, in numerous contexts, as a way into a debate about improving the effectiveness of labour law interventions, and thereby of responding to the neoliberal critique of labour law. Conversely, by no means all or even most neoliberal policy initiatives use reflexive techniques; they just as often involve the use of traditional 'command and control' approaches to the use of law as an instrument of policy. They also make assumptions about the permeability of the legal system, and its openness to economic influence in the form of market pricing and similar effects, which run counter to reflexive law theory.

The Reflexive Dimension of European Social Policy

The relationship between EU-level labour law and the labour law systems of the member states can be understood in reflexive terms. There has never been a time when the role of EU law was seen in terms of simple, top-down harmonisation of national level labour laws. At the time of the passage of the Treaty of Rome, social policy was given a marginal place in the emerging European legal order, but not because social concerns were seen as less important than the task of building an internal (or as it was then known), a common market. Instead, it was understood that the principal task of maintaining and advancing strong welfare states lay with the individual national systems. The case for general harmonisation of laws, leading to uniform legal regimes, was rejected for labour law as it was for other areas of regulatory law, in part on the grounds that social and living standards would 'level up' in an open economy based on the free circulation of goods and persons. This was not the only basis for leaving social policy to the member states, however. The original member states had each made clear political commitments, in most cases embedded in constitutional guarantees, to the protection of social rights. In addition, their economic autonomy was an important factor in limiting the role that transnational social policy would play: it was expected that, under a regime of flexible exchange rates, individual countries would not have to respond to a loss of economic competitiveness by cutting wages and social standards (Deakin, 1996). At this point, currency union, which would eventually remove this flexibility from the member states, was not a goal of the EU.

Notwithstanding the limited role of social policy in the Rome Treaty, the seeds of social Europe were sown in a number of provisions which contemplated a role for harmonising measures in addressing the possibility of social dumping. This was the basis for the adoption of the right to equal pay between women and men in Article 119 of the original EEC Treaty (now Article 153 of the Treaty on the Functioning of the European Union (TFEU)): countries which did not have effective laws against sex discrimination would, it was thought, enjoy an artificial competitive advantage over those which did, which could trigger a race to the bottom. Although this measure, and the thinking that lay behind it, was dormant for almost twenty years, they were both revived in the mid-1970s and served as the foundation for the two-pronged approach, based on Court rulings and newly adopted directives, to the enlargement of social policy which began at that time. The extension of EU-level social policy was seen as the necessary complement to the expansion of the Community's membership and the deepening of the internal market. The increase in the membership of the EEC from the original six member states to nine members in the early 1970s triggered the adoption of a social action programme which was aimed at countering the expected dislocating effects of transborder mergers and corporate restructuring. This was to lead on, by the middle years of that decade, to the first directives on collective redundancies and transfers of undertakings. In the mid-1980s, the Single Act was accompanied by new Treaty provisions aimed at stimulating EU-wide standards in the health and safety field. At Maastricht in 1992, Treaty measures taken to put in place the single currency were counterbalanced by the institutionalisation of EU-level social dialogue and the extension of powers to make labour law directives in the Social Agreement and the Protocol on Social Policy, which was formally integrated into the EC Treaty, as UK opposition was removed, at Amsterdam in 1997. Following on from these institutional changes, the 1990s and early 2000s were a period of considerable legislative activity in social policy, with the adoption of the directives on working time (1993), European works councils (1994), parental leave (1996), part-time work (1997), fixed-term employment (1999), equal treatment in employment (2000), and information and consultation of employees (2002) (see Barnard and Deakin, 2011).

The transnational labour law system which emerged from this process was very different in nature from those of the individual member states. Most obviously, it was far from being a comprehensive labour code in terms of its subject-matter. Whole areas, in particular collective labour law and legal aspects of wage-fixing, were excluded from the EU's legal powers. But EU labour law also differed in terms of the techniques it used from the labour law systems of the member states (Streeck, 1996). EU law is a hybrid of domestic and international law, which has developed over time to form a corpus of law which is largely *sui generis*. EU-level norms can have immediate implications for individual actors, including employers in the private sector, through the doctrine of direct effect, but they are principally addressed to the member states. In this sense they more closely resemble ILO Conventions and similar international law instruments, but here too there are differences. From an early stage, EU-level measures were designed to stimulate a learning process at member state level. A number of legal techniques were developed to this end. *Social progress clauses* envisaged the standards set out in directives as minima, below which member states could not go, but which they could improve on. *Non-regression clauses* stipulated that the implementation of directives at member state level should not be the occasion for a weakening of worker protection, even if the minimum set by the relevant EU measure was below the level already guaranteed by the domestic laws of the state in question. In the 1990s, new devices were added. The *controlled derogations* of the working time directive allowed for the variation of statutory standards through collective and, more controversially, individual agreement. The *fall-back provisions* of the European Works Councils directive introduced the logic of default rules, imposing a standard form of information and consultation only if the parties could not make their own agreement within more loosely defined parameters. *Negotiated laws* were recognised in the expanded role given to the transnational social partners in drafting framework collective agreements which formed the basis for the directives on part-time work and temporary employment.

As the body of EU-level labour law expanded in the course of the 1990s, the reflexive dimension of EU labour law arguably became its defining element. EU labour laws were reflexive in their formation (direct input from self-regulatory bodies), in their structure (the use of defaults and derogations), and in their implementation (stimulation of self-regulation at national, industry and firm level). Although combined with and operating alongside the deepening of the internal market programme, EU labour law was not part of a deregulatory agenda during this period. While some scope for regulatory competition between the member states was allowed, this was consistent with a 'market steering' approach in which states were encouraged to compete on the basis of respect for a core of social rights and protections (Deakin and Wilkinson, 1994). In principle, at least, the aim of social progress clauses and non-regression clauses was to rule out a race to the bottom.

Reflexive Coordination of European Employment Policies

The idea that EU law played a steering and coordinating role with regard to member state practice received further confirmation in the development of the open method of coordination ('OMC'), and the associated 'Lisbon strategy'. First announced as such at the European Council in Lisbon March 2000, the OMC has antecedents in the European employment strategy ('EES'), which was developed in the mid-1990s and formally recognised in the Treaty of Amsterdam (Mosher and Trubek, 2004; Ashiagbor, 2006). As we have just seen, the ideas underlying the OMC, in particular that of regulatory learning based on cross-national diversity, had resonances in the approach taken in the formulation of 'hard law' measures such as directives in the social policy field. Thus the OMC should not be seen as marking a fundamental departure from earlier approaches to EU-level governance and regulation (Scharpf, 1999). Nevertheless, in its emphasis on benchmarking, auditing and targeting, it gave a new emphasis to non-legal mechanisms for policy formulation and implementation.

The extension of the OMC in a multiplicity of fields over time led to an increase of complexity in its operation that triggered, in turn, new thinking about the way open coordination was working at European level. The OMC in employment was redesigned in 2003. This reform addressed problems of effectiveness, legitimacy and visibility by calling for a broader set of actors to be involved at member state level (Kilpatrick, 2006: 140–142). Concerns over the operation of the EES, such as the lack of qualitative dimensions of indicators and insufficient support for mutual learning, had previously been voiced (Schmid and Kull, 2004). The 2003 and 2004 Kok Reports (European Commission, 2003, 2004), commented adversely on the specificity of employment policy targets and democratic participation in the process. At the same time, the operation of a variety of OMCs next to each other was seen as giving rise to excessive complexity for both the European institutions and the member states. A reflexive strand can be seen in the approach to streamlining the OMC which led to policies based on the 'coordination of coordination' (Rogowski, 2007, 2008). The idea of linking the economic, employment and social OMCs in order to increase their mutual effectiveness was not, however, fully realised. In 2005, as a result of a critical assessment of the OMCs in economic and employment policies, in particular with respect to their actual effects on unemployment as well as employment rates, and with a view to enhancing the prospect of reaching the Lisbon targets (also referred to as a 'relaunch of Lisbon'), the Broad Economic Policy Guidelines (BEPG) and the Employment Guidelines were combined to Integrated Economic and Employment

Guidelines (Jørgensen, 2005). This meant the creation of a unified timeta-ble that accompanied the switch from one-year to three-year cycles that had already been agreed in 2003 (the first cycle started in 2003 and the second in 2006). The National Action Plans (NAP) for Employment and the Joint Employment Report (JER) were replaced by sections within member states' National Lisbon Reform Programmes (NRPs) and the Commis-sion's Annual Lisbon Progress Report (Armstrong et al., 2008).

'Coordination of coordination' can also be seen in the form of the ongoing streamlining of the social policy OMCs. The goal here was to modernise social protection systems by making coordination of social protection more effective. In the beginning, streamlining and simplifying of the social policy OMCs was confined to the method itself by providing a clearer definition of the scope of OMC. However, streamlining of policy coordination was expanded and started to become an ambition linked to the overarching goal of improving the quality and the stability of socio-economic governance of the EU as a whole. The right policy mix was supposed to create a 'virtuous circle' of economic and social progress (European Commission, 2003). A new *Joint Social Protection Report* of the Commission and the Council replaced in 2005 the *Social Protection in Europe* Report as well as the joint reports on social inclusion, pensions and policy cooperation in healthcare and long-term care. The member states' contribution changed accordingly. After 2006, member states prepared National Action Plans that covered all three social policy fields together. The 2007 *Joint Social Protection Report* was the first report that evaluates integrated National Reports on strategies for social inclusion, pensions, healthcare and long-term care.

There is now a growing body of research critically assessing the OMC (see Pochet, 2005; Büchs, 2007; Heidenreich and Zeitlin, 2009). Doubts have been voiced, for example about the implementation process of the EES, alleging that the production of National Action Plans was often confined to technocrats and government officials (Zeitlin, 2005). The monitoring process has been described as riddled with cultural misunder-standings and linguistic ambiguities (Barbier, 2003, 2008). Furthermore, the choice of indicators has been criticised for favouring a quantitative rate of employment (largely neglecting qualitative aspects) and alternative indicators that focus on the development of capabilities and favour an informational basis in selecting social justice have been suggested (Salais, 2006, 2007).

These doubts do not seem to have stopped the OMC playing an increasingly important role in social policy. From the mid-2000s, the Commission's overarching concern was to link European coordination effects with the reform of welfare policies at member state level. The

Commission put high hopes, in this context, on improved exchange of information and opportunities for mutual learning in order to promote national reform processes (European Council, 2006). However, the Commission's evaluation of the Lisbon Strategy led to critical insights on its effectiveness (European Commission, 2010), and the reliance on OMC as a key instrument for future EU policy-making seems now in doubt.

THE ROLE OF SOCIAL POLICY AND SOCIAL RIGHTS IN BUILDING LABOUR MARKET CAPACITIES: THE CAPABILITY APPROACH

Capabilities and Social Rights

A main contribution of reflexive law theory to the analysis of EU labour law has been the offer of an improved basis for assessing and analysing different regulatory techniques used in the legal system. In principle, it is compatible with a number of different substantive policy objectives. In the context of European social and employment policy, it has largely been deployed to implement policy goals which have been defined separately. The task of giving substantive content to social policy lies elsewhere. In this section we consider the relevance, in this context, of capability theory as a basis for the recognition of social rights and social policy more generally within the legal and institutional framework of the EU.

Sen's capability approach argues that policies and institutions should be evaluated by reference to how far they enhance individual capabilities, which he defines as the degrees of substantive freedom that enable individuals to achieve the subjectively defined states of well-being that he calls 'functionings' (Sen, 2009). Economic growth, on the one hand, and legally guaranteed rights, on the other, are only means to the greater end of securing individual well-being in this sense. Nussbaum more explicitly argues that policy should aim to fulfill certain objectively defined developmental goals which include 'life', 'bodily health', 'bodily integrity', 'play', the 'ability to control one's environment', and 'affiliation' (Nussbaum, 2000). Nussbaum's list of core capabilities can be seen as having a dual source: it is based, on the one hand, on empirical observation and experience concerning the basic conditions for human well-being in all societies, while, on the other, giving expression to social and economic rights set out in fundamental legal texts including the UN Declaration on Human Rights and the International Covenant on Economic, Social and Cultural Rights. Again, more explicitly than Sen, Nussbaum argues that legal and other institutions of a given polity should be designed with the aim of ensuring that a threshold level of well-being is achievable for all its citizens, broadly defined. The differences in emphasis between the view of Sen and Nussbaum are less important, for present purposes, than their common focus on individual freedom as the end or goal of social policy, rather than as a means to another end such as economic growth or market efficiency.

Sen's analysis places greater emphasis than Nussbaum on the value of learning and deliberation over the goals of policy and on the role of context in shaping the substantive elements of the capability approach. He does not set out in detail a conception of the goals which social policy should aim for. He does however provide some discussion on the contribution of markets in general and labour markets in particular to the enhancement of capabilities. In *Development as Freedom* (1999), he argues that individuals have reason to value certain freedoms which labour markets provide. Access to waged labour is an important capability for groups which have traditionally been subject to social discrimination and exclusion from participation in economic activity beyond the structure of the family. In Sen's work this argument is addressed to the case of developing countries in which labour markets are still in a process of formation, but the claim that labour market access is a significant capability in its own right is one with wider resonance. Sen's argument can be extended in the context of industrialised societies to argue the case for labour market institutions which provide alternatives to more traditional forms of risk allocation (social security law as an alternative to the family and access to the land), or more coercive ones (such as the poor law), and which seek to remove barriers to market access in the form of social discrimination (equal treatment law), (Deakin, 2009a). Extending this argument further, it can be argued that labour law rules with an egalitarian or solidaristic orientation support, and are supported by, democratic institutions which ensure a voice in the political process for groups most exposed to social and economic risks. This implies a role for labour law in not just mitigating the effect of social risks, but in establishing the conditions for effective deliberation in and beyond the workplace, through support for independent trade unionism and other forms of autonomous worker organisation, and for the principle of freedom of association in the context of collective bargaining and the right to strike (Kolben, 2010).

Legal Underpinnings of the Capability Approach

Sen devotes a good deal of space in his recent works (e.g. Sen, 2009) to analysing normative theories of justice, but does not go into detail on the kinds of legal techniques needed to implement policy initiatives drawing on the capability approach. Thus the kind of legal order implied by the capability approach has to be inferred from his wider body of work, and possible complementarities identified between Sen's arguments and insights from the sociology and economics of law (see Deakin and Supiot, 2009). The starting point here is to consider the role of what Sen calls 'conversion factors'. These are features of the physical or societal environment which assist the conversion of individuals' endowments into functionings. In introducing the idea of conversion factors, Sen emphasises that individual well-being is only partially linked to a given person's physical capabilities; it depends on a context which is societal, or to be more precise, institutional, in nature. Particular institutions, including those of the legal system, may assist, or frustrate, the process by which individuals realise their desired states or goals. This implies an active role for the legal system in supplementing the operation of markets.

A capability-based approach to understanding the relationship between the legal system and the market rests on three linked propositions. The first is that *markets are not self-constituting*. Markets, whether the 'labour market' understood in abstract terms, or the EU's 'internal market', are neither self-constituting nor self-generating. They rest on institutional underpinnings. Thus there is a role for the legal framework as a 'conversion factor' which both creates and also regulates market-based forms of exchange. This is not inconsistent with a reflexive approach: the relationship between the legal system and the economy is one of co-evolution and mutual constitution. The operational autonomy of the systems does not contradict their adjustment, through co-evolution, to each other's influence, and their mutual adjustment over time to a common societal environment.

A second proposition is that *the exercise of individual choice in market settings rests on institutional capacity-building*. Individual market access is not simply a matter of being left alone by the state ('negative freedom'), but of having the substantive capacity to act as a result of having access to certain social rights recognised and protected by the legal order ('positive freedom'). These include the rights recognised by private law in its limited, nineteenth-century sense, such as the right to hold property and to make contracts: *capacitas* in the narrow legal sense of the term. But they also extend to the rights which the modern welfare state seeks to guarantee, such as access to health care and education, membership of mutual or social insurance schemes for offsetting social and economic risks arising from labour-market participation, and participation in meaningful work: *capacitas* in the broad sense (Deakin and Supiot, 2009).

The third proposition is that in identifying the conditions for the effective co-evolution of market-based and law-based institutions, *a reflexive or learning-based conception of regulation or governance is to be preferred to one based on a 'one size fits all' approach.* The legal system can be understood as codifying and embedding solutions to collective coordination problems (Deakin and Carvalho, 2010). These are more likely to endure when they are the result of a learning process based on a diversity or multiplicity of viable models, and on the mobilisation of the knowledge available to the actors concerned. At this point, reflexive law theory intersects with Sen's open-ended and learning-based conception of capabilities.

The Capability Approach and the Reform of European Social Policy

The question of how to re-frame labour law rights to cope with a changing market and organisational environment was one which EU social policy began to address in the late 1990s, drawing in part on the capability approach. The Supiot Report (Supiot, 2001), commissioned by the EU and first published in French in the late 1990s, argued that labour law was under pressure from deregulatory tendencies and not because new technological or market conditions had abolished the social risks attendant on participation in waged labour. In the form of loss of income arising from unemployment, illness and old age, these risks remained as present as ever, along with the inequalities to which relations of dependence give rise. Rather, changes in technology and work organisation had produced a situation in which the paradigmatic institutions of the welfare state, including collective bargaining and social insurance, were unable to provide effective protection to more than a minority of workers. This was in large part because these institutions created rights which presupposed stable, 'permanent' employment. As a result, the Supiot report argued for a process of labour law reform which went 'beyond employment', a shift which would involve not the abandonment of the protections associated with the employment model, but their extension through a range of new conceptual techniques and policy initiatives. These included the use, within the discourse of labour law, of concepts of labour market status to replace those associated with the more limited status of the employee, and the development of social rights outside the immediate context of the employment relationship, such as 'social drawing rights' which would enable individuals to draw on resources for training and education over the course of a working lifetime.

The approach of the Supiot report was consistent with elements of a capability-based agenda to labour law reform, as set out above (pp. 238–241). This link was emphasised by the inclusion of a chapter in the report which set out the economic case for institutional investment in labour market capacities as a response to calls for increased flexibilisation. To some degree, the ideas set out in the Supiot report drew on emerging tendencies in the labour law systems of some of the member states and in EU-level developments. The concept of social drawing rights found concrete expression in those national systems which expanded access to education and training outside the workplace, introduced greater flexibility into social insurance contribution regimes in order to accommodate time spent outside formal employment, and introduced working time reforms and work-life balance laws which were designed to reconcile family time and employment-related commitments. These developments at member-state level were encouraged by initiatives undertaken within EU law, which combined the 'hard law' approach of directives with the 'soft law' approach of the OMC.

As we have already seen, directives on parental leave, part-time work and fixed-term employment were adopted in the mid to late 1990s. Their aims included the 'normalisation' of flexible forms of work and the removal of barriers to their use. This agenda implied greater legal support for the rights of parents and carers to combine employment with family commitments, hence the coupling of the two directives on the employment relationship with that on parental leave. Each of these directives contained reflexive elements: their substance was derived from framework collective agreements made by the social partners at EU level, and they provided for a number of flexible implementation mechanisms, including provision for derogations or variations of statutory standards through collective bargaining. The aims of the directives complemented those of the employment policy OMC, which, at this time, emphasised complementarities between the goals of equal treatment in employment with those of work-life balance and flexibility in the form of the employment relationship.

There is evidence of a learning effect occurring in response to these initiatives, with national systems borrowing from one another, and also modulating the impact of the directives at the level of national implementation strategies. The directives had little direct impact on the Nordic systems which had already adopted work-life balance laws providing greater protection than the minima set out in the directives. However, they had a significant impact in other systems which, in effect, borrowed elements of the Nordic approach, adjusted to local circumstances. In Germany, 'over-implementation' of the parental leave directive led to the adoption of a right to part-time work on family-related grounds (Fuchs, 2004; Falkner et al., 2005), while in Britain a more limited but nevertheless significant right to request part-time work was adopted (Deakin and Morris, 2009: 653–654). Both Germany and Britain also moved in the direction of 'leave sharing' between parents, allowing maternity leave rights to be transferred to the father as part of paternity leave entitlements, a model first developed in the Nordic countries. The fixed-term employment directive encouraged a partial liberalisation of the rules governing the adoption of fixed-term contracts in Germany, but their tightening in Britain, indicating a degree of convergence which was not directly mandated by the directive, but can be seen to have been indirectly triggered by it (Deakin, 2009b).

These developments, while significant, were perhaps isolated successes. The Supiot report set out an ambitious agenda for the transformation of national labour law systems, with the EU law acting as the catalyst for change. This wider agenda remained unfulfilled through the course of the 2000s. The enlargement of the EU to include the accession states of central and Eastern Europe was not accompanied, as in the past, by an extension of social policy competences. Nor were new social policy initiatives taken to address the restructuring that was expected to follow from the currency union and from the further deepening of the internal market programme, beyond the limited provision made for additional information and consultation rights in the directive of 2002. Without powers to adopt harmonising measures in the areas of minimum wage setting, social security and collective labour law, the EU lacked the means to address the issues set out in the Supiot report.

With little or no progress being made on new legal initiatives in the social policy area, the Commission's attention turned to the objective of reforming national labour law regimes in line with the emerging 'flexicurity' agenda. Its 2006 Green Paper on the modernisation of labour law, consistent with the approach of the employment policy OMC, highlighted certain features of national labour law systems which were compatible with a high employment rate (European Commission, 2006). These included relatively weak levels of employment protection in the Netherlands and Denmark. Little or no emphasis was placed on the high levels of expenditure on active labour market policy in these systems, or on institutional features of the national environments which supported collective worker voice, such as the Dutch version of codetermination or strong sector-level collective bargaining in Denmark. While drawing on elements of reflexive labour law, the Green Paper also introduced, for the first time, a deregulatory emphasis into the Commission's stance on the development of national labour law systems, a harbinger of things to come, as we shall now see.

NEW CHALLENGES TO SOCIAL EUROPE: THE IMPACT OF REGULATORY COMPETITION AND FINANCIAL STABILISATION

Regulatory Competition After the Court's Rulings in *Viking* and *Laval*

The Court's rulings in the *Viking* and *Laval* cases, delivered within a few days of each other in December 2007, have generally been regarded as a turning point in European social policy (see Barnard, 2008; Davies, 2008; Deakin, 2008; Rönnmar, 2008; Reich, 2008; Malmberg and Sigeman, 2008). They are important because the Court articulated an extensive role for EU-level internal market law in subjecting national labour law systems to a process of judicial review, aimed at determining their compatibility with the principle of free movement for persons, capital and goods. The core of this approach is the view that differences across national labour law systems, in the content of the protection granted to workers and unions, are capable of amounting to a 'distortion of competition' within the internal market, and must therefore be justified by reference to an alternative ground of public policy. Potentially legitimate laws can only be kept in place if they pass a strict test of proportionality, under which the measure in question must not only be aimed at fulfilling a legitimate goal of policy, but must achieve this aim by interfering as little as possible with enterprises' rights of free movement.

In taking this view, the Court overturned the uneasy compromise which had previously been maintained between national autonomy in social policy matters and the construction of the internal market through the mechanisms of EU free movement and competition law. At the time of the Treaty of Rome, as we have seen (see above, pp. 233–234), the argument that a common or internal market required full harmonisation of regulatory laws, in labour law as in other areas, had been rejected. There was an acceptance from the outset of the case for regulatory diversity, which in time came to form the basis for the reflexive approach taken to the harmonisation of labour law through social policy directives and related EU-level initiatives. The Court has now rejected this view, in favour of a position which sees uneven regulation across the internal market as a barrier to economic integration. The Court's interpretation of the Treaty provisions on freedom of establishment and freedom to supply services sees labour law regulations, more generally, as a potential fetter on the rights of enterprises to seek out and take advantage of low-regulation regimes. This principle operates asymmetrically: the Court had previously rejected arguments that under the Treaty's free movement of labour provisions, workers moving from more protective labour law regimes to less protective ones were entitled to retain the benefit of the former while working in the latter (see Deakin, 2008), and shows no sign of going back on this position. Just as significant as its development of the case law on free movement has been the Court's approach to the interpretation of directives. In *Laval* and two of the cases following it, *Rüffert* and *Luxembourg*, the Court interpreted the Posting of Workers Directive not as a floor of rights on which member states could build, but as both a floor and a ceiling, thereby in effect pre-empting state-level labour laws in this area, and confining the scope for national-level modulation of the standards contained in that Directive. The context for *Laval* was strike action taken in Sweden against a Latvian-based service provider which refused to observe the terms of local collective agreements. The argument made here was that the strike action infringed the freedom of Laval to operate in Sweden, which in this context was the 'host state', at a cost which reflected conditions in its 'home state' (Latvia). As is usual in posting cases, the workers concerned were employed by Laval under contracts of employment governed by Latvian law, and assigned temporarily to work in Sweden under a contract agreed between a local government body and a Swedish subsidiary of Laval. Under these circumstances, the Posting Directive indicates that the host state must apply certain basic terms and conditions, including minimum wages, to the posted workers, notwithstanding the application, for other purposes, of the law of the home state to their employment. However, the Directive, among other things, only requires the host state to apply basic minimum wage rates which are set out in legally binding instruments such as minimum wage legislation, or in collective agreements which have *erga omnes* effect or are otherwise regarded as generally binding on employers in a particular sector. The problem for the defendant trade unions in the *Laval* case was that Swedish law makes no provision for either legally mandated minimum wages or for sector-level collective agreements to have binding effects on all employers in a given industry. In its ruling, the Court held that Sweden was not entitled to go further than the strict terms of the Directive; hence strike action to support a sector-level collective agreement, while permitted by Swedish law, was incompatible with the Directive as well as being contrary, in this case, to the principle of free movement. In *Rüffert* the Court used similar logic to strike down a sector-level collective agreement which applied to the provision of services under public contracts, ruling that the Directive only permitted member states to enforce such agreements if they covered all employers in a given sector. In *Luxembourg* the Court nullified a number of aspects of the Grand Duchy's posting law, in the process confirming that the Directive imposed strict limits on the steps member states could take to regulate the cross-border supply of services.

The Court's restrictive approach to the interpretation of the Posting Directive is not an isolated event. In cases involving environmental protection and product safety, the Court has taken a similar view, interpreting directives as imposing a ceiling on state action. In the social policy sphere, the scope for such an approach should be limited by the use of social progress clauses in the relevant directives. As explained above (see above, p. 235), these clauses generally provide that while member states may not, unless otherwise stated, derogate from the protective standards set out in a directive, they may improve on them. The Posting Directive contained a social progress clause of this kind, which the Court, however, did not regard as having the effect normally ascribed to such clauses (see Deakin, 2008). It is possible that similar clauses in social policy directives will be approached differently in future. The Posting Directive was an internal market measure, adopted under the part of the Treaty governing free movement rather than its social policy provisions. It seems unlikely that the Court will simply ignore the 'floor of rights' aspect of social policy directives. However, it is possible that it will give social progress clauses a more limited reading. This has happened in several recent cases concerning non-regression clauses, to the extent that some commentators see these as now little more than a 'fig-leaf' (Peers, 2010).

The Court also took a narrow view of the potential of fundamental rights arguments to counter-balance market freedoms. In *Viking*, the issue was the legality of strike action designed to enforce a Finnish collective agreement following the reflagging of a passenger vessel from Finnish to Estonian law. The Court ruled that the strike amounted to a potential infringement of the employer's freedom of establishment rights, on the basis that the reflagging of the ship amounted to a cross-border transfer of establishment. In its ruling, the Court accepted that the right to strike formed part of EU law, a position since confirmed by the granting of legal force, under the Lisbon Treaty, of the EU Charter of Fundamental Rights. However, the Court concluded that strike action still had to be justified by reference to the principle of proportionality. It seems likely that both the right to strike recognised by the Court as a general principle of EU law and that contained in Article 28 of the Charter will be interpreted similarly in future, as simply one factor to be weighed in the balance when considering whether strike action unduly interferes with the free movement rights of enterprises. The Court's view is at odds with the approach to the interpretation of fundamental human rights by the European Court of Human Rights. Under European human rights law, it is departures from the principle of freedom of association contained in Article 11 of the European Convention, which extends to the right to collective bargaining and the right to strike, which must be justified by economic arguments, not, as under *Viking*, derogations from economic rights which must be justified on human rights grounds (Ewing and Hendy, 2010).

The Court's *Laval* judgment drew more or less explicitly on the idea that an 'undistorted' market space could be brought about by the elimination of regulatory differences across the member states. The deregulatory bias of the Court's emerging free movement jurisprudence provides a new source of institutional pressure on the high-regulation member states, which could tip over into a race to the bottom. It nevertheless remains open to member states to seek to amend their laws in a way that brings them more clearly within the scope of the proportionality defence, or of the exceptions to free movement allowed by directives such as the one on posting. Thus following *Laval*, the Swedish law on strike action has been amended in a measure which preserves the right of unions to take action in support of sector-level agreements but which nevertheless has led to some weakening of their position by comparison to the previous state of the law (Rönnmar, 2010). Similar steps have been taken in Denmark, while in Norway, where a version of the legal extension of sector-level agreements operates, the law has been strengthened with a similar goal in mind (Skjeie, 2010). In the German Land of Lower Saxony, the upshot of the *Rüffert* judgment has been the updating of legislation governing the extension of sector-level collective agreements to cover all employers and not just those involved in public service contracts, as allowed by the Posting Directive. The response to *Viking* has included the conclusion of a framework collective agreement by the EU-level social partners on the issue of the rights of workers affected by the reflagging of vessels, which in time is expected to be adopted as a directive (Sciarra, 2010). These developments suggest that Court-led interventions similar to those in *Viking* and *Laval* will not, in general, create a regulatory void. Member states continue to have considerable autonomy in the formulation and application of social policy, and transnational social dialogue will have a role to play in filling the gaps created by Court rulings. Nevertheless, *Viking* and *Laval* have put the reflexive, learning-based approach to European social policy under pressure, and enhanced the prospects for deregulation.

Labour Law and the Emerging Agenda of Financial Stabilisation

In practice, a greater threat to national labour law regimes than that posed by *Viking* and *Laval* is the agenda of financial stabilisation which is emerging in the aftermath of the global financial crisis and the resulting rise in national debt and public deficit levels at member state level. There is a sense in which this is just the playing-out of a process which began with the adoption of the Maastricht convergence criteria and the Growth and

Stability Pact in the early 1990s. The convergence criteria and the stability pact were designed with the aim of limiting the use of fiscal deficits at national level as a response to conditions of recession. They thereby removed one of the sources of flexibility in macroeconomic policy and planning which the member states had previously used to maintain welfare state expenditure across the economic cycle. As we have noted (see above, p. 233), this flexibility was seen as essential to member state autonomy in social policy matters at the time of the drafting of the Treaty of Rome. Thus the loss of national autonomy over economic policy, for those member states in the Eurozone, has unavoidable implications for labour law and social policy more generally.

The economic discipline implied by the convergence criteria was rein- forced by the way in which the constitution of the European Central Bank was drafted, initially in the Maastricht Treaty, and in the way that the ECB's role subsequently developed. The ECB's primary legal objective, as now set out in Article 127 of the TFEU, is to maintain price stability; it can act in support of the Union's general economic policies and other objec- tives only to the extent that they do not conflict with this goal. The ECB is thereby formally barred from performing tasks which central banks have traditionally performed at national level, including the fostering of eco- nomic growth through industrial and regional policy and the reduction of unemployment. The assumption behind the institutional design of the ECB is that once price stability is ensured through monetary policy, the market will operate spontaneously to generate the conditions for full employment (see Schettkat, 2010). Any unemployment that remains must be the result of distortions or 'rigidities' in the labour market, arising from labour laws and collective bargaining. For supporters of this approach to monetary policy, one of the benefits of currency union was expected to be an increase in the pressure on national governments to reform their labour markets with a view to removing such 'rigidities' (Alesina et al., 2010).

This hope has so far been largely disappointed, as member states have mostly resisted the temptation to use the introduction of the euro as the occasion for labour law reforms. In this context, it is striking that the financial stabilisation measures put in place for Greece and Ireland during 2010 should have made cuts in welfare benefits and labour law deregulation one of the conditions of financial support. The reforms carried out in Greece since the extension of financial support from the EU and IMF have included restrictions on the right to strike and on the application of collective agreements, while the implementation of the financial package in Ireland has been accompanied by a cut in the level of the minimum wage (European Commission, 2010a, 2010c). These are not accidental or contin- gent developments; they reflect an emerging view to the effect that the stabilisation of the single currency necessitates the imposition of stricter controls over national economic and social policy (European Commission, 2010b). This trend seems likely to result in the further marginalisation of social policy at EU level and an increase in the use of internal market law and monetary policy as catalysts for deregulation.

CONCLUSION

In this chapter we have reviewed the contribution of reflexive law to the evolution of European social policy and labour law. We have seen that reflexive or evolutionary approaches were implicit in the EU's approach to the harmonisation of labour laws from an early stage. Regulatory diversity and the possibility of member states learning from each other's experiences within the framework of transnational economic integration were built into the institutional design of the Treaty of Rome. At each successive stage of the enlargement of the Union and the deepening of the internal market programme, at least up to the early 2000s, social policy advances were also made. EU labour law nevertheless retained its distinctive form: it was not a comprehensive labour law code, more a series of techniques for coordinating the learning process around the development of labour law at national level. It also made increasing use of forms of transnational economic regulation, including social dialogue and the various manifestations of the open method of coordination, which originated in the unique institutional architecture of the EU. As these methods developed, they arguably contributed to the extension and legitimation of labour law within the wider European project, and to the embedding of the European social model.

In retrospect, the turn taken by the EU at the time of the Maastricht Treaty has had negative implications for labour law which have taken some time to come to the fore but have now done so, with the catalysts being the Court's *Viking* and *Laval* judgments and the agenda of financial stabilisation which has emerged in the wake of the global financial crisis. The programme of monetary union which was launched at Maastricht and realised a decade or so later with the adoption of the Euro has had a wider influence over EU policies and institutions. The idea has taken hold that regulatory differences across the member states pose a potential barrier to economic integration and, specifically, that rigidities induced by labour law and collective bargaining distort the operation of the internal market and impede the workings of monetary poilcy. This view conjoins the *Viking* and *Laval* rulings with the logic of the financial stabilisation agenda, both of which have been used as a pretext for deregulation.

There seems little doubt that European social policy and labour law is now at a turning point. The compromise put in place by the Treaty of Rome is unsustainable and the European Social Model is in need of reform (Moreau, 2011). If social policy is to move forward, the issue of the EU's currently limited legal powers to harmonise the law in certain core areas, including social security law and collective labour law, must be addressed. There needs to be a reassertion of the binding force of the floor of rights set by directive, a clarification of the autonomy of member states to develop their own approaches to labour law and social policy above the floor, and a strengthening of transnational social dialogue. These reforms would not, of themselves, produce new solutions of the kind needed to address the organisational and technological transformations affecting labour law, but they would help to renew the institutional architecture which has success-fully supported the evolution of European labour law to this point.

REFERENCES

Alesina, A., S. Ardagna and V. Galasso (2010), 'The Euro and Structural Reforms', in A. Alesina and F. Giavazzi (eds) *Europe and the Euro*, Cambridge, MA: National Bureau of Economic Research, pp.57–90.

Armstrong, K., I. Begg and J. Zeitlin (2008), 'The Open Method of Co-ordination and the Governance of the Lisbon Strategy', *Journal of Common Market Studies*, 46(2), 436–450.

Arthurs, H. (2007), 'Corporate Self-Regulation: Political Economy, State Regula-tion and Reflexive Labour Law', in B. Bercusson and C. Estlund (eds) *Regulating Labour in the Wake of Globalisation: New Challenges, New Institutions*, Oxford: Hart, pp.19–35.

Ashiagbor, D. (2006), *The European Employment Strategy. Labour Market Regula-tion and new Governance*, Oxford: Oxford University Press.

Barbier, C. (2003), 'Research on "Open Methods of Coordination" and National Social Policies. What Sociological Theories and Methods?', in T. Bredgaard and F. Larsen (eds) *Employment Policy from different Angles*, Copenhagen: DJØF Publishing, pp.47–74.

Barbier, C. (2008), *La longue marche vers l'Europe sociale*, Paris: Presses Universi-taires de France.

Barnard, C. (2008), '*Viking* and *Laval*: an introduction', *Cambridge Yearbook of European Legal Studies*, 10, 463–492.

Barnard, C. and Deakin, S. (2011), 'Social Policy and Labour Market Regulation', in A. Menon, E. Jones and S. Weatherill (eds) *Oxford Handbook on European Union Law*, Oxford: Oxford University Press.

Büchs, M. (2007), *New Governance in European Social Policy. The Open Method of Coordination*, Basingstoke: Palgrave.

Davies, A. (2008), 'One Step Forward and Two Steps Back: The *Viking* and *Laval* Cases in the ECJ', *Industrial Law Journal*, 37, 126–148.

Deakin, S. (1996), 'Labour Law as Market Regulation: The Economic Foundations of European Social Policy', in P. Davies, A. Lyon-Caen, S. Sciarra and S. Simitis (eds) *Principles and Perspectives on EC Labour Law: Liber Amicorum for Lord Wedderburn*, Oxford: Oxford University Press, pp.63–93.

Deakin, S. (2008), 'Regulatory competition after *Laval*', *Cambridge Yearbook of European Legal Studies*, **10**, 581–609.

Deakin, S. (2009a), '*Capacitas*: Contract Law, Capabilities, and the Legal Foundations of the Market', in S. Deakin and A. Supiot (eds) *Capacitas: Contract Law and the Institutional Preconditions of a Market Economy*, Oxford: Hart, pp.1–30.

Deakin, S. (2009b), 'Reflexive Harmonisation and European Company Law', *European Law Journal*, **15**, 224–245.

Deakin, S. and F. Wilkinson (1994), 'Rights v. Efficiency? The Economic case for Transnational Labour Standards', *Industrial Law Journal*, **23**(4), 289–310.

Deakin, S. and G. Morris (2009), *Labour Law*, 5th ed., Oxford: Hart.

Deakin, S. and A. Supiot (eds) (2009), *Capacitas: Contract Law and the Institutional Foundations of a Market Economy*, Oxford: Hart.

Deakin, S. and F. Carvalho (2010), 'System and Evolution in Corporate Governance', in G.-P. Calliess and P. Zumbansen (eds) *Law, Economics, and Evolutionary Theory: State of the Art and Interdisciplinary Perspectives*, Cheltenham: Edward Elgar.

De Schutter, O. and S. Deakin (2005), 'Reflexive Governance and the Dilemmas of Social Regulation. Introduction', in O. De Schutter and S. Deakin (eds), *Social Rights and Market Forces: is the Open Coordination of Employment and Social Policies the Future of Social Europe*, Brussels: Bruylant, pp.1–27.

European Commission (2003), 'Jobs, Jobs, Jobs. Creating more employment in Europe', Report of the Employment Taskforce chaired by Wim Kok, November 2003, European Commission, Brussels ('Kok I').

European Commission (2004), 'Facing the Challenge. The Lisbon strategy for growth and employment', report from the High Level Group chaired by Wim Kok, November, Luxembourg: Office of the European Communities ('Kok II').

European Commission (2006), *Modernising Labour Law to Meet the Challenges of the Twenty-First Century*, Green Paper, COM(2006)708, 22 November.

European Commission (2010), *Lisbon Strategy evaluation document*, SEC(2010), 114 final.

European Commission (2010a), 'Euro area and IMF agreement on financial support programme for Greece', 3 May 2010, available at http://ec.europa.eu/economy_finance/articles/eu_economic_situation/2010-05-03-statement-commissioner-rehn-imf-on-greece_en.htm (last accessed on 16 August 2011).

European Commission (2010b), 'A new EU economic governance – a comprehensive Commission package of proposals', available at http://ec.europa.eu/economy_finance/articles/eu_economic_situation/2010-09-eu_economic_governance_proposals_en.htm (last accessed on 16 August 2011).

European Commission (2010c), 'Commission and IMF issue joint statement on Ireland', 28 November 2010, available at http://ec.europa.eu/economy_finance/articles/eu_economic_situation/2010-11-28-js-ireland_en.htm (last accessed on 16 August 2011).

European Council (2006), Presidency Conclusions on the social dimension of the revised Lisbon strategy at the Informal EPSCO Council Meeting Villach, 20 January 2006, available at http://www.eu2006.bmsg.gv.at/cms/eu2006EN/

detail.htm?channel=CH0601&doc=CMS1137851810205 (last accessed on 16 August 2011).

Ewing, K. and J. Hendy (2010), 'The Dramatic Implications of _Demir and Baykara'_, _Industrial Law Journal_, **39**(1), 2–51.

Falkner, G., O. Treib, M. Hartlapp and S. Leiber (2005), _Complying with Europe: EU Harmonisation and Soft Law in the Member States_, Cambridge: Cambridge University Press.

Fuchs, M. (2004) 'Germany: Part-Time Work – A Bone of Contention', in S. Sciarra, P. Davies and M. Freedland (eds), _Employment Policy and the Regulation of Part-Time Work in the European Union_, Cambridge: Cambridge University Press, pp.121–155.

Heidenreich, M. and J. Zeitlin (eds) (2009), _Changing European Employment and Welfare Regimes – The influence of the open method of coordination on national reforms_, London: Routledge.

Jørgensen, H. (2005), 'The European Employment Strategy up for Revision – Effective Policy or European Cosmetics?', in T. Bredgaard and F. Larsen (eds), _Employment Policy from different Angles_, Copenhagen: DJØF Publishing, pp.23–46.

Kilpatrick, C. (2006), 'New EU Employment Governance and Constitutionalism', in G. De Burca and J. Scott (eds), _Law and New Governance in the EU and the US_, Oxford: Hart, pp.121–151.

Kolben, K. (2010), 'Labour Regulation, Human Capacities and Industrial Citizenship', in S. Marshall (ed.) _Promoting Decent Work: The Role of Labour Law_, report to DIALOGUE section, Geneva: ILO.

Luhmann, N. (1995), _Social Systems_, Stanford, CA: Stanford University Press.

Luhmann, N. (2004), _Law as a Social System_, Oxford: Oxford University Press.

Malmberg, J. and T. Sigeman (2008), 'Industrial Actions and EU Economic Freedoms: The Autonomous Collective Bargaining Model Curtailed by the European Court of Justice', _Common Market Law Review_, **45**(4), 1115–1146.

Moreau, M.-A. (ed.) (2011), _Before and After the Economic Crisis: What Implications for the 'European Social Model'?_, Cheltenham, UK: Edward Elgar.

Mosher, J.S. and D.M. Trubek (2004), 'Alternative Approaches to Governance in the EU: EU Social Policy and the European Employment Strategy', _Journal of Common Market Studies_, **41**(1), 63–88.

Nussbaum, M. (2000), _Women and Human Development: The Capabilities Approach_, Cambridge: Cambridge University Press.

Peers, S. (2010), 'Non-regression Clauses: The Fig-Leaf Has Fallen', _Industrial Law Journal_, **39**(4), 436–443.

Pochet, P. (2005), 'The Open Method of Coordination and the Construction of Social Europe. A Historical Perspective', in J. Zeitlin and P. Pochet in collaboration with L. Magnusson (eds), _The Open Method of Co-ordination in Action: The European Employment And Social Inclusion Strategies_, Brussels: Peter Lang, pp.37–82.

Reich, N. (2008), 'Free Movement versus Social Rights in an Enlarged Union: the _Laval_ and _Viking_ Cases before the European Court of Justice', _German Law Journal_, **9**(2), 125–160.

Rogowski, R. (2007), 'Flexicurity and Reflexive Coordination of European Social and Employment Policies', in H. Jørgensen and P.K. Madsen (eds) _Flexicurity and Beyond. Finding a new agenda for the European Social Model_, Copenhagen: DJØF Publishing, pp.131–153.

Rogowski, R. (2008), 'The European Social Model and Law and Policy of Transitional Labour Markets in the European Union', in R. Rogowski (ed.) *The European Social Model and Transitional Labour Markets: Law and Policy*, Aldershot: Ashgate, pp.9–28.

Rogowski, R. and T. Wilthagen (eds) (1994), *Reflexive Labour Law. Studies in Industrial Relations and Employment Regulation*, Deventer: Kluwer.

Rönnmar, M. (2008), 'Free Movement of Services versus National Labour Law and Industrial Relations Systems: Understanding the *Laval* Case from a Swedish and Nordic Perspective', *Cambridge Yearbook of European Legal Studies*, **10**, 493–523.

Rönnmar, M. (2010), '*Laval* Returns to Sweden: The Final Judgment of the Swedish Labour Court and Swedish Legislative Reforms', *Industrial Law Journal*, **39**(3), 280–287.

Salais, R. (2006), 'On the correct (and incorrect) use of indicators in public action', *Comparative Labor Law & Policy Journal*, **27**(2), 237–256.

Salais, R. (2007), 'Europe and the Deconstruction of the Category of "Unemployment"'. *Archiv für Sozialgeschichte*, **47**, 371–401.

Scharpf, F.W. (1999), *Governing in Europe: Effective and Democratic?*, Oxford: Oxford University Press.

Schettkat, R. (2010), 'Will only an Earthquake Shake Up Economics?', *International Labour Review*, **149**(2), 185–207.

Schmid, G. (2008), *Full Employment in Europe. Managing Labour Market Transitions and Risks*, Cheltenham, UK: Edward Elgar.

Schmid, G. and S. Kull (2004), 'Die Europäische Beschäftigungsstrategie. Perspektiven der Offenen Methode der Koordinierung', in H. Kaelble and G. Schmid (eds), *Das europäische Sozialmodell. Auf dem Weg zum transnationalen Sozialstaat*, WZB-Jahrbuch, Berlin: Sigma, pp.317–343.

Sciarra, S. (2010), 'Notions of Solidarity in Times of Economic Uncertainty', *Industrial Law Journal*, **39**(3), 223–243.

Sen, A. (1999), *Development as Freedom*, Oxford: Oxford University Press.

Sen, A. (2009), *The Idea of Justice*, London: Allen Lane.

Skjeie, T. (2010), 'European Economic Integration: A Threat to the Scandinavian Labour Law Systems?', LL.M. Dissertation, University of Cambridge.

Streeck, W. (1996), 'Neo-Voluntarism: A New European Social Policy Regime?', in G. Marks, F.W. Scharpf, P.C. Schmitter and W. Streeck, *Governance in the European Union*, London: Sage, pp.64–94.

Supiot, A. (2001), *Beyond Employment. Changes in Work and the Future of Labour Law in Europe*, Oxford: Oxford University Press.

Supiot, A. (2010), *L'esprit de Philadelphie: la justice sociale face au marché total*, Paris: Seuil.

Teubner, G. (1993), *Law as an Autopoietic System*, Oxford: Blackwell.

Trubek, D.M. and J. Mosher (2003), 'New Governance, Employment Policy, and the European Social Model', in J. Zeitlin and D.M. Trubek (eds), *Governing Work and Welfare in a New Economy: European and American Experiments*, Oxford: Oxford University Press, pp.33–58.

Zeitlin, J. (2005), 'The Open Method of Coordination in Action. Theoretical Promise, Empirical Realities, Reform Strategy', in J. Zeitlin and P. Pochet in collaboration with L. Magnusson (eds), *The Open Method of Co-ordination in Action: The European Employment and Social Inclusion Strategies*, Brussels: Peter Lang, pp.447–503.

Zumbansen, P. (2008), 'Law after the Welfare State: Formalism, Functionalism and the Ironic Turn of Reflexive Law', *American Journal of Comparative Law*, **56**(3), 769–805.

12. Employment and the social dimension of Europe: what constitutive conventions of the market?

Robert Salais

INTRODUCTION

The current global crisis has arisen from the belief in the virtues of the market as a system. Since the 1980s Europe has increasingly succumbed to this belief, either in trying to dogmatically construct the perfect market, or in allowing market participants to develop their own rules without effective oversight. Since 2000 this second register has taken hold, with the flourishing of so-called governance activities. Instead of bringing durable benefits as promised, the system as a whole has led to chaos in markets, to unemployment, to social problems and the weakening of the European project. Indeed, we are entering a new world which threatens the future of employment in Europe.

The question of employment cannot be addressed independently of the social dimension of the economy, hence implicating the conventions constitutive of the market. The employment challenge is simple. Europe must change both its market conventions and its political method. Briefly reviewing the history of market conventions in Europe, this chapter intends to show to what extent the capability approach and its combination with the transitional labour market approach could provide a suitable foundation for such a change.

Since the signing of the Treaty of Rome in 1957, the European political project has been characterised by an irreducible specificity, namely that to be legitimate and politically acceptable the justification for increased or wider European social intervention must be based on economic arguments invoking economic efficiency and competition. This holds true today as it has in the past and will in the future. This must be the starting point for any discussion. It is not enough to fight for a social dimension (some say a 'social constitution') for Europe that is independent of or counterbalances its 'economic constitution'. Contrary to widespread opinion (see Scharpf, 2002), there is no refusal to include the social sphere in the objectives of European integration. The only constraint, albeit a powerful one, is to provide meaningful theoretical and practical guidance, hence a constitutive convention which allows the 'social' to advance in step with the 'economic'. To comply with this condition, Europe should adopt a market convention that is better suited to this objective than the ones it has adopted to date. The importance of such conventions, as one will see in the following sections, is that, when established, they are subsequently interpreted to develop European legislation and propose regulations (market reforms, competition and so on). Through its jurisprudence the European Court of Justice is the most powerful interpreter of constitutive conventions.

European actors have to become aware of the plurality of conceptions of the economic and social spheres and their relationship, *in economic science itself*. Economics does not propound a single theory that brooks no challenge, the dogma of the perfect market. Why would economics be any different from other sciences, building itself through a collective process aimed at the acquisition of knowledge, combining investigation, theoretical formalisation, multiple approaches, scientific doubt, internal criticism and contradictory debate? Several conventions of the market are available to European actors, conventions that can readily become operative if a reform is engaged.

Adopting another convention is by no means impossible. The first part of this chapter points out that at least two such conventions have been successively in effect since the Treaty of Rome, first ordo-liberalism and then the single market since the 1980s. The second part of the chapter shows the inherent limits of the strategy aimed at integrating the social under the control of the single market. The third part advocates a market convention that combines the ordo-liberal philosophy with the capability approach. The implementation of economic freedoms should be subordinated to the respect of two fundamental principles, a principle of justice (revisiting the equal treatment requirements as equality of capabilities between persons) and a principle of democracy (democratic deliberation of collective choices). It is also suggested below that the goals of the transitional market approach can be dynamically reformulated via an extension of the capability approach.

FROM ORDO-LIBERALISM TO THE SINGLE MARKET

Broadly following the Ohlin Report produced by ILO in 1956,[1] the Spaak Report and the EEC Treaty concluded that there was no need to endow the European Community with the power to legislate in the social field (De Schutter, 2005). Not because national prerogatives had to be preserved in these matters, but because in the opinion of the expert group:

> International competition in a common market would not prevent particular countries from raising workers' living standards and there is no sound reason to think that freer international markets would in any way hamper the further improvement of workers' living standards as productivity rises, through higher wages or improved social benefits and working conditions. (Ohlin, 1956: 115)

There were, however, two exceptions justified by the risk of distortion of competition, i.e. equal pay between men and women, and paid leave (Articles 119 and 120 EEC Treaty). The fear was that if within a given industry or sector differences in these domains were too great between countries it would lead to a situation of unfair competitive advantage. Finally, one must recall that the Treaty establishing the European Coal and Steel Community (ECSC) in 1951 which in many ways prefigured the Treaty of Rome, had among its objectives 'to participate at the request of governments, to study the possibilities for reuse in industry existing or creating new activities, the labour made available by the changing market or technological changes'.[2] Such tasks, now called 'restructuring', were assigned to the European Social Fund (ESF) by the Treaty of Rome and later were integrated under the objectives of Structural Funds.

The social preoccupation was therefore present from the start. In addition to Articles 119 and 120 EEC Treaty, Article 117 EEC Treaty expressed 'the need to promote better living conditions and labour for their harmonisation in progress'. The modest initial status of these Articles should not mask the fact that from the outset they correspond to a fundamental rule of equal treatment, considered from two points of view, static and dynamic. The historical importance of equal treatment is that it can be analysed using a capability approach, as we will see later. According to the capability approach, two persons are treated equally if in their living and working conditions they enjoy the same *real* freedom of choice and action. This has not been and still is not the dominant interpretation (which remains the fight against discrimination), but it continually emerges in EU legislative work, for instance whenever equality between men and women is an issue.[3]

Legal and Institutional Provisions Awaiting Interpretation

Overall, the reasoning underlying the Treaty of Rome is economic in nature, based on the theory of comparative advantage in international trade. The chain of causation adopted in 1957 linking economic and social issues is robust and simple. Economic efficiency gains are expected from trade liberalisation through a better allocation of production factors in a common market; these gains can be used to finance social progress. But a correct interpretation of this reasoning requires that we refer back to the economic, social and political conditions that prevailed in the immediate post-war period. There were no precise notions anticipating what economic integration, enlargement to other countries or globalisation might be. National economies were still closed economies. The opening of national borders within a wider community, thus promoting trade, was meant to encourage national economies to specialise in their strengths for the benefit of all, for growth, productivity and employment. The priorities were to progressively introduce free movement of goods and to establish a system ensuring that competition was not distorted (Part One. Principles, Article 3 EEC Treaty). The abolition of obstacles to the free movement of persons (limited to workers), services and capital between member states is also part of Article 3 EEC Treaty, but at that time had few practical consequences. The language of competition that is used did not focus on prescription, but on freedom and fair play.

In short, these 1957 provisions called for an interpretative theory capable of enabling and implementing European rules which, in case of dispute, would help found the proper decisions, in other words a constitutive convention. At this time, that constitutive convention was borrowed mostly from ordo-liberal economic theory.

'Market' is such a dazzling term that it blots out the background which gives it meaning. One should grasp the magnitude of change for Europe stemming from the passage from an ordo-liberal theory to a theory of a 'unique' market. As noted by Alain Supiot, for such a market to be deployed, a space must be created that is devoid of all the singularities that could impede the perfect liquidity of economic exchanges.[4] First we recall that ordo-liberalism is concerned not with the market, but with the overall economy and that, for it, economy should be considered as a spontaneous order regulated by the state. Secondly, we argue that advances in the social domain under the Delors presidency and the Single European Act and the Charter of Fundamental Social Rights amounted to a Pyrrhic victory concealing submission to a convention of the market that later proved hostile to the social dimension, even if nothing seemed lost at the time.

Ordo-liberalism: The Economy as a Spontaneous Order Regulated by the State

In reconstructing the European project as an 'economic constitution', ordo-liberalism has provided the conceptual and legal resources needed to establish a competition policy. As Joerges and Rödl have written, the Community has acquired the legitimacy of a 'law-based order committed to guaranteeing economic freedoms and protecting competition by supranational institutions'.[5] This framework is limited to some general rules organising the common market so as to enable the future European economy to be deployed as an efficient and spontaneous order for Europe and to benefit from economic growth. These rules are: guaranteed economic freedoms, open economies, rules of non-discrimination, commitment to undistorted competition. The European economy as a spontaneous order cannot but suffer from the development of European discretionary economic policies (that is to say, policies that focus on particular areas and intend to pilot them from above). Beyond the fact that they are unfounded in law, such policies are inefficient, for they impede the autonomy and freedom of coordination of economic actors. On the basis of this argument, the ordo-liberals later criticised the move toward the single market (see below). Given the current state of the European project, we must leave them the benefit of the doubt. However, two of the so-called current deficits of Europe, the social and democratic ones, arose from this initial foundation of the market. For the ordo-liberals, the social should be dealt with at the national level, the proper echelon for redistributing the wealth created. And an economic order based on European law did not need to gain democratic legitimacy. Valuable in the 60s and the 70s, these claims can no longer be sustained.

Ordo-liberalism can be compared with the economics of conventions.[6] This approach deals with coordination between people and its underlying constitutive rules. Conventions are defined as a system of mutual expectations backed by common knowledge which allows individuals and actors to interact in specific situations, including work or the market. A constitutive convention of the market is in this view shaping a common understanding among its actors (as well as of those in charge of assessing or judging the situation) of what is the market, its relevant features and its right way of functioning. Both the ordo-liberal school and the economics of conventions attach great importance to mutual coordination and transaction networks. They differ, however, in their appreciation of justice and democracy in collective choices, concerns which the economics of conventions want to integrate in European economic policy making (see comments below).

As in the economics of conventions, ordo-liberalism emphasises mutual expectations and freedom of action as the basis for economic efficiency. Institutions and the state are present as coordinating instances to ensure the inclusion of the common good, to recall the rules and to provide procedures for fair rulings in case of conflict. Indeed, as developed by its founders, ordo-liberalism is not a philosophy of the market, let alone the neoclassical perfect market.[7] It is a theory of the state, a state regulator of a spontaneous order. This is precisely what those who built Europe in its early years have failed to perceive. To understand the practical implications of this observation one has to go back to Germany in the 1950s and 1960s and acknowledge that ordo-liberalism is linked to the historical mode of socio-economic development that produced the 'German miracle'. The decentralised industry of southern and western Germany, which was at the core of that miracle, was an economy composed of dense networks of companies, territorially anchored, self-coordinated and capable of endogenous development. To efficiently support it, the central government restricted its intervention to setting some basic rules of conduct designed to allow 'self-coordination from below' and to enforcing them (Streit and Mussler, 1995: 7). These rules had to be sufficiently universal for economic actors to adhere to them.[8] They had to provide moral incentives in order for actors to deploy, spontaneously but responsibly, their coordination conventions:

> Self-coordination takes place within a network of transactions among autonomous individuals or legal entities. The network itself is very complex and ever changing. Furthermore it is highly informative in that, along every transaction, information relating to the subjective assessment of scarcity is produced, processed and disseminated. (Streit and Mussler, 1995: 7)

This transposes into theory the effective operation of what Herrigel (1996) calls the decentralised German industrial order.

Ordo-liberalism includes investment in specific assets and innovation (hence quality) among positive factors for economic competition. In this view it is important to protect 'free and equal trade'. The rules it advocates are intended to secure trust, to allow transactions among equals (hence the objective of fighting against the formation of monopolies or dominant positions). The freedom in question is not that of neo-liberal opportunism. This is a responsible freedom, conscious of the 'good' functioning of a spontaneous order, understood as public order. As employment comes within the national purview, the member states are considered as having full latitude to socially embed the market in their own ways. Under the Treaty of Rome they pledged, however, to observe a universal social rule, that of equal treatment (that in 1957 had just two applications, in the areas of pay and working time) and to integrate it into their national model.

The pursuit of economic integration should have achieved progress towards a truly European production system. To that end, the European Community should have promoted, above all, the development of common economic and social conventions at industry, occupational and country levels in Europe (conventions with regards to product quality, labour conventions). This has been partly achieved (see below), but within an interpretive framework that has corrupted the efforts undertaken. Instead of concentrating on the building of a common economy, priority was given to building a single market. The European project shifted in the 1980s (the Thatcher and Reagan years) from the perspective of economics as spontaneous order to a constructivist approach to market.[9]

In this context economic freedoms were redefined as a regulatory straitjacket, the aim of which was to construct a single market affording perfect liquidity and complete substitutability between workers, between products, between services and between movements of capital. The 1985 White Book on Completion of the Internal Market can be read as a deliberate movement towards institutionalising standard economic rationality, and the 1992 Treaty of Maastricht as a break with the ordo-liberal economic constitution. Why did this occur under the chairmanship of a prominent social-democrat, of a great European figure like Jacques Delors? The hypothesis that deserves further inquiry is that this was the political price, probably higher than expected, that Jacques Delors had to pay to advance the vision he had at heart, a social Europe (Didry and Mias, 2005; Didry, 2009). He rightly understood that a supranational entity cannot be legitimate without the democratically obtained support of the people, and that a necessary step in this direction was to demonstrate that the European Community could bring added social value, which could not be provided by the member states.

Conventions of Product Quality and the Threat Posed by the Single Market

By signing the Single European Act in 1986 the member states agreed to go forward in the fight against the 'obstacles' hindering free trade. This concept of 'obstacles' changed drastically in meaning and scope. At issue are Articles 28 and 81 of the Treaty and the threat they pose to implementing standards, e.g. conventions defining the quality of products. No market can work unless suppliers and users agree on the qualification and use of the products produced and sold. If a German special machine producer has a global market without any real competition, this is not because the producer has imposed a monopoly, but because the shared view of users is that the product's technical specifications and performance are better and more efficient. Other competitors have to do better and convince the market; it is not up to public authorities to condemn the market standard in the name of a dogmatic and blinkered conception of competition and market functioning. But Articles 28 and 81 lead to this result, the first condemning restriction on imports, the second condemning distortion of competition.[10]

Article 28 EC in effect extends the prohibition of quantitative restrictions on imports to 'all measures having equivalent effect'. This encompasses specific but essential dimensions of conventions designed to ensure quality, health and safety. The famous decision handed down by the ECJ in the case of *Cassis de Dijon* (C 120/78) had challenged the German legislative ban on imports of Cassis de Dijon because its alcohol content contravened national legislation on occupational health and safety. This decision could have opened the way to a possible route, later recommended by the 1985 White Paper, that of mutual recognition (every member state recognising the others' laws) as long as different national approaches provided the 'same level of protection'. But the ECJ rejected this path (C 188/84 *Commission v France*), which, in practice, reveals rather than resolves the incommensurability of national laws. In this case, protection against accidents related to the use of wood-working machines was ensured by measures in France and Germany that were so different (improving the protective equipment of machines for France, better training the workers for Germany) that the Court refused to consider them as equivalent.[11] More generally, the Court began to track any trace of 'public' and therefore 'national' intervention in the establishment and role of these standards, and to take such intervention as evidence of an effect equivalent to a restriction of imports. But the Court had to accept, ruefully, that many standards were 'private' in nature. Then along came Article 81, relating to rules on competition, which prohibits as incompatible with the common market:

> ... all agreements between undertakings, decisions by associations of undertakings and concerted practices which may affect trade between Member States and which have as their object or effect the prevention, restriction or distortion of competition within the common market.

Although its original purpose is the prohibition of cartels, Article 81 led to including quality conventions among the factors distorting competition, for they could be read as concerted practices having as their effect to distort competition.

The combination of Articles 28 and 81, applied literally, would have led to the elimination, as 'obstacle', of any collective definition of quality conventions, in line with a utopian but totalitarian vision of a perfect market, in which price is the only legitimate form of competition. In addition, the rigid opposition made between public and private identifies the state as a factor that disturbs the market and that should be removed or neutralised. We are far from the ordo-liberal approach. Deprived of quality conventions for its products, the European economy would have been led to ruin in the long run. However, the Court and the Commission were reluctant to seek another path, proving that in the 1980s they began to be anchored in a top-down constructivist approach aiming to build the perfect market.[12]

After having oscillated between various regulatory impulses, the so-called New Approach was launched in 1985. Through sectoral Directives, the Community intervention set forth a number of essential requirements that states were allowed to impose on their products. Recognised European standards bodies were given the task of developing European standards in compliance with these requirements. These bodies involve all stakeholders: governments, state agencies, producers, users, consumers, unions. Greater flexibility was given to member states to implement these standards or, in the case of no standards, to develop their own standards under these requirements, subject to the principle of mutual recognition. The rule was to achieve consensus.[13] A codicil was added to Article 81, specifying exceptions to the principle of competition that would be tolerated, if duly proven (for instance agreements aimed at improving economic efficiency or consumer satisfaction).[14] Concerns of health and safety were placed at the top of the agenda and seized by Jacques Delors as an opportunity to legislate on working conditions and environment (12 social directives among the 16 adopted during his presidency). This return to reality was welcomed as a change in perception of technical standardisation: 'From an activity by nature generating technical barriers to trade, it has become a privileged instrument of economic integration, serving the internal market, and competitiveness of European enterprises', according to Repussard (1994) then Secretary General of the European Committee for Standardization. Helmut Reihlen, long time Director of the Deutsches Institut für Normung (DIN) and influential actor in the European standardisation process qualified the New Approach as a way 'to overcome bureaucracy and "parliamentary paralysis"'.[15]

But this is not the end of the story. The New Approach was in practice neither deregulation nor privatisation. One could even say that it borrows some of its features from ordo-liberal recommendations. By involving economic and social actors and national authorities, it recognises the de facto primacy of quality conventions as well as the autonomy exercised by actors in reaching an agreement on European standards. But it is not in any case self-regulation by the market. The public actor is responsible for defining the goals and the processes. Yet, in another turn-around, the

Commission now interprets the New Approach as self-regulation by the market, from which European or national law should abstain. So reviewed and betrayed, the New Approach is touted as the model for European governance. As Schepel (2005: 73) says: 'In the bitter debates of Community competencies versus member states' sovereignty, the idea of European-wide industry self-regulation disarms both sides by introducing the notion that bottom-up integration generates its own normative frameworks.' But the weakening of nation states, which conforms to the strategic interests of the Commission, comes at the price of a similar weakening of the Commission, as seen during the economic crisis. Overall, the public actor is marginalised in its various incarnations.

THE LIMITS OF A STRATEGY AIMED AT INTEGRATING THE SOCIAL UNDER THE SINGLE MARKET

The establishment of a European Charter of Fundamental Rights was the path chosen in 1989 to foster a concept of social citizenship and to include it in the political agenda within the single market. The idea was to find for the social sphere a subordinate but still legitimate place within a structure whose economic basis remained untouched. Various pitfalls threatened this strategy and are now threatening to scuttle it. Is it possible not to stay at a purely rhetorical reference to fundamental rights? Can one prevent them from being instrumentalised and their ethical sense perverted? How to move beyond the status of a mere *market citizenship*, created by the fundamental economic freedoms, which essentially recognises individuals as *units of a production factor*,[16] instead of as *persons* who enjoy citizenship status and rights independent of current work and market conditions?

We have already seen, in the case of products, the unresolved swinging between the dogmas of constructivism and of laissez-faire economics. Twenty years later, what can be said about the gains and the losses? Do gains exceed losses? These questions are raised by three examples: the process of establishing a charter of rights; the jurisprudence of the ECJ regarding the status of social rights; and the submission of social policy and employment to criteria for economic performance, disconnected from any concern for social justice.

The Establishment of a Charter of Fundamental Rights

The dilemma regarding the status of social rights was well summarised by Poiares Maduro in 1999.[17] Are these rights instituted only to provide a playing field for the deployment of fair competition or, more broadly, are they meant to include criteria for solidarity and distributive justice, independent from free competition objectives, in the scope of European integration? In the first case, social rights derive a fragile and subordinate legitimacy from the market; in the second they impose their logic in European integration.

To overcome this dilemma, the European Community should have sought, not to follow its own path but, as suggested by several committees,[18] to incorporate directly into the Treaty the fundamental rights to which member states were already committed in the framework of international organisations: ILO Conventions, the European Convention of Human Rights, the Social Charter of the European Council. Thus the respect and realisation of these fundamental social rights would have truly become the principles constitutionalising a European welfare state and guiding its future development.[19] This option was not chosen. Margaret Thatcher made sure of that (the UK has never, to date, agreed to sign any charter of fundamental rights whatsoever, binding or not). The ECJ had expressed its opposition to this solution, stressing that the Community had its own legal personality, separate from other international organisations.[20] Ultimately most member states wanted to retain control over the social.[21]

So Europe chose its own path, trying to achieve a common position by internal consensus. Thus it is no surprise that the 1989 European Charter of Fundamental Social Rights (a great political success in other respects) is far less ambitious than the Social Charter of 1961: it contains no right to work, no right to collective bargaining or right to fair compensation, and in the end its scope is largely restricted to the employment relationship. Combined with the Commission's aggressive use of its right of initiative, the Charter has nevertheless provided support for a series of action programmes. Considering the rather hostile political context, its outcome is important: 16 social guidelines adopted under the Delors Presidency, a half-dozen afterwards. But the momentum has slowed. Difficulties have emerged, e.g. the fact that the right to strike and salary issues are firmly excluded from the Community's competencies. Intended to bring a renewed impetus, the social dialogue institutionalised to establish and, if agreed, implement Framework Directives has faltered in recent years. The Commission has taken it as an excuse not to exercise its right of initiative.[22] However European social dialogue remains active at the sectoral level. The Charter of Fundamental Rights of 2000 is even more limited in the social field, but it is more complete regarding political freedoms and citizenship status. However from the outset human rights have remained outside the core institutional architecture of Europe, added but not really incorporated (De

Schutter, 2005: 284). And the obligations that may arise from them, such as the Charter of Fundamental Social Rights, do not concern the member states, they only apply to the Union when it acts in its areas of competence (Kenner, 2003: 531).[23]

Are Social Rights Obstacles to Fundamental Economic Freedoms?

One is tempted to blame the increased weight of the new ex-socialist member states in the composition of the ECJ, or the rise of neo-liberalism, but it remains clear that from the outset the ECJ has not found in the Treaties and European texts any solid basis for placing social rights on an equal footing with economic freedoms. Its judgement methodology is biased by the orientations of meaning induced by the convention that the market should be a space devoid of all features that could impede its perfect liquidity.

The legitimacy of social goals is not disputed as such, rather the question is whether social rights can be invoked to justify restrictions on the full exercise of economic freedoms. This leads the Court, following the principles of proportionality and necessity, to try to assess in each case whether the negative economic impact expected as a result of these restrictions exceeds the value attached to the respect for social rights. Several questions ensue. Are social rights fundamental in nature? If so, is their validity limited to the national level or does it extend to the European level? In areas recognised by the Treaty as being of exclusive national competence (such as the right to strike or wages), should not member states, when implementing rights, still respect the primary (the Treaty) and even secondary (regulations and directives) Community law? These questions have been raised, more or less successively, in the rulings handed down by the Court. Recent ECJ jurisprudence reinforces subordination to economic freedoms.

Only in duly proven exceptions are social rights allowed to impede the application of economic freedoms, which means that subordination is the rule. Witness the cases (*Commission v. France*, C-265/95) and (*Schmidberger*, C-112/00). In the latter case, a Dutch international transport firm was prevented from crossing a bridge, due to a demonstration by Austrian environmental protection groups. Although the demonstration had been authorised, the firm appealed to the Court, arguing that it had suffered from restriction on the principle of free movement of goods. Following the firm's reasoning, the Court ruled that the fact that Austrian authorities had refrained from intervening was equivalent to a quantitative restriction of imports, and hence incompatible with the principle of free movement of goods. How then can the protection of fundamental rights (freedom of expression and assembly) guaranteed by Articles 10 and 11 (ECHR) be reconciled with this principle? The Court acknowledged that the issue went beyond the mere enforcement of rights and addressed their potential scope. But, referring to the 'interests' involved and balance between them, the ECJ ruled: 'the interests involved must be weighed having regards to all the circumstances of the case in order to determine whether a fair balance was struck between these interests.' The legal language used here is contaminated by conventional economic rationality. This reasoning conceives action as strategic and governed by economic interest, even if it professes ethical or moral motives. As De Schutter remarks, the Court thus precludes a priori the language of human rights.[24]

Indeed, the Court is reluctant to recognise social rights as fundamental. The *Albany* (C-67/96) case, for example, was ultimately about whether the right to collective bargaining is a fundamental right and could justify a restriction on free competition within the single market. Although many articles in the Treaty promote social dialogue and encourage understanding the right to collective bargaining as a fundamental right in several European Charters, the Court replied no, with two arguments. For the Court, the European Social Charter – the only charter the Court retained – compiles the listed rights not as enforceable fundamental rights but as policy goals which the states may choose to pursue, or not. For the Court the legal immunity potentially enjoyed by collective bargaining, despite the barriers to competition that it implies, is limited to agreements on 'core subjects such as wages and working conditions and which do not directly affect third parties or markets'. Collective bargaining on working time is suspect because it works in practice: 'as cover for a serious restriction of competition between employers on their product markets'.[25]

Some recent cases have marked an inflection or a hardening in favour of the supremacy of fundamental economic freedoms.[26] In *Viking* (C-438/05), a shipping company in Finland re-registered its boats under the Estonian flag and replaced the Finnish crew with an Estonian one, in order to circumvent Finnish collective agreements on wages and employment conditions. The company filed a complaint against trade unions, arguing that the threat of collective action and the activities of the International Transport Workers Federation (ITF) aimed at organising a joint response among workers in Finland and Estonia were incompatible with the exercise of the firm's right to freedom of establishment (Art. 43 EC). While recognising as fundamental the right to collective action (right to strike included), the Court held that its exercise at national level should nevertheless comply with Community law (here the freedom of establishment) and ruled in favour of the company. It even set forth an extremely restrictive interpretation of the 'social purpose' of the European Community (former Article 2 EC Treaty, now, in substance, Article 9 TFEU, and Article 151 TFEU, formerly 136 EC Treaty: 'improved living and working conditions, so as to make possible their harmonisation while improvement is being maintained, proper social protection and dialogue between management and labour') as the foundation of union action.[27] In virtue of the principle of proportionality, it limited the legitimate objectives of this action to protecting existing jobs, leaving the national courts to judge whether the action undertaken went beyond what was necessary in the light of this objective.[28]

The case of *Laval* (C-341/05) concerned the application of Directive 96/71 on posted work, in addition to freedom to provide services (Article 56 TFEU, formerly 49 EC Treaty). A subsidiary of a Swedish firm had won a competition to build a school on the outskirts of Stockholm. Registered in Riga under Latvian law, the subsidiary decided to employ Latvian workers as posted workers in Sweden, but with Latvian working conditions and wages. The Directive requires that member states ensure that conditions for posted workers employed in their territory comply with national standards, under law or under collective agreements provided the latter are subject to a procedure extending them as law, which is not the case in Sweden where, on the contrary, the autonomy of collective bargaining is guaranteed by law. The ruling found the Swedish standards non-applicable by lack of extension of collective agreements. But the Court went even further, declaring unlawful the actions of Swedish unions to support the transnational nature of their agreements. It restricted the legitimacy of union action on posted work to the respect of minimum working conditions. In so doing, it transformed the European principle of minimum harmonisation into a principle of maximum harmonisation, excluding de facto the stipulation 'while improvement is being maintained' stated in Article 151 TFEU, formerly 136 EC Treaty. As in *Viking,* the Court undermines the recognition of the right to strike as a fundamental right at the national level, although the Treaties explicitly exclude it from Community competence. Lastly, it claims to give a particular element of European secondary law (a Directive) a legal status equivalent to the Treaties. Any piece of European secondary law could thus, in its view, successfully challenge, in the name of economic freedoms, social models democratically developed at national level.[29]

All these shifts in ECJ jurisprudence reveal the inherent dangers of a convention of the market that removes social or national specificities as obstacles to perfect economic competition. Not only is the social challenged as a foundation of European integration, the very principle of democracy is called into question as well through its achievements. Similar deviation can be seen in the implementation of reforms of social policy and employment. The question is no longer 'hard' versus 'soft' law, for the same dangers are now found in soft law and its main tool, the open method of coordination.

The Open Method of Coordination and Performance Criteria

The European Employment Strategy (EES) illustrates the emerging effects of a soft law instrument, the coordination of national policies via monitoring of performance indicators.[30] Priority is given to quantitative performance at the expense of social justice and quality of jobs.

Employment is an area where the Community lacks competence. Nonetheless we see a potentially intrusive approach in an area where member states believed they were only modestly involved, in recognising it as of 'a matter of common concern' (Article 146 paragraph 2 TFEU, formerly 126 paragraph 2 EC Treaty). Via techniques borrowed from the private sector (guidelines, benchmarking, best practices, evaluation by performance indicators), in practice the Commission has introduced a conception of the labour market equivalent to the neoclassical perfect market, that is, once again, a space free of social and legal 'rigidities' that would hamper the adjustment of supply and demand. Beyond rhetoric exposed in the guidelines, the EES prefers flexibility to security, focusing on individual employability, on accelerated return to work whatever the job, on the weakening of legal and social protection. Such biases appear in the set of indicators chosen to evaluate national performances. These indicators deny any serious approach based on the quality of work, concentrating instead on maximising the gross rate of employment[31] and the rate of quick return to employment whatever the job or the 'other equivalent measure' offered to the applicant. The consequences that can be easily imagined are promoting bad jobs at the expense of good ones, contrary to the Lisbon Strategy objectives.

Research that deals only with political procedures has missed the basic issues, i.e. the cognitive instruments used and their role (as exemplified by indicators). These are measuring instruments that call for quantitative responses: performance indicators, statistical tables, reports to be sent each year by national administrations. National answers are subjected by the Commission to evaluation, ranking, reviews and recommendations. In a nutshell, the whole process creates incentives for the member states to favour bad jobs which improve their employment performance more easily and at lower cost.

Globally speaking, the EES framework is linked with the system of vertical coordination piloted by the monetary policy and the broad guidelines of economic policies, the gross employment rate being key for evaluating national macroeconomic performance.[32] However, it is virtually impossible to compare the results with what they would have been in the absence of coordination, especially as monitoring indicators promotes public policies which directly target increasing scores at the expense of real improvement in people's circumstances. The rise of the gross employment rate since 1997 claimed by the European Commission is dubious, depending as it does on the conventions adopted for defining jobs. The Commission chose the broadest possible definition: is regarded as a job any paid task performed at least one hour during a reference week. When adjusted for the decreasing number of hours actually worked per person annually, the 'rise' appears as stagnation. Evaluated in terms of the quality of jobs created, the assessment would be even more severe. Likewise, the democratic quality of the procedures can be criticised, as they are essentially carried by a small group of high-level civil servants, with no democratic elaboration and approval.

Overall, achievements have reinforced *market citizenship* rather than social citizenship. There are, however, three notable exceptions: equality between men and women, European Works Councils, information and consultation of workers. They demonstrate that another path remains possible. Initiatives in these areas have kept alive the fundamental goals of justice and democracy, because, potentially at least, they are based on other constitutive conventions of the market.

SUBORDINATING THE LABOUR MARKET TO THE GOALS OF JUSTICE AND DEMOCRACY. WHAT CONVENTIONS?

Now that the single market is largely established, is it not time to return to a few simple basic rules that would truly create a European economy? Priority should be given to bottom-up self-coordination for the economic and social fabric. The objectives of the founding fathers of ordo-liberalism have lost none of their relevance, quite the contrary given the complexity of modern economies, and the flexibility, creativity and forms of competition through quality and innovation which drive them. They would have the additional advantage to bring the state back in and to legitimate its necessity and role. But they must be reformulated and extended. In effect, there are fundamental flaws in the economic freedoms as stated in the Treaty.

These flaws appear in full light, when interpreted by the dogma of the single market. Human beings are there reduced to the status of objects or flows. Like goods, services and capital, they are treated identically and at the same level. But human beings cannot be so reduced. The economy, as well as society, does not work as a mechanical machine. Economy is the outcome of human beings who coordinate their production and market activities, who are motivated not only by instrumental interests, but also by aspirations for freedom to choose and to act, for personal accomplishment and democratic participation. Reconfiguring the European market order into an economic order requires the addition of two fundamental principles, a principle of justice and a principle of democracy. The challenge is to achieve conceptions of freedom and responsibility (the principles of action of ordo-liberalism) that would be based on justice, democracy and personal accomplishment (the capability approach).

Real Freedom, Responsibility and Capability

The capability approach derived from the works of Amartya Sen is a philosophy of freedom, but not freedom which is imposed on everybody from outside (as in market dogma).[33] Freedom has to be effective for everybody. Creating the conditions for freedom to be effective should be both the goal and the engine of economic and social development. It requires, as Sen (1999) demonstrates, the mobilisation and extension of all freedoms (civil, political, economic, social) at the same level and pace. The political issue is to improve for all European citizens their power to act, to choose and achieve what they value and choose to do, that is to give them capability. To be efficient and fair Community resources must be oriented (and often re-oriented) towards capability development. To this end the definition, content and distribution of collective resources require effective, rigorous, constructive and contradictory public debate and democracy. Public action should no longer be restricted to general considerations (that are often too close to ideological statements) and delve into concrete circumstances, their diversity from one territory to another, from one community to another, from one problem to another. In this way European citizens will have real and accrued freedom, which in return would require them to exercise a sense of responsibility towards the Community and its common goods. To have full on-the-ground effect, Europe must involve all relevant actors with equal consideration and not fear disagreement. On the contrary, disagreement helps us to understand problems as they actually exist, not as one would like to imagine them (see Besson, 2003).

The market for Amartya Sen is not a rational or mechanical construction, but a living fabric of human, economic and social relationships in which freedom and responsibility should progress at the same pace. And it must be subordinated to higher economic, social and political ends. Consequently, in Sen's works the founding principle of the social is not to repair the damage done by the market, but to prevent it insofar as possible, which implies acting upstream, in work and in life. Although starting from different premises, there is a subtle kinship here with ordo-liberal ideas. In order to be fair, market and more general economic relationships should be relationships between equals. However ordo-liberalism failed to take into account that formal equality in law is not sufficient. Many factors inherent to situations of life and work lead to unequal outcomes, despite equal rights. For example, a married woman with young children has less chance of finding any job, let alone a good one, than a bachelor with the same skills applying for the same job. Inequalities of power in the labour market relationship and within firms should be offset or neutralised wherever possible. Such inequalities in capabilities (and in opportunities) cannot be corrected on the market alone, but primarily upstream in situations of life and work.

One can see such ideas implicit in the 3rd Action Programme (1991–1995) of the Delors Presidency, although they were not really exploited. The programme stipulates that the implementation of the law 'cannot alone secure the *de facto* equality of opportunity'. 'What was required was specific action aimed at improving the situation of women in practice' (Kenner, 2003: 139).[34] Their implementation would also require innovation in the ECJ method of interpretation. As Tamara Hervey (1994: 403–406) pointed out the ECJ is unable to consider gender equality in a manner appropriate to real life, due to its methodology. The ECJ follows a formalist 'like as like' approach and focuses on finding a comparator (a man in a similar situation in terms of the general categories used by the ECJ) or operates with general reasons such as the state of the labour market. It thereby loses sight of what is specific and pertinent to the situation of women, and to the need to restore gender equality: for example pregnancy, giving birth, having to work part-time due to family constraints. One can appreciate the bias of the ECJ approach in the case of *Stoeckel,* which condemned in 1991 the banning of night work for women (prohibited under conventions of the ILO) by applying the principle of gender equality.[35]

Adding Principles of Justice and of Democracy

Following Amartya Sen and the capability approach, rules are needed to implement principles of justice and democracy and to guide actors' conduct that affects aspects of work and life. Such rules should be universalising, as defined above by Streit and Mussler (1995: 7), hence abstract, open and unambiguous, in order not to impinge on the autonomy of conventions between actors. This requires a legislative framework strongly rooted in European law at the same level as economic freedoms. It also means that these rules should be implemented *in situ* through democratically formed procedures of assessment and of deliberation that promote effective learning by all stakeholders (in firms, territories, sectors, etc.). Such procedures should be also stipulated by European law.

The capability-based principle of justice is to ensure that all persons dispose of an area of effective free choice and action, at all times and in all places. This space must be real and concrete, that is to say, it must provide resources in a format and in circumstances such that they lead to genuine effective freedom, and over time, to capability development of the person. This is how the principle of equal treatment should be implemented in Europe.

The capability-based principle of democracy is to ensure that decisions relative to work organisation, placement, evaluation, and, more generally, all economic decisions having effect on employment, are subject to democratic procedures, wherever they are made. These procedures should be such that all stakeholders, particularly those affected by these decisions, are present and can make their voices heard, and have their proposals, when judicious, taken into account in the most balanced way possible. Works councils, the right to information and consultation are first steps in this direction in Europe.

Implementing the Principle of Justice: Combining the Capability and Transitional Labour Market Approaches

The conjunction of the two approaches discussed in this book – capability and transitional labour markets – can be formalised in a very simple way.[36] It sharply contrasts with the path chosen by the European Employment Strategy (EES). We look first at the EES and then develop the combined approach.

The EES focuses on individual employability. Let p_i be the probability of employment for an individual i. The overall employment rate, the main target of the EES, can be written as the sum of the individual probabilities of N number of individuals that make up the population of working age. Employability, in other words, is seen as dependent on properties intrinsic to each individual: natural characteristics (sex, age, location), or over which the individual has responsibility and control (motivation, cost-benefit calculation, investment in human capital, etc.). Let us call this set of properties e_i.

The EES target can be written: $\max \sum_{i=1}^{N} p_i(e_i)$. The EES applies a utilitarian model, creating inequality and inefficiency. The choice of labour market rules (rules of hiring or dismissal, job quality, employment incentives and refusal penalties, management rules for agencies) are designed to maximise the sum of individual employabilities. This leads to greater selectivity in hiring (priority to the most employable), weakens the rules for dismissal (the most employable will quickly return to employment whatever happens), qualifies any task as employment, encourages the best and penalises the others. This choice sacrifices the people who are the least well placed on the job market, precisely those who instead should be granted more favourable rules. The quality of jobs is not taken into consideration, because it makes hiring and firing more difficult, involves higher wages and provides negotiating power to workers. This static approach neglects the applicants' professional career. Its focus on unemployed workers and their rate of return to employment is an additional factor of inefficiency. The EES ignores the majority of the population of working age, those already employed and those who are inactive (mostly women who do not work). But the probability of *remaining employed*, for example from one year to the next, could well have a major positive impact on the overall employment rate. Remaining employed does not mean keeping the same job, it also involves mobility, but mobility that is anticipated and prepared, to advance passage through the labour market.

The suggested alternative strategy combines the capability and transitional labour market approaches. In such a strategy and in order to join together, the TLM approach should have to shift its focus from employability to capability, and the CA approach to extend its concern to transitions on the labour market. It will run in the following way.

It sets as its target: $\sum_{i=1}^{N} \max c_i(s_i)$, where c_i is the capability for employment of the individual i and s_i the set of relevant variables relative to his or her life and work situation, what Sen call the *focal features*. The capability for employment c_i of the individual i corresponds to the scope of employment opportunities that, at a time t, are really available to the individual and that he or she can freely choose, either in job or in transition. In other terms, the design of these opportunities (on-the-job policies, active labour market policies) should also dynamically provide and develop this capability. Maximising that capability for *each person* will ensure a real concern about inequalities between people. The action variables of employment policies are no more, or marginally, individual employability; more broadly they become the *focal features* of situations s_i (for examples for such focal features, see Bénédicte Zimmermann's chapter, this volume).

Such a strategy would address all people of working age (in employment or in transitions, being unemployed or returning to employment). We have no room to develop, just to quote three illustrations.[37] In firms, jobs should be designed and organised with regard to their capability building (experience, skills, training) and professional development (a valuable professional future) for those holding the positions. Companies must be proactive, not in relation to job cuts to come, but in creating jobs, internally or in their sector, to address new product demand, technologies and markets. On the labour market, the priority for all agencies dealing with welfare, training, job placement, etc. should be to create an enabling environment for every jobseeker (coherent satisfaction of needs, not of employment but for housing, health, training, etc.) creating conditions for sustainable inclusion. To help women with children enter the workforce or remain in employment, priority should be given to trajectories that maintain effective freedom of choice between family life, raising children and work which here again, involves a set of coordinated policies (family policy, childcare, transportation, housing, planning) and of work organisation policies.

The overall employment rate which would be obtained would be the joint product of increased capability, better jobs, professional development and effective free choice for all. This strategy would be more socially just and more economically efficient than the present one. It clearly breaks with the dominant orientations we have already analysed. Implementing such an alternative strategy requires commitment from all actors – European institutions, member states, enterprises, local authorities, professional organisations, not-for-profit groups and, not least, the European citizens. The substantive issue to be dealt with is the lack or insufficiency of democracy, whenever collective choices are to be made.

The Principle of Democracy: Civil and Social Criticism as the Political Engine of Europe

Europe must change its policy approach. The European bureaucratic machinery wrongly led us to believe that progress can arise only from consensus. However, in practice, the European project has progressed only under pressure from critics, internal and external. For this criticism reflects a need for fair European solutions. We have seen that in the 1980s powerful economic interests compelled the Commission and the ECJ to, momentarily, come around to a more realistic approach to markets as they really work. During the same period a truly committed President of the Commission, Jacques Delors, advanced the cause of social Europe. Another example is that of European works councils: they would not have come into existence without the social movement in Vilvoorde in 1997. Nothing can be worse than the growing general indifference to Europe as political project.

The time is past when unions could accept long-term wage gains lower than productivity increases in exchange for the social dimension of Europe.[38] Without active intervention by employees and their representatives, professional development will never be truly taken into account. No objectives for territorial development or job creation will be set without economic rights of action and sufficient resources for local communities and authorities. Neither real freedom of choice in employment, nor capability-providing trajectories for inclusion will come into existence without representation and rights of action for jobseekers at the level of each agency and employment area, etc. All of this calls for living democracy practices in Europe, wherever, at all levels, collective decisions are to be taken in economic, financial, political and social domains. Such is the message delivered by Amartya Sen's works.

As James Bohman (2004, 2007) demonstrates, introducing deliberative democracy is essential to give Europe a new start. Unfortunately there is to date little thinking that, in European matters, avoids the traps of governance and consensus. However, effective democracy and critics need each other. Much is to be thought and done in that direction.

To conclude, we will take the example of the European social dialogue and its relationship to the reinforcement of social and civil criticism. The European social dialogue as a mechanism for preparing Directives and their framework is an illustration of the problems confronting effective deliberative democracy. In the examples quoted above, the Commission, the ECJ (and the member states) have consistently returned to their old practices once the pressure let up. In light of the persistent failure to implement a process of fundamental rights, as well as the use of methods of governance in favour of market neo-liberalism since 2000, the social and civil movement can no longer remain locked into a pure internal participatory approach in the myriad of bodies, committees, forums, programmes and other similar initiatives that flourish under the control of European and national authorities. The configuration of roles is now such that this position leads almost automatically to the weakening of the European project and to the marginalisation of the social and civil movement.

Deliberative democracy, thus, cannot be achieved by acting out a play with a script and rules of the game written in advance and without the knowledge of the actors. Each player must participate actively in choosing the agenda, writing the play and setting the stage. It follows that the participation in internal deliberation within European bodies must rely on external criticism, and the two must advance along the same path. So far, due to their mode of institutionalisation within the EU process, the European social and civil actors have yet to prove by their practice to be representative of European workers and citizens. They will have to fight to become truly and democratically legitimate, if they want to be able to influence the fate of Europe. Hence their strategic priority should be to engage European citizens in a collective process of social and civil criticism about the impacts, negative and positive, of Europe on their lives and work.[39] And to demonstrate in this process their ability to create a political agenda and knowledge of social realities with which European citizens can identify and in which they could actively participate.

NOTES

1. In 1956 Bertin Ohlin (1899–1979), a Swedish economist, led a group of ILO experts charged with considering the social aspects of the emerging 'European arrangement for closer economic cooperation'. Ohlin was a macroeconomist and belonged to the Wicksell school.
2. ECSC Treaty, Title III. Economic and social provisions, Article 46.
3. See Lewis and Giullari, 2005.
4. Supiot, 2008 and 2010.
5. Joerges and Rödl, 2008.
6. On economics of conventions see, among others, the special issue of Revue économique, **40** (2), 1989; Orléan, 1994; Storper and Salais, 1997; Salais et al., 1998; Eymard-Duvernay, 2006.
7. This excludes variants influenced by Hayek or neo-classical economics. See Eucken, 1948a and 1948b, Müller-Armack, 1947; also Vanberg, 2004. The problem, however, with the analysts of ordo-liberal thinking is that they limit themselves to internal debate in economic theory or policy, without examining its practical foundations. One should not forget that all theories are embodied in the realities and problems of their own time.
8. 'The most suitable rules of conduct are universal, i.e.:
    -   they are abstract in the sense of being applicable to an unknown and indeterminable number of persons and bodies;
    -   they are open in the sense of describing merely those actions which are not allowed and thus leave to individuals to discover and take unprecedented action;
    -   they are certain in the sense that individuals can trust in their continuance and are able to identify in practice those actions which are not allowed.' (Streit and Mussler, 1995: 8)
9. One must remember that Sir Leon Brittan, Commissioner at the General Directorate for Competition Policy and who triumphed over Jacques Delors in impeding any European industrial policy (Ross, 1995) had previously been Margaret Thatcher's Home Secretary, active in the fight against striking miners in 1984, a conflict which was a turning point for the Conservative revolution in Britain.
10. When the Commission and the Court refer to the *technical or quality requirements,* they are in fact discussing conventions of product quality, but without understanding their economic significance: 'The Commission is referring in particular to rules covering the composition, designation, presentation and packaging of products as well as rules requiring compliance with certain technical standards.' European Commission, 1980.
11. Schepel, 2005: 39–42, that we reformulate in a convention's approach.
12. In a 1981 decision that fortunately had no successors (*Dansk Supermarked* C 58/80), the Court stated, 'It is impossible in any circumstances for agreements between individuals to derogate from the mandatory provisions of the Treaty on the free movements of goods.' (quoted in Schepel, 2005: 46, footnote 38).
13. See Kessous, 1997.

14. The tortuous wording of this codicil is interesting: 'The provision of paragraph 1 may, however, be declared inapplicable in the case of:
    - any agreement or category of agreements between undertakings,
    - any decision or category of decisions of associations of undertakings,
    - any concerted practice or category of practices, which contributes to improving the production or distribution of goods or to promoting technical or economic progress, while allowing consumers fair share of the resulting benefit, and which does not: a) impose on undertakings restrictions which are not indispensable to the attainment of these objectives; b) afford such undertakings the possibility of eliminating competition in respect of a substantial part of the products in question.' See European E & M Consultants, 2005.
15. Reihlen, 1990, quoted in Schepel, 2005: 65.
16. 'Entitled to move from their State to another member state exclusively by virtue of their being workers, self-employed or providers of services, that is *qua* units of a production factor', ECJ Judge Mancini, 1989 address at Harvard University (quoted by Kenner, 2003: 118).
17. 'For those who argue in favour of a model of European integration restricted to economic integration, the goal is to maximise wealth (efficiency) through free trade and market integration. Social rights may be required, but only as a form of securing a level playing field and fair competition. For those who argue in favour of a model of political integration, wealth maximisation has to be complemented by some criterion of solidarity and distributive justice in the new political community. Social right will be a requirement of independent and fair competition arising from membership of that political community' (quoted in Kenner, 2003: 110).
18. See for example the Opinion on the social aspects of the internal market (European social area) of the Economic and Social Committee (rapporteur Beretta) (European Commission, 1987) and later the report of the Expert Group on Fundamental Rights, chaired by Spiros Simitis (European Commission, 1999), *Affirming Fundamental Rights in the European Union: Time to Act*.
19. In German legal thinking, a *Sozialstaat* requires the state to create a just social order. That would have helped to create 'a European sphere of entitlements to a decent livelihood' (Leibfried and Pierson, 1992: 336).
20. Opinion 2/94 of the ECJ.
21. As became evident during the negotiation of the Maastricht Treaty (Salais, 2001).
22. Of the 47 proposals of the Platform for Action of the Delors Presidency, only 27 were submitted to the European Council. Today around 20 have been converted into Directives.
23. The ECJ should nevertheless be required 'in performing its judicial role, to have cognisance of the rights in the Charter'.
24. De Schutter, 2005: 291–293.
25. De Schutter, 2005: 315–318. Denying that collective bargaining is a fundamental right renders collective rights uncertain and contradicts the mechanism of social dialogue in the Treaty. European actors are entitled to negotiate collective agreements with the aim of transforming them into directives, after approval by the European Council. Thus they are entitled to make Community law, and not just limited to negotiating between strategic interests.
26. For *Viking* and *Laval*, we summarise here the conclusions of Joerges, 2007, and Joerges and Rödl, 2004, 2008. See also the comments in Chapter 11 by Simon Deakin and Ralf Rogowski.
27. Another interpretation, truly in line with the 'social purpose', is provided by the capability approach. See the discussion earlier.
28. The court, an English tribunal, held that this action was not necessary. According to Joerges and Rödl, 2008, the Attorney General Maduro now supports the view that transnational industrial action constitutes a violation of fundamental rights (Opinion 23 May 2007).

29. Attorney General Poiares Maduro went further in a recent opinion (*Kadi*, 16/1/2008) by subordinating the application of international law (in this case a resolution of the Security Council of the United Nations which, according to the claimant, undermined many of his fundamental rights) to the Community legal order: 'International law can permeate that order only under the conditions set by the constitutional principles of the Community.' (para. 24).

30. This briefly summarises a series of works: Salais, 2004b, 2006a, 2006b and 2007.

31. This rate is calculated by counting each job as one unit, whatever its duration, the nature of the employment contract, the wage level, the degree of security or insecurity regarding the future, etc.

32. The annual European calendar initially provided for discussing economic policy, employment and social policies at different times in the year, leaving room for criticism from advocates of social causes. Today the calendar schedules all the debates at the same time, with the effect that the voices of proponents of social concerns are stifled by the focus on finance and the economy.

33. A single reference: Sen, 1999. Many other references to that book can be found in Chapters 6 and 7, by Bénédicte Zimmermann and Jean-Michel Bonvin respectively, this volume.

34. COM (90) 449, adopted as a Council Resolution on 21 May 1991.

35. Tamara Hervey (1994) argued instead for a differentiated approach, critical and dynamic in terms of substantive equality (not unlike the capability approach).

36. See Salais, 2004a, and Leonardi, 2009.

37. Extensively developed in Chapters 3, 6 and 7 by Günther Schmid, Bénédicte Zimmermann and Jean-Michel Bonvin respectively (and, in historical matters, in Chapter 8 by Noel Whiteside, all this volume).

38. As it was still the case during the first social dialogue at Val Duchesse (6 November 1986) that developed a joint cooperation strategy for growth and employment.

39. Such a process should combine deliberative inquiry and the creation of a public, as already imagined by John Dewey at the beginning of the last century. See Bohman, 2004 and Salais, 2009.

REFERENCES

Besson, S. (2003), 'Disagreement and democracy: from vote to deliberation and back again?', in J. Ferrer and M. Iglesia (eds), *Law, Politics and Morality: European Perspectives I*, Berlin: Duncker & Humblot, pp.101–135.

Bohman, J. (2004), 'Realizing deliberative democracy as a mode of inquiry: pragmatism, social facts and normative theory', *Journal of Speculative Philosophy*, **18** (1), 23–43.

Bohman, J. (2007), 'Democratizing the transnational polity: the European Union and the presuppositions of democracy', RECON On-line Working Paper, 2007/2.

Dehousse, R. (2002), 'Misfits: EU law and the transformation of European governance', Jean Monnet Working Paper 2/02, Florence: European University Institute.

De Schutter, O. (2005), 'The implementation of fundamental rights through the Open Method of Coordination', in O. De Schutter and S. Deakin (eds), *Social Rights and Market Forces: Is the Open Method of Coordination of Employment and Social Policies the Future of Social Europe?*, Brussels: Bruylant, pp.279–343.

Didry, C. (2009), 'L'émergence du dialogue social en Europe: retour sur une innovation institutionnelle méconnue', *L'Année Sociologique*, **59**(2), 417–447.

Didry, C. and A. Mias (2005), *Le moment Delors. Les syndicats au cœur de l'Europe sociale*, Brussels: PIE-Peter Lang.

Eucken, W. (1948a), 'The social question', reprinted in H.F. Wänsche (ed.) (1982) *Standard Texts on the Social Market Economy. Two Centuries of Discussion*, Stuttgart, New York: Gustav Fischer, pp.267–275.

Eucken, W. (1948b) 'What kind of economic and social system', reprinted in A. Peacock and H. Willgerodt (eds) (1989), *Germany's Social Market Economy: Origins and Evolution*, London: Macmillan, pp.27–45

European Commission (1980), Communication from the Commission concerning the consequences of the judgment given by the Court of Justice on 20 February 1979 in case 120/78 ('Cassis de Dijon'), Official Journal C 256 , 03 October1980, 2–3.

European Commission (1985), 'Completing the Internal Market,' White Paper, COM(85) 310, June, Brussels.

European Commission (1987), Opinion on the social aspects of the internal market (European social area) of the Economic and Social Committee, Rapporteur Beretta, Brussels, November.

European Commission (1999), 'Affirming Fundamental Rights in the European Union: Time to Act', Report of the Expert Group on Fundamental Rights, President: Spiros Simitis, Brussels, February.

European Commission (2007), 'Opportunities, Access and Solidarity', Communication, COM(2007) 726 final, Brussels, November.

European E & M Consultants (2005), 'Article 81(3) EC-Treaty', Competition Competence Report, May.

Eymard-Duvernay, F. (ed.) (2006), *L'économie des conventions, vingt ans après*, Paris: La Découverte.

Herrigel, G. (1996), *Industrial Constructions: The Sources of the German Industrial Power*, Cambridge: Cambridge University Press.

Hervey, T. (1994), 'The future for sex equality in the European Union', in T. Hervey and D. O'Keefe (eds), *Sex Equality Law in the European Union*, Chichester: John Wiley, pp.399–413.

Joerges, C. (2007), 'Integration through de-legalisation? An irritating heckler', EUROGOV Working Paper, 07/03.

Joerges, C. and F. Rödl (2004), 'The "Soziale Marktwirtschaft" as a model for social Europe?', in L. Magnusson and B. Strath (eds), *A European Social Citizenship? Preconditions for Future Policies in Historical Light*, Brussels: PIE-Peter Lang, pp.125–158.

Joerges, C. and F. Rödl (2008), 'On the "Social Deficit" of the European Integration Project and its Perpetuation through the ECJ Judgements in *Viking* and *Laval*', RECON Online Working Paper, 2008/06.

Kenner, J. (2003), *EU Employment Law: From Rome to Amsterdam and Beyond*, Oxford: Hart Publishing.

Kessous, E. (1997), 'Le marché et la sécurité. La prévention des risques et la normalisation des qualités dans le marché unique européen', thesis, Paris: EHESS.

Leibfried, S. and P. Pierson (1992), 'The Prospects for Social Europe', in *Politics and Society*, **20**(3), 333–366.

Leonardi, L. (2009), 'Capacitazioni, lavoro e welfare. La ricerca di nuovi equilibria tra stato e marcato: repartire dall'Europa', *Stato e mercato*, **85**(1), 31–62.

Lewis, J. and S. Giullari (2005), 'The adult-worker-model family, gender and care: the search for new policy principles and the possibilities and problems of a capabilities approach', *Economy and Society*, **34**(1), 76–104.

Möschel, W. (2001), 'The proper scope of government viewed from an ordoliberal perspective: the example of competition policy', *Journal of Institutional and Theoretical Economics*, **157**(1), 3–13.

Müller-Armack, A. (1947), 'The Social Aspect of the Economic System', reprinted in H.F. Wänsche (ed.) (1982), *Standard Texts on the Social Market Economy. Two Centuries of Discussion*, Stuttgart, New York: Gustav Fischer, pp.9–21.

Ohlin, B. (Rapporteur) (1956), 'Social Aspects of European Economic Co-operation', Report by a Group of Experts, Geneva: ILO.

Orléan, A. (ed.) (1994), *L'analyse économique des conventions*, Paris: Presses Universitaires de France.

Revue économique (1989), 'L'économie des conventions', Special issue, **40**(2), March.

Ross, G. (1995), *Jacques Delors and European Integration*, New York: Oxford University Press.

Salais, R. (2001), 'Filling the gap between macroeconomic policy and situated approaches to employment. A hidden agenda for Europe?', in B. Strath and L. Magnusson (eds). *From the Werner Plan to the EMU. In Search of a Political Economy for Europe*, Second Edition, Bruxelles : PIE-Peter Lang, pp.413–446.

Salais, R. (2004a), 'Social Europe and the Capability Approach', Paper delivered at the 4th International Conference on the Capability Approach: Enhancing Human Security, 5–7 September 2004, University of Pavia, available at http://www-3.unipv.it/deontica/ca2004/papers/salais.pdf (accessed 17 August 2011).

Salais, R. (2004b), 'La politique des indicateurs. Du taux de chômage au taux d'emploi dans la stratégie européenne pour l'emploi', in B. Zimmermann (ed.), *Les sciences sociales à l'épreuve de l'action. Le savant, le politique et l'Europe*, Paris: Editions de la MSH, 287–331.

Salais, R. (2006a), 'Reforming the European Social Model and the politics of indicators: from the unemployment rate to the employment rate in the European Employment Strategy', in M. Jepsen and A. Serrano (eds), *Unwrapping the European Social Model*, Bristol: The Policy Press, pp.189–212.

Salais, R. (2006b), 'On the correct (and incorrect) use of indicators in public action', *Comparative Labor Law & Policy Journal*, **27**(2), 237–256

Salais, R. (2007), 'Europe and the deconstruction of the category unemployment', *Archiv für Sozialgeschichte*, **47**, Special Issue on 'The crisis of the social state', 371–401.

Salais, R. (2008), 'Capacités, base informationnelle et démocratie délibérative. Le (contre-) exemple de l'action publique européenne', in J. De Munck, and B. Zimmermann (eds), *La liberté au prisme des capacités. Amartya Sen au-delà du libéralisme*, Paris: Editions de l'EHESS (Raisons pratiques 18), pp.297–329.

Salais, R. (2009), 'Deliberative democracy and its informational basis: what lessons from the Capability Approach', *Contribution*, SASE Conference, Paris, 16–18 July, available at http://halshs.archives-ouvertes.fr (accessed 17 August 2011).

Salais, R., Chatel, E. and Rivaud-Danset, D. (eds) (1998), *Institutions et conventions. La réflexivité de l'action économique*I, Paris: Presses de l'Ecole des Hautes Etudes en Sciences Sociales.

Scharpf, F. (2002), 'The European Social model: Coping with Diversity', Working Paper 02-8, Max-Planck Institute for the Study of Societies, Cologne.

Schepel, H. (2005), *The Constitution of Private Governance. Products Standards in the Regulation of Integrated Market*, Oxford: Hart Publishing.

Sen, A. (1999), *Development as Freedom*, New York: Anchor Books.

Storper, M. and R. Salais (1997), *Worlds of Production: The Action Frameworks of the Economy*, Cambridge, MA: Harvard University Press.

Streit, M. and W. Mussler (1995), 'The Economic Constitution of the European Community: From "Rome" to "Maastricht"', *European Law Journal*, 1(1), 5–30.

Supiot, A. (2008), 'L'inscription territoriale des lois', *Esprit*, November, pp.151–170.

Supiot, A. (2010), *L'esprit de Philadelphie. La justice sociale face au marché total*, Paris: Seuil.

Vanberg, V. (2004), 'The Freiburg School: Walter Eucken and Ordoliberalism', Freiburg Discussion Papers on Constitutional Economics 04/11, Universität Freiburg.

Zimmermann, B. (2009), *Ce que travailler veut dire. Une sociologie des capacités et des parcours professionnel*, Paris: Economica.

Index